11,000ers The of the Canadian Rockies

Bill Corbett

Rocky Mountain Books

VANCOUVER • VICTORIA • CALGARY

Rocky Mountain Books
#108 – 17665 66A Avenue
Surrey, BC V3S 2A7
www.rmbooks.com

Library and Archives Canada Cataloguing in Publication

Corbett, Bill
   The 11,000ers of the Canadian Rockies / Bill Corbett. — Updated ed.

Includes index.
ISBN 978-1-897522-40-0

   1. Mountaineering—Rocky Mountains, Canadian (B.C. and Alta.)—Guidebooks. 2. Mountaineering—Rocky Mountains, Canadian (B.C. and Alta.)—History. 3. Rocky Mountains, Canadian (B.C. and Alta.)—Guidebooks. 4. Rocky Mountains, Canadian (B.C. and Alta.)—History. I. Title.

FC219.C67 2009   796.52209711
C2008-907146-8

Library of Congress Control Number: 2008942457

Front Cover: Lyells 4 and 5 (rear). Photo: Sandy Walker.
Back Cover: South Ridge of The Helmet, Kain Face of Mount Robson in the background. Climbers: Glen Boles (l), Forbes Macdonald and Roman Pachovsky.

All photos by the author unless otherwise indicated.

Rocky Mountain Books acknowledges the financial support for its publishing program from the Government of Canada through the Book Publishing Industry Development Program (BPIDP), Canada Council for the Arts, and the province of British Columbia through the British Columbia Arts Council and the Book Publishing Tax Credit.

Printed in Canada on 50% recycled paper.

Contents

*To Forbes and Roman, for launching me on the
quest, and to Nancy and Colin for helping me finish.*

See www.billcorbett.ca for updates

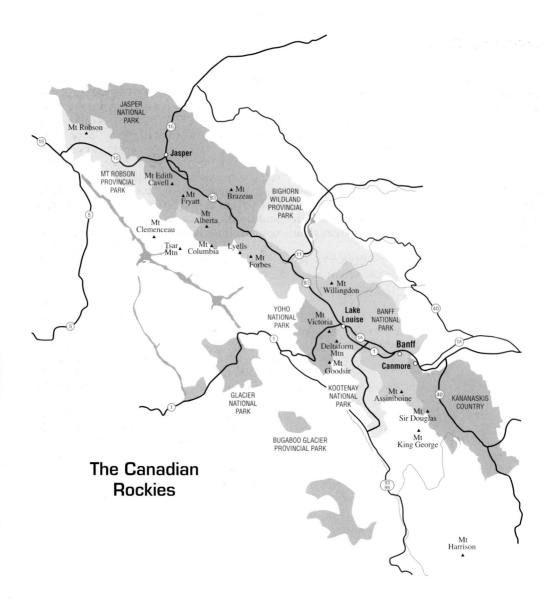

The Canadian
Rockies

Disclaimer

There are inherent risks in mountaineering. While the author has done his best to provide accurate information and to point out potential hazards, conditions may change owing to weather and other factors. It is up to the users of this guide to learn the necessary skills for safe mountaineering and to exercise caution in potentially hazardous areas. Climbers using this book do so entirely at their own risk and the author and publisher disclaim any liability for injury or other damage that may be sustained by anyone using the access and/or mountaineering routes described.

Introduction

This book celebrates the high peaks of the Canadian Rockies and the often-forgotten history of those who made pioneering ascents on them. It also provides detailed descriptions of how to get up the standard and other good, moderate routes on these big mountains.

Specifically, this book focuses on the Rockies' peaks that exceed 11,000 feet or 3,353 metres in height. The 11,000ers, as these 54 peaks are commonly known, are spread out along and near the spine of the Rockies from Whitehorn in the northwest to Mount Harrison, more than 400 kilometres to the southeast.

The 11,000ers contain many of the most spectacular and best-known of the mountains in the Canadian Rockies and in their entirety represent a majestic tapestry difficult to surpass anywhere in the world. Besides their height, they often boast big faces, soaring ridgelines and—because of their elevation and latitude—significant amounts of encircling glaciation. It takes little convincing for mountaineers to attempt the obvious classics of this group such as Robson, Assiniboine, Athabasca, Edith Cavell, Alberta or Temple. These brand-name peaks are magnets for aspiring and seasoned mountaineers from around the world.

But many less-heralded 11,000ers are also well worth a visit—for the quality of rock (such as the West Ridge of Fryatt), for a big glacial expedition (Clemenceau) or for the spectacular scenery. Even peaks like Willingdon or Recondite, mostly tedious scrambles on loose rock, are situated in superb wilderness areas where few backpackers or climbers venture. Nancy Hansen, one of a handful of people to have climbed all the 11,000ers, estimates she ran into other climbers on only four of her 54 ascents.

If you climb many of the peaks in this book, you will explore a broad swath of the Rockies and be lured into many of its untrammeled corners. Indeed, the approaches and the often exquisite high campsites on the more remote expeditions are sometimes more memorable than the climbs.

Despite the infrequent visitors to many of the 11,000ers, the self-propelled access is mostly quite reasonable. All but a handful can be accessed by excellent paved highways, the few exceptions usually being good gravel logging roads. Likewise, the approaches on foot or ski are virtually all one day or less and mostly on good human and sometimes game trails, through relatively open forest. Only a couple of these peaks require nasty bushwhacking. Of course, if you're approaching 11,000ers outside the national parks, the more expensive option of hiring a helicopter is also available, though it does diminish the wilderness exploration aspect of these expeditions.

The 11,000ers

In descending order of height

Mount Robson – 3954 metres (12,972 feet)
✓Mount Columbia – 3747 (12,293)
✓North Twin – 3730 (12,237) – highest peak entirely in Alberta
Mount Clemenceau – 3658 (12,001)*
✓Twins Tower – 3640 (11,942)
Mount Alberta – 3619 (11,873)
✓Mount Assiniboine – 3618 (11,870) – highest peak in the southern Rockies
✓Mount Forbes – 3612 (11,850)
✓South Twin – 3580 (11,745)
✓Mount Goodsir, South Tower – 3562 (11,686)
✓Mount Temple – 3543 (11,624)
Mount Goodsir, North Tower – 3525 (11,565)
✓Lyell 2 (Edward Peak) – 3514 (11,529)
✓Lyell 3 (Ernest Peak) – 3511 (11,519)
Mount Bryce, Southwest Peak – 3507 (11,506)
✓Lyell 1 (Rudolph Peak) – 3507 (11,506)
✓Hungabee Mountain – 3492 (11,457)
✓Mount Athabasca – 3491 (11,453)
Mount King Edward – 3490 (11,450)
✓Mount Kitchener – 3480 (11,417)
Mount Brazeau – 3470 (11,384)
✓Mount Victoria, South Summit – 3464 (11,365)
✓Snow Dome – 3451 (11,322)
✓Mount Andromeda – 3450 (11,319)
✓Stutfield, West Peak – 3450 (11,319)
✓Mount Joffre – 3450 (11,319)
Resplendent Mountain – 3426 (11,240)
Tsar Mountain – 3424 (11,233)
Deltaform Mountain – 3424 (11,233)
✓Mount Lefroy – 3423 (11,230)
Mount King George – 3422 (11,227)
The Helmet – 3420 (11,220)
Mount Sir Douglas – 3406 (11,174)
✓Mount Woolley – 3405 (11,171)
✓Lyell 4 (Walter Peak) – 3400 (11,155)
Lunette Peak – 3400 (11,155)
Whitehorn Mountain – 3395 (11,138)
✓ Mount Hector – 3394 (11,135)
✓Lyell 5 (Christian Peak) – 3390 (11,122)
✓Stutfield, East Peak – 3390 (11,122)
✓Mount Victoria, North Summit – 3388 (11,115)
Mount Alexandra – 3388 (11,115)
Mount Goodsir, Centre Peak – 3384 (11,102)*
✓Mount Willingdon – 3373 (11,066)
✓Diadem Peak – 3371 (11,060)

Mount Bryce, Centre Peak – 3370 (11,056)
Mount Huber – 3368 (11,050)
Mount Edith Cavell – 3363 (11,033)
Mount Fryatt – 3361 (11,027)
✓Mount Cline – 3361 (11,027)
Tusk Peak – 3360 (11,023)*
✓West Twin – 3360 (11,023)*
✓Mount Harrison – 3359 (11,020)
Recondite Peak – 3356 (11,010)

* The Centre Peak of Mount Goodsir, West Twin and Tusk Peak were not included in the original list of 51 peaks that exceeded 11,000 feet. Tusk was previously thought to be below 11,000 feet, West Twin was unnamed, though listed in *The Rocky Mountains of Canada–North* guidebook and Centre Goodsir was not listed in *The Rocky Mountains of Canada–South*. Some would argue the latter two are not peaks at all but merely an extension of the South Twin and a bump in the col between the North and South Goodsirs, respectively. The most recent Imperial topo map doesn't show a 12,000-foot contour on Mount Clemenceau.

Near 11,000ers
Queens Peak – 3350 (10,991) – this height may be exaggerated as the attached Alexandra, listed at 3388 metres, seems significantly higher
Mount Saskatchewan – 3342 (10,964)
Mount Barnard – 3339 (10,955)
Willingdon South (Crown) – 3337 (10,948)
Mount Freshfield – 3336 (10,945)
Mount Murchison – 3333 (10,935)
Cataract Peak – 3333 (10,935)

Honourable Mentions
Mount Chown – 3331 (10,928)
Mount Shackleton, Centre Peak – 3330 (10,925)
Cromwell – 3330 (10,925)*
Catacombs Mountain – 3330 (10,925)
Unnamed (near Andromeda) – 3330 (10,925)
Oppy Mountain – 3330 (10,925)
Mount Amery – 3329 (10,922)

* Newer, metric maps show a 3360-metre (11,023-foot) contour on Cromwell and a 3350-metre (10,990-foot) contour on Mount Warren; the former is listed as 3330 metres and the latter only 3300 metres in *The Rocky Mountains of Canada-North*. Indeed, my handheld GPS readings from standing on these two summits is 11,006 feet for Cromwell and 11,030 for Warren, indicating the latter is a solid 11,000er candidate and the former is in the ballpark.

Why are these peaks high?

In 1827, when Scottish botanist David Douglas mistakenly estimated that Mounts Hooker and Brown were some 16,000 to 17,000 feet in elevation, he wasn't entirely wrong—his estimate was just a few million years too late.

At their greatest height, reached some 60–70 million years ago, many Canadian Rockies' peaks were probably on the order of 8,000 metres (26,250 feet) high, or about the same elevation as today's Mount Everest and other giants of the still-young Himalayas. Over the subsequent geological eons, the erosive powers of glaciation, running water and melt-freeze action—along with subsidence from the sheer weight of these mountains—brought the 11,000ers down to roughly their current height by about 60,000 years ago.

But not all Rockies peaks have eroded equally. According to geologist Ben Gadd, the two biggest, interacting forces in shaping individual mountains and determining their height have been the angle of their sedimentary bedrock and the effects of glaciation. During the ice ages, thick valley glaciers cut away at the slopes of the peaks, a lot of them made of rock layers tilted at a considerable angle. As the glaciers melted, the support for these undercut slabs was removed, causing massive rockslides that lowered the height of these peaks.

By contrast, today's higher peaks in the Canadian Rockies nearly all have horizontal or gently-tilted layers. This horizontal bedding is clearly visible in big peaks such as Robson, Assiniboine, Temple and Deltaform. Such flat-lying layers were much more resistant to undercutting during this period of extensive glaciation. Thus, the angle of the bedding planes—not the age, type or hardness of rock—is the primary factor in determining how high these peaks are today.

Many high peaks with horizontal bedding are found along the Continental Divide, which separates Alberta from British Columbia. It's also the crest of the main ranges, one of three long, narrow geological zones in the Canadian Rockies. The other two zones are the foothills and the front ranges, both found east of the main ranges. The rock of the foothills and front ranges is far more tilted and bent than the rock of the main ranges, so it has eroded more rapidly, leaving the main ranges generally higher.

The biggest collection of 11,000ers in the region is the dozen such peaks situated on and around the Columbia Icefield, which—no surprise—lies on the largest expanse of flat-lying rock in the Rockies. Similarly the Rockies' highest peak, Mount Robson, features a broad span of horizontal layers, even though it sits in a geological hole—the middle of a syncline, or down fold in the rock.

Glaciation is also responsible for the horn shape of such 11,000ers as Assiniboine, Tsar and Whitehorn. Here, glacial cirques on all sides of a peak have carved the rock into steep walls separated by sharp ridges, or arêtes.

As well, glaciers in the Canadian Rockies have carved existing river valleys into the deep, steep-sided glacial troughs we see today, providing the great, visually arresting topographic relief on many of the 11,000ers. For example, the difference in elevation between the valley floor and summit of Mount Robson is more than 3,000 metres, over a horizontal distance of only a few kilometres.

Even though the Colorado Rockies boast as many 14,000-foot peaks as the Canadian Rockies have 11,000-footers, none of those southern peaks come close to matching Robson's base-to-summit rise in elevation, and certainly not over such a short distance. In combination, these two factors—greater relief and steeper slopes—make it a lot more difficult to climb our 11,000ers than the 54 peaks that constitute the Colorado 14,000ers. Indeed, two men climbed all the "fourteeners" in 16 days; by far the quickest ascent by one person of all the 11,000ers is more than seven years.

How accurate are the summit elevations?

A very brief examination of our barometers showed that Mount Murchison would have to suffer the degradation which, sooner or later, is the lot of most mountains in this region… Possibly some future mountain explorer will bring it down further still until, as some American geographer predicted would one day be the fate of these mountains, it becomes a hole in the ground.
Norman Collie and Hugh Stutfield, 1903

In the monthly newsletter of the Calgary Section of the Alpine Club of Canada, a debate once raged for several issues over how many 11,000ers there actually were in the Canadian Rockies. Part of the discussion examined which peaks were true summits or just bumps on the ridge of a higher mountain. But the primary argument revolved around the accuracy of the official measurements of these peaks, given in metres above mean sea level. If accurate within about five metres, only a couple of peaks might be thrown out or added. But extend that margin of error to more than 10 metres and suddenly seven peaks (including Edith Cavell and Fryatt) could lose their 11,000er candidacy, while two might gain admission. If you had to climb everything 20 metres or less below the mark, just to be sure, another six peaks would be added to your list.

So just how accurate are the given heights for these peaks? Unfortunately, there's no easy, all-encompassing answer. Some are undoubtedly very accurate, others somewhat less so. It depends on the details of how they were measured, and more specifically on how much error can be expected in their height estimates.

In the early days of Rockies mountaineering and exploration, the amateur climbers were the mapmakers. On his 1902 expedition through the Rockies, James Outram packed a mountain transit with a tripod, a Watkin mountain aneroid, a pocket barometer, a sextant, a clinometer and a small plane table – plus a horse to carry them all. The scientific ardour of these pioneers helped lower the estimated height of many peaks. In the 1850s, for example, Palliser Expedition explorer James Hector estimated Mount Murchison's height to be 13,500 feet and said local Indians believed it was the highest peak in the Rockies. After standing on its summit with a barometer in 1902, Norman Collie revised the elevation to 11,300 feet; today's given height is 10,935.

Greater precision was brought to the job by professional surveyors, especially those who mapped the Alberta-B.C. boundary along the Continental Divide from 1913 to 1925. This magnificent effort—rivaling the climbing and exploration of pioneers such as Collie, Outram, Ostheimer and their guides—produced meticulous maps along the spine of the Rockies, from the U.S. border to north of Jasper. These maps provided the first reliable set of elevations for many of the 11,000ers (later surveys filled in some of the gaps, especially east of the divide).

When boundary survey leader Arthur Wheeler measured Mount Robson in 1911, he took readings from adjacent peaks, buttressed by very accurate benchmarks in the Fraser Valley. Still, he found that without a distinct signal, such as a rock cairn, on Robson's summit, his deduction of 13,068 feet was not absolute. "It is the fate of great peaks to have their reputed heights brought down, and I fancy that more extended observations will find Robson no exception to the rule," he observed. After more precise mapping in the early 1920s, Wheeler lowered the elevation to 12,972 feet, which remains the accepted height, ending all hopes of a 13,000er in the Canadian Rockies.

The next mapmaking breakthrough was aerial photography, translated into stereoscopic models. While many of the early surveyors' summit estimates remained essentially unchanged, others were adjusted up or down using this method. Although this technology has continued to evolve over the years, maps produced since the early 1970s have yielded roughly the same accuracy. Incidentally, the heights listed in the two *The Rocky Mountains of Canada* guidebooks were taken from the official topo maps of the 1960s.

When making maps from aerial photographs, mapmakers first establish vertical control points—recognizable features such as a lake or peak for which the elevation is known. These control points, however, are usually only accurate within about two to four metres, depending on the method used (by contrast, a benchmark from a ground-based survey is much more accurate; unfortunately, there are not a lot of them in the Rockies). The control point is then transferred to an air photo and aerotriangulated and is used as the basis for adding contour lines and spot heights to the map. But the processes of aerotriangulation, line plotting and printing all add little bits of error.

What this means is contour lines on 1:50,000 topo maps for the 11,000ers are roughly accurate to within half of the contour interval. For a map with 40-metre contours, the vertical accuracy is thus about 20 metres. The accuracy of spot elevations is about one-third the contour interval—within about 13 metres on the same map. Again, the elevation accuracy of a specific peak could be better or worse, depending on the accuracy of the control point.

Around 1990, the B.C. government began producing a series of Terrain Resource Information Management (TRIM) maps, on a 1:20,000 scale with 20-metre contour lines, covering the province (roughly 30 of the 11,000ers are either in B.C. or on the Alberta-B.C. border). These TRIM maps were generated from digital elevation models, based on aerial photography taken in the mid-1980s. They are said to have an elevation accuracy of about five metres for both contour lines and spot elevations. In some cases, the heights they list for 11,000ers are somewhat different than the official guidebooks—for example, 3442 metres for Athabasca, versus 3491 in the guidebook, and 3442, versus 3423, for Lefroy. The TRIM map lists Mount Huber as only 3348 metres (20 below the guidebook listing), which if accurate would drop it from the 11,000er club.

The newer, metric maps add to the confusion, changing the height of some 11,000ers and even offering two new candidates to the group, Mount Warren and Cromwell. Whether these changes are the result of newer, more accurate information or reflect a greater range of error because of the larger contour interval is hard to say. Muddying things even further are the 11,000er offerings of the *Atlas of Canada* (produced by Natural Resources Canada), which have variations, from the guidebook, as large as 70 metres and which lists Goodsir's North Tower as higher than the South Tower. Some of these are clearly wrong.

Science does have a more precise answer, called the Global Positioning System (GPS), which may eventually resolve this puzzle. If you carry a pocket GPS unit to a summit and can contact sufficient satellites, a pretty good elevation measurement can be attained, though probably in the same range of error as the map (indeed, my GPS reading on the summit of Sunwapta Peak was within a few metres of the guidebook listing of 3315 metres, compared with the the *Atlas of Canada* listing of 3360 metres, the lat-

"The Roof," upper SE Ridge of Mt. Robson. Photo: Doug Fulford.

ter which would make it an 11,000er). A much better answer is differential GPS, where a ground station is located within a reasonable distance of the peak. If simultaneous readings are taken from this station and from a sophisticated portable GPS unit on the summit, the result should be vertically accurate within centimetres.

The only problem, aside from accessing this expensive equipment, is having someone haul at least several kilograms of GPS gear in a pack to the summit, while a second person monitors the ground station. This might not be too arduous for straightforward, accessible peaks like Athabasca or Temple, but are there any volunteers for Alberta or Recondite?

In the meantime, it's probably best to go with the heights listed in the *The Rocky Mountains of Canada* guidebooks, which seem the most accurate as a whole. These are the ones I've used in this book.

Opposite: A near 11,000er, the gorgeous Mt. Shackleton, from Tusk Pk.

A short history of the 11,000ers

The history of alpine climbing in the Canadian Rockies has always been closely tied to the 11,000ers. The earliest mountaineers were almost exclusively after these big virgin peaks, bagging all but a handful of them by the late 1920s. Over the ensuing decades, the 11,000ers remained in the forefront as climbers put up new and increasingly harder routes. As attention turned in the 1960s to north faces and winter ascents, the giants of the Rockies were again most often the testing grounds.

It all started with a myth. Passing fur traders and early explorers noticed these high peaks but lacked the inclination or time to scale any. The exception was Scottish botanist David Douglas (the Douglas fir is named after him), who made the second recorded ascent of a Canadian Rockies peak in 1827, while crossing Athabasca Pass, south of Jasper, with Hudson's Bay Company traders. He named the peak Mount Brown and claimed its height was 16,000 or 17,000 feet, "the highest yet known elevation in the northern continent of America." He estimated a nearby peak, which he named Mount Hooker, was nearly as high.

The publication of this news created a furor in Europe and North America, as these alleged giants soared above the Alps' highest peak, Mont Blanc (15,780 feet). "A high mountain is always a seduction but a mountain with a mystery is doubly so," wrote Toronto geology professor Arthur Coleman, the first explorer to seriously search for these monsters. But when he arrived at the pass in 1893, he was mystified to find no nearby peak higher than about 9,200 feet. Douglas had apparently relied on someone's earlier and vastly inflated estimate of Athabasca Pass's height, though he also didn't notice other area peaks were much higher, including Hooker, which in reality is nearly 10,800 feet.

The Brown-Hooker myth was exposed, but it had fired imaginations for so long that American explorer Walter Wilcox and British climber Norman Collie felt compelled to do their own searches a few years later. A thorough review of Douglas's writings finally convinced Collie that Coleman was right. But by then, the early mountaineers were already enthralled by this magnificent wilderness with all these big, gorgeous, unclimbed peaks.

Coleman, more an explorer than a climber, never got up any of the big peaks he approached, including Mounts Clemenceau (1892), Brazeau (1902) and Robson (1907-08).

Joseph Hickson (l.) and guide Edward Feuz, Sr. (Courtesy Whyte Museum of the Canadian Rockies).

Guide Hans Fuhrer (l) and 19-year-old Alfred Ostheimer III, along with Jean Weber (r) in 1927.
Photo: A.J. Ostheimer Collection (Courtesy Whyte Museum of the Canadian Rockies).

Wilcox, Samuel Allen and other members of Yale University's Lake Louise Club were slightly better mountaineers, finding the easy way up Mount Temple in 1894, thus bagging the first Canadian Rockies 11,000er.

Ironically, it was the 1896 death of a much finer American climber, Philip Abbot, on Mount Lefroy that prompted the introduction of Swiss guides and thus changed the face of subsequent Rockies climbing. Armed with guide Peter Sarbach, a team led by Collie and American Charles Fay easily scaled Lefroy and Mount Victoria's South Summit the next year, though Collie may have been Sarbach's technical equal. Indeed, Collie and compatriots Herman Woolley and Hugh Stutfield ventured north unguided the following year, getting up Mount Athabasca and two other 11,000ers.

A fellow Brit, the lanky James Outram, arrived in the Rockies in 1900, ironically to recover from "a brain collapse from overwork" as an Anglican vicar. Apparently, running up a rapid succession of big peaks was just the cure. Whereas Collie seemed as interested in exploring and mapmaking as getting up these untrodden peaks, Outram was more narrowly focused on the prize. Though he lacked the financial resources of his more well-heeled British and American counterparts, his first ascent of Mount Assiniboine in 1901

prompted the Canadian Pacific Railway to put Christian Kaufmann, the finest of the early Rockies' guides, at his disposal the next year.

The skill of Kaufmann, the ambition of Outram and the apparently inexhaustible energy of both produced their magical summer of 1902. In a few weeks, they made first ascents of five 11,000ers including Mount Columbia, Mount Forbes (along with Collie's party) and Mount Bryce, the latter by far the hardest Rockies' climb of its time and still a stiff test. This peakbagging binge seemed to satiate Outram, who never climbed seriously again. The next year, Kaufmann added to his resume, guiding first ascents of three of the southern Rockies' hardest, loosest peaks—Goodsir's South Tower, Hungabee and Deltaform, all with American Herschel Parker—before returning to Switzerland for good with his guiding brother Hans.

As more of these big southern mountains were climbed, focus shifted to the Canadian Rockies' highest peak, Mount Robson, resulting in agony and ecstasy for two men. Reverend George Kinney's obsession with this mountain led to three long expeditions and many heroic attempts, mostly in foul weather. After a desperate push for the top with Curly Phillips, Kinney claimed victory in 1909, but others soon doubted whether they actually made it to the

13

top. Four years later, Robson became Austrian guide Conrad Kain's crowning moment, as he led two amateurs up the 50-degree Northeast (Kain) Face and then went down the other side of this massive mountain.

The years following World War I were dominated by Americans Howard Palmer and Monroe Thorington—who collaborated on the first Canadian Rockies guide book—and Joseph Hickson, the only Canadian to play a prominent role in the first ascents of 11,000ers. A frontpiece photo on Thorington's and Palmer's book inspired an unwieldy team of six Japanese climbers and three guides to make the audacious 1925 ascent of the hardest 11,000er, Mount Alberta.

On the first ascent of three of the Lyell peaks in 1926, Thorington was guided by Edward Feuz, Jr. and joined by 18-year-old Alfred Ostheimer III, who proved the inheritor of Outram's peak-bagging crown. A year later, this energetic, ambitious Harvard student teamed with another great guide, Hans Fuhrer, to climb 30 peaks in 60 days, including first ascents of four 11,000ers on the Columbia and Clemenceau Icefields. But like Outram before him, he suddenly disappeared from the climbing scene.

With today's equipment, training and shunning of guides by top climbers, there is a tendency to downplay the achievements of these early Rockies mountaineers. But they truly pushed the known limits. Though they often had a month or more at their disposal, they had to travel long distances on horseback—with much bushwhacking, routefinding and river fording—just to reach mountains with no known route of ascent. They often ended up climbing the loosest route on the mountain, equipped with only a hemp rope, hobnailed boots and no protection. Consider that Kain, with neither crampons nor ice screws, had to cut 600 boot-sized steps to get up the steep, icy Northeast Face of Robson. Today, anyone who climbs long, loose routes like Mount Bryce's Northeast Ridge or Mount Forbes's collapsing Southwest Ridge truly appreciates how skilled and physically and mentally tough these pioneers were.

The majority of the loftier mountains (in the Canadian Rockies) will not test the skill of the modern Alpine gymnast very severely.
Norman Collie and Hugh Stutfield, 1903

With the close of the golden age of big-peak first ascents around 1930, there was little exploratory climbing during the Depression years. Notable exceptions were Hans Wittich and Otto Stegmaier claiming the East Ridge of Temple (IV, 5.7) in

1931, Hans Fuhrer guiding a party up the Fuhrer (North) Ridge (IV, 5.4) of Robson in 1938 and Rex Gibson and Sterling Hendricks becoming the first to ascend all four 12,000-foot peaks (Robson, Columbia, North Twin and Clemenceau). The early 1930s also marked the introduction of ski mountaineering in the Rockies, with ascents of such 11,000ers as Resplendent, Edith Cavell and many of the Columbia Icefield peaks. The war years and early 1950s were an even drier stretch, ending with Don Claunch, Mike Sherrick and Harvey Firestone finally getting up Robson's Wishbone Arête in 1955, more than four decades after guide Walter Schauffelberger's heroic attempt.

The next frontier was the big north faces, starting with legendary figures Yvon Chouinard and Fred Beckey leading the first climb of Edith Cavell's north wall. Brian Greenwood, the finest local climber of his generation, upped the ante with his and Charlie Locke's ascent of Temple's glacier-capped North Face in 1966. In the early 1970s, George Lowe and companions (including North American climbing historian Chris Jones) raised the bar much higher with daring ascents of north walls on Mount Alberta and Twins Tower, the latter still perhaps the hardest alpine climb in the Rockies. Transplanted South African David Cheesmond later spurred local efforts to this level, leading first ascents of Robson's Emperor Face, Goodsir South Tower's North Face and the East Face of Assiniboine.

Winter ascents were also *de rigueur* during this period, starting with Fred Beckey and Leif -Norman Pattersen's ascent of Robson's Kain Face in 1965, followed by Greenwood, Locke and Chic Scott claiming Hungabee's standard route the following winter. American Himalyan superstar Carlos Buhler really pushed those limits in 1976 and 1977 with dead-of-winter, multi-day epics on the north faces of Temple and Deltaform.

The next evolution on the 11,000ers was mixed alpine ice routes, centred on the big ice faces of the Columbia Icefield near the Icefields Parkway. Jeff Lowe and Mike Weis started with a first ascent of Mount Kitchener's Grand Central Couloir (V, 5.9, A2, WI5) in 1975, followed by Tobin Sorenson's and Jack Robert's winter climb of the same route in 1978. John Lauchlan and Jim Elzinga made the first winter ascents of both Mount Kitchener's Ramp Route (V, 5.8, A1) in 1977 and Snow Dome's Slipstream (IV, WI4) in 1979. Cheesmond teamed up with Barry Blanchard and Tim Friesen to complete Andromeda Strain (V, 5.9, A2, WI4) in 1983.

In the fall of 2002, Blanchard, the first great Canadian-born climber of big alpine faces in the Rockies, finally finished the 2200-metre Infinite Patience (VI, WI5, M5, 5.9) route up the Emperor

Face using the latest techniques in mixed climbing. This is the future frontier for the 11,000ers, as today's rising stars—many of them based in Canmore—bring their often acrobatic ice and mixed skills to the big walls and ridges of the Canadian Rockies.

More detailed accounts of the first ascents can be found under each of the 11,000ers. The amateurs who climbed these pioneering routes were often articulate writers, and it's one of the pleasures of writing this book to revive portions of their accounts from dusty alpine journals.

The 11,000er Club

Many readers of this book will choose to climb only the easiest, most accessible or most famous of the 11,000ers. Others will content themselves with those that offer solid rock or snow/ice routes, good ski runs or big glacier expeditions. This book is not intended as a tick list, a holy grail to those wanting to climb all the 11,000ers. But if you choose to do so, be forewarned that it takes a lot of perseverance and single-mindedness, likely over more than a decade. To climb all these peaks, Nancy Hansen estimates she drove 26,000 kilometres (3,000 on logging roads), hiked 2,000 kilometres and climbed 120,000 vertical metres.

As of early 2004, six climbers are known to have climbed all the 11,000ers. The torchbearer was Don Forest, who didn't start climbing until his early 40s but quickly made up for lost time with his boundless energy and enthusiasm. Climbing many of these peaks with a loose collection of Calgary-area mountaineers known as the Grizzly Group, Don climbed Lunette Peak, his last 11,000er in 1979. He subsequently became the first, and perhaps still the only, person to climb all 16 of the 11,000ers in B.C.'s Interior Ranges, and he scaled Mount Logan at the age of 71. Don died suddenly in late 2003, at the age of 83, while ski touring. It would be a fitting tribute if all the 11,000ers in the Canadian Rockies became collectively known as "the Forests."

Rick Collier followed in 1994, climbing his last five 11,000ers in a sudden flourish. Rick has also climbed such far-flung giants as the highest peaks in Canada (Logan) and South America (Aconcagua). In 2004, he was nearing the completion of a more impressive and likely never to be repeated feat—scaling all the nearly 600 named peaks in the southern Canadian Rockies.

I was the third to finish, in 2002, only because my 11,000er mentors, Forbes Macdonald and Roman Pachovsky, got stymied for many years by their last and most difficult peak, Mount Alberta, which they finally summited in August, 2003. Forbes and Roman were unusual in that

Don Forest. Photo: Glen Boles.

they climbed all but a handful of these peaks together. They were also notorious for scaling many of the more remote 11,000ers in about half the usual time. I accompanied them on one such trip, for example, in which we climbed all five Lyell Peaks and Mount Forbes in a four-day, self-propelled push, including the drive from and back to Calgary.

Nancy Hansen, who climbed all these peaks in less than half the time of her predecessors, became the first woman to climb all the 11,000ers, finishing with Mount Forbes in September, 2003. As well, she climbed many of these peaks by harder routes, including the East Ridge of Temple, the complete West Ridge of Mount Fryatt, the North Ridge of Mount Cline, and the East Ridge of Sir Douglas.

Jason Thompson completed the quest in 2005 and Colin Jones in 2007. Perhaps one or two others have quietly and anonymously finished as well.

How to use this book

These mountains make the Colorado 14,000ers look like a walk in the park.
Calgary climber and author Alan Kane

It's been said that if you can climb in the Canadian Rockies, you can climb anywhere in the world. That's because there are so many variables to deal with, most beyond your control.

First and foremost is the nature of the rock, which is predominantly limestone. While it can rear up in solid faces, the limestone encountered on most of these 11,000er routes tends to be shattered and loose. This can range from the merely tedious—big scree slopes or low-angled ledges covered in rubble—to the truly frightening—steeper lines where protection and solid holds are scarce for long, run-out stretches—though the rock tends to be reasonable where belayed climbing is needed. About the only good news is limestone, unlike granite or quartzite, is usually not much worse when wet. Mostly, it just takes getting used to, which means Rockies' newcomers are well advised to start with something considerably below their usual climbing comfort level.

Then, there's the weather. Other than the infrequent big high-pressure system, the weather is unpredictable from day to day, often changing several times within a day. Two pieces of hard-earned advice: Don't trust a forecast more than a couple of days into the future and, particularly on peaks with long approaches, leave yourself enough time to have two shots at the summit. This strategy includes attempting the summit on your approach day if the weather's good and you have sufficient time and energy to get up and down safely. As well, be prepared for snow or at least freezing rain any time of the year. Fresh or remnant snow, for example, can turn a pleasant, near scramble on the North Ridge of Mount Assiniboine into a scary siege.

Other objective hazards while climbing Rockies 11,000ers include rock and serac fall, crevasses and avalanches (no snakes or poisonous insects, though). This means always wear a helmet, unless you're wandering across a big glacier, and beware of steeper slopes with fresh or softening snow. As well, glaciers are receding rapidly in the Canadian Rockies, throwing more yawning crevasses and steep, serac-like formations at climbers. A growing number of approaches and routes are thus becoming more problematic and some are already nearly impassable in dry years, such as the approach to the West Ridge of Whitehorn Mountain.

Routefinding is another challenge on these big peaks. While the "cattle track" can be followed up the standard, North Glacier route on Mount Athabasca, many 11,000er routes see little traffic, and cairns may be nonexistent or misleading. Big, low-angled face routes often involve wandering back and forth looking for the best line, which can vary significantly depending on conditions. Detours are also common on ridges to circumvent steep steps. The bottom line is don't turn off your brain and blindly follow the route description.

Unlike, say, the cushy Alps, approaches to the 11,000ers are often a full day on foot, with lots of elevation gain and perhaps some route finding and river crossings thrown in, all with a big pack. Fortunately, the travel is mostly along some sort of trail and through open, often spectacular country, with little of the bushwhacking that ranges to the west are infamous for.

So what skills are needed to climb the 11,000ers? Virtually all the routes described in this book require no more than intermediate technical climbing or backcountry skiing ability. What you need is the wide range of skills and experiences to handle technical rock, glaciers and snow or ice slopes of 35 to 50 degrees; sometimes you'll encounter all three on a single climb. You should also be adept at navigation, crevasse rescue, avalanche assessment and rescue (particularly on ski trips) and wilderness first aid.

Beyond skill, there are a couple of things that will largely determine your success at getting up many of these 11,000ers. The first is fitness and endurance. Reaching and climbing many of these peaks involves long days, considerable packs and lots of elevation gain, often on backsliding scree or post-holing snow. The second prerequisite is mental. While many of these routes are not technically difficult, they demand an ability to move efficiently, and usually unroped, over long stretches of fourth-class terrain that is exposed, loose and hard to protect. A final necessity is self-reliance. Because many of these peaks are far from civilization and thus rescue, you have to be prepared to look after yourself, though a satellite phone can be used to summon the cavalry in an emergency.

As part of each peak entry, there is a short summary of what is involved in getting up the described routes. This summary is divided into six categories:

First Ascent

This lists the date, the climbers (with the guides' names italicized) and the route of the first ascent of the peak. Wherever possible, the exact date and full names of the climbers are given. Subsequent first ascents of other routes on the mountain are mentioned in the history section.

Routes Described

For every peak but one (Mount Athabasca) in this guide, there are one to two routes described in detail. If just one route is listed, it is generally the standard and most straightforward one up the mountain. A second, usually somewhat harder, route is added if it offers good, interesting and/or especially scenic climbing. In a few cases, this second route is similar in grade to the first and merely provides a different line up the peak. Recommended routes are noted as such in italics. There are no described routes beyond the ability of experienced intermediate Rockies' climbers. While some expert routes are mentioned in passing or in the history section of each peak, none are described in detail.

Grades

Each described route is assigned a grade, which collectively should be taken as a very general guide to the technical and objective difficulties one might expect on these routes under reasonable conditions. Snow or ice on rock routes, faces covered in deep, wet snow or thin snow over crumbly ice can make the climbing much harder.

The ratings used here are a combination of overall grades—the National Climbing Classification System (NCCS), in Roman numerals I to VI - and technical rock grades, using the Yosemite Decimal System (5.0-5.14) for sections requiring belayed climbing. Many of the routes have just an NCCS rating, while those with technical rock will show a combined grading, eg. II, 5.3.

The Yosemite system rates the hardest move on a climb and is well understood by most North American climbers. On alpine climbs, it can be somewhat misleading. On the South Ridge of Tusk Peak, for example, a rock grade of 5.4 is given, even though there are only a couple of moves that require a belay, on a section that can be avoided entirely. By contrast, there is sustained, loose rock climbing on Mount Alberta's East Face, even though most of it falls well below the given grade of 5.6/5.7. Read the route descriptions under each peak for a more detailed description of what to expect.

The NCCS overall grade considers such things as the length of the route in distance and time, the average difficulty and hardest pitch, how sustained the difficulties are, the difficulty of retreat and descent, and the remoteness of the mountain. It then weighs these technical and objective difficulties to come up with a grade. The definition of the resulting grade is hopelessly vague, eg. a Grade I is a "route that includes a technical portion (of any difficulty), which generally requires only a few hours." In this book, readers can generally assume the following:

I An easy, generally low-angled route that can be climbed in a few hours, with almost no technical difficulties expected. Examples: Southwest Ridge of Mount Temple, South Slopes of Mount Kitchener, North Ridge of North Twin (though some may say the length and objective hazards of the approach on the latter two might justify a II rating).

II A moderate climb, with some technical difficulties, on rock, snow and/or ice that may require most of the day to get up and down. The large majority of routes in this book fall into this rather loose category. Examples range from the straightforward North Glacier of Mount Athabasca to the steeper West Face of Mount Lefroy to the big, remote and wandering West Face of Mount Clemenceau.

III An advanced, fairly technical climb on steep terrain that will likely consume most of the day. Example: North Face of Mount Athabasca (III, 5.4/5.5).

IV A long day on a long route with sustained technical climbing. Examples: Kain Face of Mount Robson, East Ridge of Mount Temple (IV, 5.7).

V Steep, sustained technical climbing in a remote setting. Be prepared for a bivouac. The East Face of Mount Alberta (V, 5.6/5.7) is the only described route in this book thus graded.

Gear

This is a quick but by no means exhaustive summary of what technical gear most parties will need to get up a route. Some people will choose to take more, others less, depending on current conditions and their comfort level. A typical alpine rack might consist of a small selection of nuts, half a dozen camming devices, half a dozen runners and webbing and cordelette for building anchors and rappel stations; in some cases, pitons and a hammer are also needed. It's assumed that climbers will know what other basic gear to take (always wear a helmet when climbing anything but a low-angled glacier route in the Rockies). If you don't know what "glacier gear" means, you probably shouldn't be on a glacier; carrying a few ice screws on a glacier trip is almost always a good idea. Pickets tend to work better than deadmen in the Rockies' snow pack; in winter or powdery snow, either may provide only illusory protection.

Maps

These are the 1:50,000 federal topographic maps that in most cases are indispensable to finding your way to and up these routes. In some cases, an additional map is listed for the vehicle access to the approach and climb. While some of these maps are still available in Imperial (feet) measurements, they are steadily being replaced with metric versions, the most recent which have abysmal contour intervals of 40 or, in some cases, 50 metres (which translates to an interval of 131 and 165 feet, respectively, compared with 100 feet for the old Imperial maps).

That brings me to the metres/feet conundrum of this book. Canada has long been officially metric, but for an even longer time the peaks in this book have been widely and affectionately known as the 11,000ers, indicating their height in feet. No one refers to them as the 3,353ers, the metric equivalent of 11,000 feet. To produce a nice, catchy round number, you'd either have to go up to 3,400 metres (only 34 peaks on that list) or down to 3,300 metres, expanding it some 100. I have thus landed squarely in the middle of this debate, using metric numbers generally and Imperial ones in historic references. If you want to convert metres to feet, multiply by 3.2808 (3.3 rounded off); for feet to metres, multiply by .3048.

Grid References

Throughout the text are six-digit grid references (eastings, or horizontal numbers, before northings, or vertical), which usually provide the most accurate means of indicating a location on the map. Unfortunately, this creates another dilemma. The old, mostly imperial 1:50,000 maps used North American Datum 1927 (known as NAD 27), while the new, mostly metric, ones use 1983 datum (NAD 83), which more precisely locate those one-kilometre blue grid boxes on the map; the bottom of the map will tell you which system is being used. Thus the grid references are slightly different for NAD 83

maps than for NAD 27 ones. These differences won't matter much if the grid reference is given to provide a rough location, but it can matter if you're trying to find a col or the start of an indistinct ridge.

Because every 1:50,000 topo map referred to in this book (except for 82 J/2 Mount Peck, used for climbing Mount Harrison) is now available only in NAD 83, I've chosen, for consistency, to provide all grid references in this newer format. What this means is people with older, NAD 27, maps will have to make slight adjustments when using the grid references. Each map's conversion numbers are slightly different (they're listed on the bottom of the new maps), but on average you'll add about 80 metres to the easting and subtract about 200 metres from the northing when using a NAD 27 map. That means if the grid reference given is 452856, those with NAD 27 maps will have to change that reference to 453854.

Season

This provides a rough guide to when these peaks and routes are usually in shape and most often climbed, though some can be ascended in winter or during the shoulder seasons. The summer alpine season in the Canadian Rockies is notoriously short, with many big peaks having too much snow on them to climb until the second or third week of July. By mid-September, the rock routes are often too snowy or too icy or the days too short. Add unpredictable weather, and it's easy to see why it's generally hard, unless you're obsessed, to get up more than a handful of 11,000ers in a summer. The good news is there are more than a dozen 11,000ers one can tackle on skis, adding a couple of spring months to the climbing season.

Time

It's with considerable reluctance that I suggest time frames for climbing peaks. Under good conditions, fast, competent parties might climb some of these routes in half the suggested time, especially if they choose not to rope up on ones like the East Ridge of Mount Edith Cavell or the Southeast Ridge of South Victoria. By contrast, bad conditions can add hours to a climb, particularly if the party is inexperienced, large or occasionally off route. The listed hours are only intended as a rough guideline of what a fit team might take to get up and down a route under reasonably good conditions.

Opposite: The magnificent N Ridge of Lyell 4 from Lyell 3. Photo: Nancy Hansen.

Robson Group Approaches

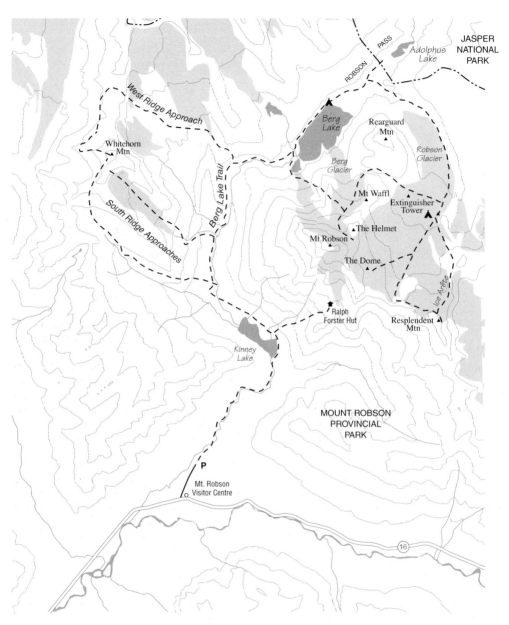

The Robson Group

Perched on the northwest lip of the Canadian Rockies, the four 11,000ers in Mount Robson Provincial Park are far removed from the other high peaks of the range. After driving an hour northwest of the low mountain town of Jasper (500 metres lower than Lake Louise) and descending steadily for the last 10 minutes into the depths of the Fraser River Valley, it's surprising to see any 11,000ers at all, let alone be confronted by the sudden, monstrous mass of Mount Robson.

While Robson is the obvious jewel and the highest peak in the Rockies, the surrounding three 11,000ers are also gorgeous, glaciated gems. Three of the four peaks are clustered above the heavily-fractured cirque at the head of Robson Glacier—Robson in the middle, connected by cols to The Helmet to the northeast and to Resplendent Mountain to the southeast. To the near west lies Whitehorn Mountain.

The glaciated view of these peaks from Berg Lake is matched by the 3,000-metre rise of Robson's south flanks, as seen from the highway visitor centre. This base-to-summit uplift, over a horizontal distance of only three kilometres, is not far below that of Mount Everest and is unrivalled in the Canadian or U.S. Rocky Mountains.

The reasons for this are a combination of geology and erosion. As geologist and explorer Arthur Coleman noted in the early 1900s, Robson is ironically the lowest structural point in the region, at the bottom of a synclinal fold. But the "slightly compressed and, therefore, strengthened parts of the syncline" have over time suffered less from the destructive forces of glaciers, weather and runoff than the "more expanded and shattered forms around it, once probably parts of anticlines," Coleman wrote. In particular, Robson's colourful, horizontal bands of limestones and quartzites, clearly visible in its southwest flanks, are much more resistant to erosion than surrounding peaks with tilted bedding planes. The great depth of the valley below the South Face is largely the result of the tremendous eroding action of the Fraser River over the ages.

Access From Jasper, drive 89 km west on Highway 16 to the Mount Robson Viewpoint and Visitor Centre. Go 2 km north to a parking lot beside the Robson River. The approaches for all four 11,000ers in this group start up the Berg Lake Trail, which leaves from this parking lot. Bicycles are allowed on the trail as far as the Kinney Lake Campground (7 km, 130 metres of elevation gain), though descending cyclists should take care to respect the many hikers going to and from Kinney Lake. See the individual peak descriptions for approach details.

Mount Robson Visitor Centre It's a good idea to call the visitor centre (250-566-4325) before leaving home to check on current climbing conditions, which can be much different than elsewhere in the Rockies. One problem particular to this area is it often doesn't freeze at night, even at high elevations, before mid-August. When arriving, it's worth checking the centre's collection of climbing route photos and descriptions.

Facilities A gas station next to the visitor centre has some groceries, with more extensive supplies available in Jasper or in Valemount, B.C, to the near west. There's roadside camping near the visitor centre and eight backcountry campgrounds along the Berg Lake Trail, the latter requiring an overnight permit (fee) from the visitor centre. While most sites at these backcountry campgrounds are first come, first served, a limited number can be reserved (phone toll-free 1-800-689-9025 or check www.discovercamping.ca). The Ralph Forster Hut, at the base of Mount Robson's South Face route, is also available on a first-come, first-served basis (see page 28)

There is a voluntary self-registration box for climbers at the Berg Lake trailhead. Two ranger stations are located along the Berg Lake Trail, at the Whitehorn campground and at the north end of Berg Lake. To fly in to the Robson Glacier area, phone Yellowhead Helicopters (250-566-4401) in nearby Valemount, B.C.

Mt. Robson in 1988 from Resplendent Mtn. A. Icefall approach.
B. Alternative approach. C. The Dome. D. Kain Face.

Mount Robson
3954 metres (12,972 feet)

Mount Robson is truly the Monarch of the Canadian Rockies. It stands more than 200 metres higher than any other 11,000er and is the only near 13,000er. Robson is awesome from any aspect, with the Everest-like 3000-metre rise of its southern wall and the spectacular shattered glaciers and huge faces on its northern flanks. Where other 11,000ers are lucky to be blessed with two good climbing routes, Robson boasts half a dozen classic lines, ranging from the storied Kain and North Faces to the mammoth Wishbone Arête and Emperor Ridge, capped with their feathery ice gargoyles.

Robson is a big, serious mountain that should never be taken lightly. As two hardened Brits who spent four days climbing the Emperor Ridge and descending the Kain Face put it: "The scale and sense of commitment was far greater than we had ever experienced in the Alps." While the South, Kain and even North Faces can offer straightforward step kicking up solid snow, things can quickly go awry when climbing conditions deteriorate, crevasses beckon or Robson's notoriously bad weather moves in. Suddenly, you're a long way from the safety of camp and a candidate for one of the many epics on this mountain.

Conditions on Robson can vary tremendously from year to year, with approaches and route sections in good shape one year and impassable the next. After some wet springs and early summers, the mountain never gets into climbing shape. Consider that in 2000 only two of 41 parties made it to the summit by any route. Even in normal years, only about 15 per cent of aspiring teams succeed, in part because many parties' ambition exceeds their skill and experience.

The South Face is the quickest and easiest way up the mountain, with a mid-mountain hut from which to launch a summit bid. Be prepared, though, for a nearly 1700-metre scramble on the approach up dry slopes to the Ralph Forster Hut. Objective hazards on the route include crevasses and serac fall, particularly while crossing the notorious Schwartz Ledges. While the upper face below the summit roof is generally no more than 40 degrees, it's a long, long ways down the Great Couloir if you slip. The long hours on this route can thus be mentally taxing, especially under marginal conditions or in a whiteout.

The Kain Face, which follows the first ascent line, is the classic route on the mountain, with great positions in a spectacular setting. This route can be broken into three distinct sections. The first is the long approach up the Robson Glacier, capped by picking one's way through the shifting icefall (often the crux of the expedition) to a base camp on The Dome. The second is the 300-metre Northeast (Kain) Face, which can range from a staircase of steps to hard ice to, worst, soft snow over crumbly ice. I've seen a party waltz up this 40 to 50-degree slope in an hour, while another spent more than half a day gingerly down climbing and lowering while the surface snow slithered around them. The third section is the Southeast Ridge, which can spring a surprise when one steeper step is riddled with crevasses or guarded by ice formations.

After all the effort of getting up any route on Robson, the actual summit—a little snow bump on a bit of broader ridge—is a bit anticlimactic. The summit views, which are all down, are also not as good as from the surrounding peaks, though the glimpse down the fantastically feathered Emperor Ridge is unique. But the warm glow of knowing you made it all the way up, and down, this big and most challenging of mountains lasts a long time.

Deciphering the true origins of Robson's name can be as difficult as climbing the mountain. Theories range from 19th-century fur traders Joseph Robson and Colin Robertson to newspaper publisher and later B.C. premier John Robson. No one knows for sure, but Robson is neither as aptly descriptive as one early name, Cloud Cap Mountain, nor as evocative as the Shuswap term *Yuh-hai-has-kun*, meaning Mountain of the Spiral Road, for the distinctive coloured rock bands on the South Face.

History
Mount Robson was brought to wider attention by the 1865 publication of William Milton's and Walter Cheadle's book *The North-west Passage by Land*, in which they described a "giant among giants and immeasurably supreme" and estimated the peak's height at "ten thousand or fifteen thousand feet." Although geological surveyor James McEvoy whittled that elevation down to 13,700 feet in 1898, the interest of mountain explorers was soon whetted.

The early attempts on Robson are unmatched in Rockies' history for hardship and struggle, courage, foolhardiness and controversy. The first protagonists were brothers Arthur and Quincy Coleman and Reverend George Kinney, who made two long treks to Robson from Lake Louise in 1907 and 1908. Bad weather limited the first trip to exploring the mountain's base, and frequent storms frustrated the 1908 climbing forays, which included a trip to the top of The Dome and a solo ascent by Kinney to a height of some 3200 metres on the northwest slopes.

In the spring of 1909, Kinney heard that a renowned British team, led by Arnold Mumm and Leopold Amery, had designs on the virgin summit. So he quickly set out alone from Edmonton equipped with three packhorses, three months of provisions and $2.85 in his pocket. En route, he enlisted 25-year-old outfitter Curly Phillips, who had no climbing experience and a stick cut from the bush in lieu of an ice axe. After many aborted attempts and close calls with avalanches, their provisions were down to subsistence stews of marmot and grouse. In a last desperate effort, they scaled the difficult west side of the mountain below the upper Emperor Ridge.

"On all that upper climb we did nearly the whole work on our toes and hands only," Kinney wrote. "The clouds were a blessing in a way, for they shut out the view of the fearful depths below. A single slip any time during that day meant a slide to death. At times the storm was so thick that we could see but a few yards, and the sleet would cut our faces and nearly blind us. Our clothes and hair were one frozen mass of snow and ice."

Once on the summit ridge, they floundered through the "treacherous masses" of crystal-like gargoyles and at last, in dense cloud, claimed the summit. A few years later, however, Phillips apparently admitted he and Kinney were stopped by a small dome just shy of the actual top.

Though controversy still rages over whether the summit was actually reached, Kinney's claim had been generally discounted by 1913, when the Alpine Club of Canada set up its annual camp below Robson. This marked Austrian guide Conrad Kain's finest moment as he cut some 600 ice and hard snow steps while leading Albert MacCarthy and William Foster (both later on the first ascent of Mount Logan) up the Northeast Face and Southeast Ridge. Stepping onto the summit at 5:30 p.m., Kain turned and said, "Gentlemen, that's so far as I can take you."

Robson was mastered, but the adventure was not over. Kain was half snow blind, the rope and the climbers' damp clothing were almost frozen and their ascending steps had melted away. They traversed the mountain as Kain, again cutting steps, sought a safe way down the fractured glacier on the unknown south side. After bivouacking on a rock ledge above 3000 metres, they limped back to camp, 30 hours after departing from the Extinguisher Tower.

The ascent of Robson was the first major ice climb in North America, its Kain Face route not repeated for another 40 years. But at the same 1913 camp, guide Walter Schauffelberger nearly trumped Kain. He led two amateurs in only 14 hours to within about 100 vertical metres of the summit via the Wishbone Arête (IV, 5.6), by far the hardest route undertaken in the Rockies to that time. They were turned back only by slow, difficult step cutting on the summit ridge and an approaching storm; they bivied part way down the ridge. A year later, Schauffelberger died in an avalanche while skiing in Europe.

In 1924, Kain led the first ascent of the South Face, left of the Hourglass variation that he descended in 1913. In 1938, Hans Fuhrer guided J.W. Carlson and William Hainsworth up the Fuhrer Ridge (IV, 5.4) from the Robson-Helmet Col. Again, this mixed ice/snow and rock route was well ahead of its time.

The Wishbone Arête—a long, narrow and tremendously exposed route, featuring rotten rock on its lower stretches and a labyrinth of overhanging ice gargoyles near the top—resisted many efforts until 1955, when Americans Don Claunch, Mike Sherrick and Harvey Firestone got up it in three intense days, with Claunch carrying a bible throughout. In sharp contrast,

Guide Conrad Kain (l), Albert MacCarthy and William Foster after their 1913 first ascent of Mt. Robson. Photo: Byron Harmon. (Whyte Museum)

A. Robson Glacier. B. Resplendent Mtn. C. The Helmet. D. Mt. Robson. Photo: Glen Boles.

Joe Josephson and Larry Stanier did the route in the dry summer of 1998 in less than 48 hours, including the drive from and back to Canmore.

The Northwest, or Emperor, Ridge (V, 5.6,), perhaps the biggest ridge climb in the Rockies, was nearly scaled in 1930 by Robert Underhill and Lincoln O'Brien. But it, too, repelled all attempts until unheralded Americans Tom Spencer and Ron Perla finally made it up in 1961. More than 30 rope lengths were needed to overcome the long stretch where ice pinnacles were perched on a knife-thin rock ridge. Their technique was to establish a solid axe belay on an ice block and then thread the rope on alternating sides of subsequent blocks. Occasionally, they chopped away overhanging portions of blocks, with several ice pitons used for direct aid.

"We were almost grateful for the cloud cap, for during occasional partial clearings the terrifying exposure from our knife-thin ridge was revealed," Spencer wrote. "Kinney Lake was visible 8,000 feet below on our right. The Northwest and North faces fell away for about a mile at an angle in excess of sixty degrees."

While on the Emperor Ridge in 1930, Underhill looked over at the 1000-metre, 50-degree North Face (IV) and declared it "was out of the question: besides carrying the cornice, it presents one of the most sheer and stupendous precipices one is likely to see—far more impressive than the north wall of the Matterhorn or the wall of the Eiger stretching down to Grindelwald." In 1963, Washington climbers Dan Davis and Pat Callis marched up the lower face in good snow, but the sting was in the tail.

"By the time we reached the rock band, it had become light, and we could see how steep and exposed the face is," Davis wrote. "It gave us quite a sensation to be able to look so nearly straight down on our camp from high up on the face. Unfortunately from here on we found ourselves on loose, insecure powder snow over glare ice." They belayed this treacherous section for 12 pitches to the summit Emperor Ridge, climbing the upper part "on all fours as much as the angle of the face would permit."

In 1986, four climbers on the North Face encountered a "vertical wall of Styrofoam cups" just below the summit ridge and were forced to wait several days for help. Rescue wardens climbed to the top in bad weather and, after bivouacking in a crevasse, hauled the climbers up onto the narrow ridge. During a momentary break in the weather, the climbers and one warden were whisked away by helicopter, earning the pilot an award for this dangerous airlift in high winds, poor visibility and at a high elevation. An ensuing storm forced the remaining wardens to spend two more days in a crevasse before climbing down. In 2003, the late Calgary climber John Ionescu soloed this route and then went down the South Face in 35 hours, car to car.

In recent decades, top alpinists seeking new challenges on Robson have turned to the enormous Emperor Face, rising sheer above the Mist Glacier between the Emperor Ridge and North Face, which it dwarfs in scale. In 1978, Mugs Stump and Jim Logan pioneered a route (VI, 5.9, A2) up its right side in four days. Three years later and right after warming up on the Wishbone Arête, David Cheesmond and Tony Dick went up a similarly-graded rib to the left. In typical Cheesmond fashion, the three-day ascent was described in three sentences in the *Canadian Alpine Journal*.

In late October 2002, an all-star team of locals Barry Blanchard and Eric Dumerac and Frenchman Philippe Pellet pushed the limits even further with their 2200-metre Infinite Patience (VI, WI5, M5, 5.9) route up the Em- peror Face, to the right of the Stump-Logan line. The fifth attempt by Blanchard, the climb took three days over steep mixed terrain, with Pellet dropping both his ice tools on the way up, forcing those who weren't leading to follow with a single axe.

Robson has also seen its share of winter ascents. In 1965, the Kain Face was ascended by a party of four, including Seattle's legendary Fred Beckey and Leif-Norman Patterson, on his fourth winter attempt.

In the summer of 1983, Peter Chrzanowski climbed the peak and then skied down the Southeast Ridge (less than 10 metres wide in places) and the steep Kain Face. In September 1995, Troy Jungen and Ptor Spricenieks made the ultimate Rockies' extreme ski descent, plunging down the 1000-metre North Face.

Below the N Face of Mount Robson.

Routes

First Ascent July 31, 1913: Albert MacCarthy, William Foster, *Conrad Kain* – Northeast Face/Southeast Ridge (Kain Face)

Routes Described Northeast Face/Southeast Ridge (IV) *Recommended*, South Face (IV)

Gear Rope, glacier gear, crampons, two ice tools including a longer axe, ice screws, pickets

Map 83 E/3 Mount Robson

Season late July to early September

Time South Face: Trip – About 3 days
Climb – 10-14 hours return from hut
Kain Face: Trip – About 5 days
Climb – 9-14 hours return from The Dome

Northeast (Kain) Face/Southeast Ridge

Approach Some parties break this approach into two days, stopping at the end of Berg Lake the first and then ascending to The Dome the second. Others make a long, one-day push to the Extinguisher Tower, often launching a summit bid from there. A third option is to fly to the Rearguard Meadows along the upper Robson Glacier, though some folks consider that cheating (Phone Yellowhead Helicopters at 250-566-4401).

From the parking lot, follow the 22-km trail to the end of Berg Lake (800 metres of elevation gain, 7-8 hours to the Rearguard Campground). To reach the Extinguisher Tower (another 2-3 hours with a heavy pack), continue past the lake and go right on the Snowbird Pass trail, which skirts the left edge of the Robson Glacier. Where the trail bends uphill toward Snowbird Pass, drop onto the glacier, regaining a trail left of the glacier less than 2 km from the Extinguisher Tower. Go back on the glacier just before the tower (campsites on gravel moraines below the tower), and head southwest towards the Robson Cirque.

The most direct line from here is to pick your way up through a right-trending icefall, left of the Dome, which at times can be a minefield of crevasses and seracs and exposed to avalanches. If the icefall, aptly named the Mousetrap, looks too dangerous, swing south and ascend to the Robson-Resplendent Col (GR 579848) and scramble west along the lower part of the ridge (one short fourth-class bit of rock, a bit tricky with a heavy pack) and then drop down onto the flatter glacier and traverse right to The Dome, a snow hump below the Kain Face (about 7 hours from Berg Lake, longer via the col route). The Dome is incorrectly marked on the topo map

and is actually about 1 km to the northeast at an elevation of 3070 metres. *Route* A pre-dawn start is recommended, to avoid avalanches on the face. The climb itself should be abandoned if there is much fresh snow on the face.

From The Dome, angle up right and start ascending the Kain Face, crossing a sometimes problematic bergschrund about a third of the way up. Continue up the face on snow and/or ice (up to 50 degrees) on a line between the ice bulges on the right and exposed rock on the left, topping out where the cornices are thinnest. Then follow the Southeast Ridge, which steepens as it goes over "The Roof." One steep, icy step can pose problems, depending on ice formations, and sometimes requires a short detour to the left. Above, the angle relents and the ridge widens, with a final stroll to the summit.

Descend the same way. One rappel may be required for the steep step on the ridge. Depending on conditions and skill, the Kain Face can be descended by down climbing, lowering or rappelling, usually from Abalakov anchors. If the face is dangerously soft, you may have to wait till evening or even morning to safely descend. Similarly, the icefall below The Dome is best descended very early in the morning.

South Face

Approach The approach to Ralph Forster Hut gains 1700 metres of elevation in some 3 km up a dry, unrelentingly steep slope above Kinney Lake. Carry plenty of water.

From the parking lot, hike or mountain bike along the Berg Lake Trail to Kinney Lake, going over a treed shoulder along the east shore. About five minutes beyond a gravel beach, the trail crosses the bottom of a large gully known as the Great Couloir (about 6 km from the trailhead). Though it can be hard to find the start of the Forster Hut approach, work your way up a treed slope just right of this gully and pick up an indistinct trail that climbs up, and slightly right, through bush and a fire-swept slope and then up a short rock band with a fixed chain. Continue up through more trees, interspersed with short rock steps, angle left up a big scree slope and then scramble more directly over down-sloping, gravel-covered rock left of a black wall. A black headwall just below the hut can be ascended directly or circumvented by traversing right on scree and then going up left of a small peak. In the latter case, climb a 10-metre chimney (5.3)

S Face of Mount Robson. A. Little Robson. B. Schwartz Ledges. C. SE Ridge.

and follow the ridge crest left to the hut (about 8 hours from the trailhead).

Ralph Forster Hut Located on Robson's South-Southwest Ridge at an elevation of about 2500 metres (GR 558847). First come, first served, sleeps six comfortably, eight very cozily. Bring your own stove and fuel, along with camping gear if you think the hut might be full. Drinking water is from remnant snow or a small stream across scree north of the hut.

Route From the hut, dash under or through serac debris and scramble up Little Robson on a mix of good and loose rock, interspersed with scree (about 2 hours). At the top of Little Robson, rope up and cross the glacier, climbing an inverted snow V just to the right of the infamous Schwartz Ledges, named for guide Hans Schwartz of Jasper, who reached the summit a record 10 times. Traverse left across a short, icy gully to gain the ledges, which can range from wide and easy when dry to downright frightening when covered in snow or ice. The big danger is icefall from seracs overhanging the ledges, so traverse them as fast as you safely can. Once beyond serac danger, continue a rising traverse

left to regain the glacier. Avoid the temptation to head straight up a small bowl (steeper and slower, especially when icy) and continue traversing to reach a lower-angled snow ridge, which is followed on a rising line right.

Beyond, there are two options. One is to head straight up the remaining South Face on snow and/or ice (about 40 degrees) right of small rock outcrops. A final traverse right and then one back left puts you under the summit roof, which is pierced via a short climb, often through crumbly ice. The summit is just beyond, to the left. The second option is to traverse right on a wide, low-angled snow bench, intercepting the Southeast Ridge above the top of the Kain Face. Follow the ridge as described above.

Descent If snow or ice conditions are good, the most direct, though steeper, descent is back down the South Face. Otherwise, descend the Southeast Ridge to near its bottom and then traverse on the bench back to the lower South Face. Some folks have avoided the Schwartz Ledges on the return by making a long rappel (two ropes needed) off an ice block west of the old Hourglass route, but this shortcut is also exposed to serac fall.

Whitehorn Mountain

3395 metres (11,138 feet)

Whitehorn is the most northerly of the 11,000ers, separated from the Robson massif by the Robson River spilling through the Valley of a Thousand Falls. But it is the commanding presence of nearby Mount Robson that truly isolates Whitehorn, a handsome peak that would draw considerably more attention if located elsewhere.

Like a number of other pyramid-shaped peaks in the Rockies, Whitehorn's summit block is a horn, carved on four sides by the glaciers that now lie as receding remnants around it, still bedeviling climbers seeking a straightforward approach. Its most impressive aspect, the steep, triangular Northwest Face, is balanced by a long glacier flowing southeast, which can be viewed head on from Kinney Lake or in profile from near Berg Lake. Of course, the view from Whitehorn's summit of Robson's immense West Face and Emperor Ridge is one of the grand sights in the Rockies.

The West Ridge is the standard line of ascent— mostly on snow or scree, with some moderate rock climbing near the top. But the circuitous approach and descent make for a very long day and often a bivouac, even from a high camp. As one early West Ridge climber, Winthrop Stone, noted: "Although we had been climbing up or down fully seven hours, we now for the first time were facing directly toward our goal, having skirted the mountain for half its circumference, crossed two glaciers, traversed one and attained the crest of the second of the four ridges which flank the peak."

Glacial recession has made the normal approach to the West Ridge increasingly problematic and perhaps impassable in a dry year. While not listed in *The Rocky Mountains of Canada-North* as a route, other than as a "not recommended" descent, the neglected South Ridge offers by far the most direct line up and down the mountain, if you don't mind scrambling up loose, exposed and largely unprotectable rock.

The name Whitehorn, applied by surveyor Arthur Wheeler in 1911, is perhaps the most descriptively self-explanatory of all the 11,000ers. It refers to the peak's glacial cap, most prominent on the northwest side.

History

Conrad Kain was one of the most accomplished and versatile guides in Rockies history, taking climbers safely, and with much humour, up some of the hardest snow, ice and rock routes in the range. But during a 1911 reconnaissance of the area with the Alpine Club of Canada, a bored Kain made an impromptu and secretive solo dash up Whitehorn. One of the few written accounts by a guide, Kain's tale is remarkable for its freshness and immediacy, though it was no doubt polished when translated into English. It is well worth quoting in detail.

"I left camp at half-past one (p.m.) to climb Mt. Whitehorn. I went so fast that it would not have been possible to take anyone with me. I crossed the glacier to a moraine and followed the rocks, which led me directly to the pass. From there, I had to descend three hundred feet. After a very dangerous threading of the numerous crevasses, I reached the southwest ridge [actually the West Ridge]. Rain and thunder! I thought of turning back but decided to go on, for I knew that it was my only opportunity to climb the mountain. I followed the ridge right to the summit without much difficulty. The climb reminded me very strongly of the scramble on Mount Stephen."

Approaching W Ridge (right skyline) of Whitehorn Mtn. Photo: Nancy Hansen.

Whitehorn Mtn. From Mt. Robson.
A. SE Glacier. B. W Ridge approach.

Kaïn recorded his ascent on a slip of paper inside a matchbox wrapped in a handkerchief, which he placed in a hastily constructed "stone man" below the summit. He built a second, better-protected cairn "because I knew that people would not believe I had reached the summit." Then he began his descent.

"The route of return was the same, but more dangerous. Before I came to the pass, the sun sank behind the mountains. I should have liked to see the sun two hours longer. I thought that I could yet cross the glacier by daylight. To my astonishment, I found that the snow bridge, which had brought me on the rocks, was broken. I had hard work to get on the glacier. I was quite helpless in the rain. I wanted to stay on the glacier overnight, but I could not stand it longer than ten minutes, and the cold warned me that I must go on, whatever happened.

"My one bit of good fortune was the lightning, which showed me the way. Step by step, I had to feel with the axe to find whether I was on the edge of a crevasse. Very often the axe fell right through and, more than once, I thought: 'This is the last step.' I tried again to stay overnight on the glacier, but in five minutes I would have been frozen stiff from head to foot. I felt indescribably glad when I found rocks under my foot; I yodeled with delight…

"At daybreak, I came into camp, in pouring rain. I found my supper by the fire and ate it for breakfast. I laid aside all my wet clothing and, without a sound, went into the tent and to bed without disturbing anyone. I slept for a short time. Mr. (George) Kinney felt in my bed to see if I was there. Without saying a word, he clapped me on the shoulder and I pointed in the direction of Whitehorn.

"I had absolutely no pleasure in that climb. The time was too short and the dangers were too great. Two days later, I went over the glacier and saw my tracks, and I think there was only one chance in a hundred of anyone coming through safe. I was appalled when I saw the dangerous crevasses. It was one of the craziest and most foolhardy undertakings that I ever made in the mountains, and all my life I shall remember the ascent of Whitehorn. As I found no stone-man or any other sign of man, I believe that it was the first ascent."

The disgruntled head of the reconnaissance trip, Arthur Wheeler, decreed it wasn't a first ascent since it went unwitnessed. But when Walter Schauffelberger guided the second ascent two years later, he found and brought down the matchbox.

At the same 1913 ACC camp, Kain guided a large party that climbed the West Ridge and then split in two, descending the Southeast Glacier and South Ridge, respectively, thus making the first traverse of the peak. In 1938, Hans Fuhrer guided a group past the big notch in the Southeast Ridge, which was then followed by short, steep rock pitches and traverses to the summit.

Two more routes were put up within two weeks in 1973. Jeff Lowe and Mike Weis ascended the 500 vertical metres of snow and ice on the lovely Northwest Face (III), while Jock Glidden and Dave Hamre climbed the rock, ice faces and snow ribs of the North Ridge in 11 pitches, traversing left under the "White Horn" to gain the summit (III, 5.4).

Routes

First Ascent August 12, 1911: Conrad Kain, alone – West Ridge

Routes Described South Ridge (II, 5.3), West Ridge (II, 5.4)

Gear	Rope, glacier gear, ice axe, crampons, small rock rack for both routes
Map	83 E/3 Mount Robson
Season	July to September
Time	Trip – 3 days
	Climb – 14-plus hours return from a high camp on the West Ridge, somewhat shorter on the South Ridge

South Ridge This route can be tackled from two approaches, the Southeast Glacier or from below the bottom of the South Ridge. The start for both routes is the same, following the Berg Lake Trail for some 9 km to beyond the far end of Kinney Lake.

If the Southeast Glacier is likely to be dry and broken up, it can be avoided entirely. Shortly after crossing to the left (west) side of the Robson River, north of Kinney Lake, go left up a major scree slope for a few hundred metres and then bushwhack left for a short distance. Continue carefully traversing left across hard-packed, exposed ground to gain a treed shoulder right of a waterfall (GR 506855), visible from the valley bottom on the Berg Lake trail. Drop into a drainage, which is followed northwest to reasonable bivy sites, though you may have to go a ways farther to find water, around GR 482873 (about 7 hours from the trailhead). From here, scramble north over a couple of moraines to intersect the lower South Ridge, which is then followed to the summit.

If the Southeast Glacier appears navigable, continue up the Berg Lake Trail, leaving it just before the bridge that crosses to the Whitehorn campground (11 km) and briefly following the left bank of the Robson River. Shortly before a side stream emerges from the west, head left up scree and a small drainage to reach a high-walled canyon. Follow the canyon floor until it's possible to gain slopes above its left wall (it is also possible to scramble up slopes before the canyon, following cairns). Continue up through scree and scrub brush and then traverse to the right beneath seracs at the toe of the glacier, crossing the stream that drains from it. Scramble up through a low cliff band, by way of a shallow drainage, on small, edgy holds (slippery when wet) to gain the lower right side of the glacier (GR 502878), with good bivy sites nearby (about 4 hours from the Whitehorn campground). Head

SE aspect of Whitehorn Mtn.
A. SE Glacier. B. S Ridge.

northwest up the long, low glacier, angling left towards its centre to avoid major crevasses. Depending on crevasse conditions, intersect the South Ridge either at a relatively flat spot (around GR 482894) or higher up.

Regardless of which approach you take, the upper South Ridge is fairly narrow, rising in a series of small, fourth-class steps, with loose, dinner-plate rock that is difficult to protect. It is followed for about 250 vertical metres to the summit, with about one pitch of roughly 5.3 climbing getting onto the summit block.

Descent While going down the ascent route offers the fastest and most direct line off the mountain, it involves down climbing on loose, exposed rock, with at least one rappel near the top. It is also possible, but much, much longer, to descend the upper West Ridge (up to six half-rope rappels) and once the angle eases off, at about 2,800 metres, traverse under both the West Face and then the South Ridge to regain the upper Southeast Glacier at a col (GR 483884).

West Ridge From the parking lot, follow the Berg Lake Trail for 16 km to the Falls of the Pool. Head a short distance west from the main trail to pick up a parallel horse trail, which is followed

Ascending S Ridge of Whitehorn. Mtn. Photo: Nancy Hansen.

north for about 2 km At about GR 523900, leave the horse trail and bushwhack over a ridge to the northwest, crossing below a finger of glacier to reach beautiful bivy sites (GR 508907), with impressive views of Mount Robson's Emperor Face (about 7 hours from the trailhead).

Continue west-northwest, crossing a glacial stream (may be tricky at high water) at around 2,100 metres. Head northwest to gain one of two right-trending and much-crevassed glacial shelves, both leading to a col (GR 485921). While the upper bench generally has better snow cover, it is threatened by serac fall. The choice of which to follow changes from year to year, depending on conditions; it may be best to go up the lower bench and down the upper. In dry years, both may prove hazardous or even impassable.

From the col, descend southwest on snow beneath a rock tower and then swing south towards a glacier (unmarked on map) below Whitehorn's northwest side. Some fourth-class rock gains the glacier, which is ascended to reach the West Ridge at about 2700 metres. Follow the ridge up snow or scree, bypassing small cliff bands on the right. A short, somewhat loose rock step (5.3/5.4) is tackled in two pitches, both starting in left-hand corners. More scrambling leads to a second wall (about 5.4), starting on the right and following ledges and cracks to a crest, which is followed over one awkward bulge. Easier ground above leads to the summit.

Descend the same way, with up to half a dozen single-rope rappels on the upper West Ridge. Once off the ridge, either down climb or rappel the rock wall to reach the Northwest Glacier.

Opposite: S Ridge of The Helmet, Mt. Robson's Kain Face behind.

The Helmet
3420 metres (11,220 feet)

The Helmet may appear an insignificant, glaciated bump cowering in the eastern shadow of mighty Mount Robson. But it is well worth climbing, for two reasons. One, the views are among the most spectacular in the Rockies—primarily the front-row spectacle of the towering walls of Robson's North and Kain Faces and the long glaciated bench rising to Resplendent Mountain's summit.

Two, the approach via the Robson Glacier leads to an enchanting campsite just off its western edge. It is an unexpected refuge of green in a sea of ice, with two small lakes feeding a tent-side stream, whistling marmots in abundance and a collection of strange gray boulders that look like giant stromatolites, formed from dome-like accumulations of compressed, ancient algae; in western Australia, some stromatolites are more than 3.5 billion years old. This lovely base camp could also be used to climb Resplendent.

The standard route up The Helmet is a delight, wandering up the Berg Glacier—where in dry years, some big crevasses can be the crux—and passing beneath the immense east flank of Robson. From a col connecting to Robson's Northeast Buttress, steep snow slopes lead to an elevated traverse below huge cornices along the South Ridge. Peter Chrzanowski skied down this face in 1987.

In 1908, explorer Arthur Coleman named the peak for its resemblance, from below, to a Roman soldier's headpiece. He called the mountain a "striking point of rocks," although other than the North Face, it is almost entirely covered in glacial snow and ice. Indeed, once past the scree slopes near camp, climbers never set foot on rock all the way to the summit.

History

There seems to be no record of the first ascent of The Helmet. In 1928, Georgia Engelhard and guide Hans Fuhrer climbed it, went home and didn't write about it. They may have figured it was a mere hump off the shoulder of Robson and, despite the lovely views, hardly worth filling the pages of the *Canadian Alpine Journal* over.

Engelhard and Fuhrer were definitely worth writing about. A New Yorker, Engelhard made 15 visits to the Canadian Rockies and Selkirks, putting up 32 first ascents before retiring to Switzerland with husband and fellow climber Tony Cromwell. Fuhrer was one of the last great guides at the close of the Rockies' golden age of mountaineering. Best known for his blitzkrieg first ascents on the Clemenceau and Columbia Icefields with Alfred Ostheimer III in 1927, he also led the 1938 first ascent of Robson's Fuhrer Ridge, ahead of its time as a steep, sustained rock and ice climb (IV, 5.4). This route, too, started from the Robson-Helmet Col, and perhaps his 1928 ascent of The Helmet sparked the desire to tackle this hard line.

In 1934, the Southeast Ridge was climbed, via The Dome below Robson's Kain Face, by Max Strumia and William Hainsworth. On the same trip, they made the first ascent of the connecting Mount Waffl, named for their climbing companion Newman Waffl, who died in an avalanche while trying to solo Robson in 1930.

Route

First Ascent July 1928: Georgia Engelhard, *Hans Fuhrer* – South Ridge

Route Described South Ridge (II) *Recommended*

Gear	Rope, glacier gear, ice axe, crampons, perhaps a few ice screws and a couple of snow pickets
Map	83 E/3 Mount Robson
Time	Trip – About 3 days
	Climb – 8-10 hours return from Robson Glacier camp, a little longer from Berg Lake camp

Approach From the parking lot, follow the Berg Lake Trail for 18.5 km until just shy of the lake (6-8 hours). From here, there are two options:

A more direct but less aesthetic approach departs the Berg Lake Trail just before the lake and crosses the braided Robson River, usually knee deep in mid-summer. A camp in the flats is usually situated here. From the southwest end of a small lake below the Mist Glacier, go up a moraine to its end and then scramble up and left, crossing a major gully at a narrow point. Continue up and left on a rock buttress to its top, exiting on its right to gain the middle of the Berg Glacier across from Mount Waffl and ascend it to intercept the approach below.

An alternative approach, while considerably longer, leads to the lovely meadow campsite between Rearguard Mountain and Mount Waffl. Continue to the end of Berg Lake and go right on the Snowbird Pass trail, which skirts the left edge of Robson Glacier. Where the trail bends uphill toward the pass, drop onto the glacier, regaining a trail left of the glacier less than 2 km from the Extinguisher Tower. Go back on the glacier just before the tower and shortly thereafter traverse southwest all the way across the more level and less crevassed glacier to reach the meadow on its west side (GR roughly 576893,

4-5 hours from Berg Lake). From this camp, traverse west, dropping to a small lake and then crossing scree slopes to reach the Rearguard-Waffl Col and the edge of the northeast arm of Berg Glacier. Cross the glacier under Mount Waffl to intersect the approach above.

South Ridge The Berg Glacier below the northwest wall of The Helmet is heavily crevassed, which can pose serious routefinding problems and has turned back some competent parties in dry years. Continue a long, steady climb up the glacier—nearly 1,000 metres of elevation gain in all and heavy going, with some risk of avalanche if the snow is soft. The route passes almost below the immense North Face of Robson and then angles left to the Robson-Helmet Col.

The bergschrund that spans the bottom of The Helmet's Southwest Face can be gaping and is sometimes best crossed just beyond, and on the downhill side of, the col. From the col, ascend 40-degree snow and/or ice slopes towards the crest of the South Ridge and then make a long, rising traverse left to the summit (sometimes icy), staying well below a giant cornice.

Descend the same way.

The Helmet.

Opposite: A. Resplendent Mtn. B. The Helmet C. Robson-Helmet Col. D. Fuhrer Ridge, Mt. Robson. Photo: Don Beers.

Upper slopes of Resplendent Mtn., Mt. Robson's Kain Face in rear. Photo: Nancy Hansen.

Resplendent Mountain
3426 metres (11,240 feet)

As the name suggests, Resplendent Mountain is a handsome snow peak, with a cascading north glacier and precipitous East Face. Its shining, chiselled summit is best seen from the eastern flanks of Robson or distant valley floors.

Ironically, climbers approaching from Robson Pass can't see anything more than the mountain's tip until they're well up the Robson Glacier. But the long glacial trudge up the standard route is rewarded by the outstanding views of towering Robson and the exhilarating final walk along the steeply-angled, corniced summit slope. This aerial walk is immortalized in Byron Harmon's famous 1913 photo of Conrad Kain guiding four tightly-bunched climbers descending from a summit encircled in clouds. The poster of this shot, with the hand-tinted colour added much later, graces many mountaineers' walls.

Resplendent is often climbed in conjunction with Robson's Kain Face from a camp near the Extinguisher Tower, halfway up the east side of the Robson Glacier. More often than not, it's a fine consolation prize when hopes of claiming Robson are abandoned.

It is also an outstanding ski ascent in early spring, refreshingly free of the summer hordes of tourists and climbers. The descent of the North Glacier is a long, fast run, particularly for those adept at skiing roped up. The overlooked Ice Arête is also a superb snow and rock route—with exciting positions on an exposed, narrow ridge—and is deserving of more attention from intermediate alpine climbers.

Resplendent's simple, descriptive name was applied by peripatetic mountain explorer Arthur Coleman, who was obviously dazzled by the peak's glittering appearance when he first spied it in 1907, on the first attempt to climb Mount Robson.

History

During their 1910 expedition to the Robson area, Norman Collie, Arnold Mumm and guide Moritz Inderbinen made an unsuccessful attempt on Resplendent. Bad weather, too, plagued their efforts on their primary goal, Mount Robson, though they did make first ascents of Mumm Peak and Mount Phillips.

Like Kain's solo climb of Mount Whitehorn on the same expedition, the first ascent of Resplendent could be attributed to insurrection. On the 1911 exploratory trip into the Robson area, leader and martinet Arthur Wheeler apparently promised Kain, George Kinney and perhaps Harmon a shot at Robson. But no doubt wanting to save this prize for an upcoming Alpine Club of Canada camp, he procrastinated, to the point that the frustrated and independent-minded Kain decided to do some peak bagging.

The official story of the first ascent of Resplendent—supplied by Wheeler, as the climbers left no written account—was that Kain and Harmon ventured out from their Robson Pass camp one cloudy day to get photos of the crevasses and snow formations in the Robson amphitheatre. The photo opportunities were poor, the story went, but they somehow managed to wander up Resplendent. The more likely truth is the photo shoot was a pretext for illicitly claiming a virgin summit.

"It proved to be altogether a snow and ice climb, and Conrad reported having seen some of the greatest ice cracks he had met with throughout the course of his professional experience," Wheeler wrote. "The crest of the mountain he described as an immense cornice reaching far out into space over the depths below."

Harmon, the Alpine Club's official photographer in its early years, left a more lasting impression with his photos of Resplendent, particularly of one ascent during the 1913 Alpine Club camp. The results are all the more impressive considering the load he carried up such mountains—a large, wooden tripod, a five-by-seven view camera and glass plates. Though film was at a premium, Harmon took several shots of this climb from a nearby vantage point, capturing perfectly, in the one famous photo, the light and the position of climbers, suspended amidst clouds and leaning on their alpenstocks ahead of a relaxed Kain.

Numerous ascents of Resplendent were made at that 1913 camp, including a new route up a fine rock and ice arête northeast of the summit. A Conrad Kain-guided party actually descended this Ice Arête on the second ascent of Resplendent. Two days later, the route was ascended, with Walter Schauffelberger guiding C.H. Mitchell, John Watt and H.H. Prouty. "If the combination comprising the rock and ice arête is included in the ascent," Mitchell wrote, "the day's work will take on a different character and be exciting as well as somewhat more arduous than if confined to the snow" of the standard route. In 1973, Jeff Lowe and Mike Weis climbed the East Spur, a fourth-class snow and rock route that rears up to 5.7 rock near the summit.

In 1932, Rockies ski pioneers Joe Weiss and Rex Gibson trudged in from Jasper to ascend Resplendent on skis, with the aid of seal skins. But they discovered, inscribed on the wall of the Berg Lake cabin, a message from Pete Parsons of Oregon, claiming a late February climb in 1930, making Resplendent the first of the 11,000ers to be ascended on skis.

"It was blowing hard and 5 below zero F. in the bright sunshine on top, so I just ate a bit of lunch and took some pictures, and then came back down to the skis in 35 minutes and coasted down to the flat in 40 minutes more," the note read. "It took me 5-1/2 hours to climb up to the top. A beautiful day and sure had some sport." Soon thereafter, Parsons drowned while running rapids on the Peace River.

5.4 rock on Resplendent's Ice Arête.
Photo: Nancy Hansen.

Routes

First Ascent August 1911: Byron Harmon, *Conrad Kain* – Northwest Slopes

Routes Described Northwest Slopes (II), Ice Arête (III, 5.4) *both Recommended*

Gear Rope, glacier gear, ice axe, crampons; also a small rock rack, a few ice screws and a second ice tool for the Ice Arête

Map 83 E/3 Mount Robson

Season July to September on foot, March to early April on skis (extending into May if you fly in and out)

Time Trip – 3 days

Climb – Northwest Slopes: About 8 hours return from a camp near the Extinguisher Tower

Ice Arête: 10-11 hours return from Extinguisher

Approach From the parking lot, follow the 22-km trail to the end of Berg Lake (7-8 hours). You can camp here, at the Rearguard Campground, but it adds a good two hours each way to and from the Extinguisher Tower, which provides a better bivy site for climbing the peak. Continue past the lake and turn right on the Snowbird Pass Trail, which skirts the left edge of the Robson Glacier. Where the trail bends uphill toward Snowbird Pass, drop onto the glacier, regaining a trail farther along and dropping back onto the glacier just before the Extinguisher Tower (campsites on gravel moraines below the tower).

Ski Approach Most years, a ski ascent of Resplendent should be undertaken no later than early April because of snow melt on the lower approach to and beyond Kinney Lake. (A later-spring alternative is to carry one's skis up these lower sections or take the lazy option and fly to Robson Pass. Phone Yellowhead Helicopters at 250-566-4401.) It takes a full day of skiing to reach a camp near Robson Pass or, preferably, higher up along the eastern edge of the Robson Glacier opposite Rearguard Mountain. In spring, the lower section of the glacier can be followed along its left side to the Extinguisher Tower.

Northwest Slopes Note: The same route is followed on foot or skis. From the Extinguisher, head southwest toward Robson Cirque, swinging right to avoid large crevasses below Resplendent's glaciated Northwest Ridge. Ascend steeper snow slopes to the south (some large

Resplendent Mtn. A. NW Slopes. B. Ice Arête.

Ice Arête on Resplendent Mtn. Photo: Nancy Hansen.

crevasses), angling left below the Robson-Re-splendent Col (GR 579848) to reach open, more level slopes west-north-west of the peak. These slopes are followed to the summit block (skis abandoned here), which rises more steeply to the summit crest. Take care to stay well below the cornices on your left, stopping just below a final one that overhangs the steep East Face.

Ice Arête The Ice Arête is a narrow ridge of rock and, usually, snow that primarily follows a rising line south from the Extinguisher to the summit of Resplendent. Just past the Ex-tinguisher, turn left, ascending the glacier and snow slope to the ridgeline, gained near a shal-low saddle. The ridge is easy at first but soon narrows and is interrupted by gendarmes, with most of the difficulties passed on the right. The rock gets increasingly better as the climbing gets harder, up to 5.4 in difficulty. Beyond the rock, the "ice arête" is fairly narrow but will seem considerably less exposed than the rock. It leads to a broad stretch of low-angled glacier that is crossed on a right-trending line to a short, steep face. Cross the bergschrund and climb two pitches of 50-degree snow or ice to intercept the summit ridge of the normal route.

For both routes, **descend** by the Northwest Slopes route. Skiers should avoid the temptation to ski these splendid upper slopes unroped, as the spring snow cover hides some considerable crevasses.

39

Mount Edith Cavell

3363 metres (11,033 feet)

Edith Cavell is the signature peak of the Jasper area. Its gorgeous, symmetrical North Face rises high and gleaming white above the west side of the broad Athabasca Valley. Because it stands alone, the peak can be seen from several aspects and a considerable distance.

Cavell's East Ridge is one of the classic alpine climbs in the Rockies, with blocky quartzite rock and superb positions on the upper ridge. The solid holds and reasonable grade make this an excellent moderate route, so much so that the mostly walk-up West Ridge should be reserved only for a descent.

Still, the East Ridge's lichen-covered rock can be dangerously slippery when covered in snow or ice, and climbers should wait until the route is reasonably dry, usually by mid-summer. The relatively high number of rescues, forced bivouacs and 16-hour days attest to the troubles inexperienced parties can encounter under marginal conditions or if they pitch out most of the exposed ridge. By contrast, experienced mountaineers often go unroped up the dry ridge, which is similar in character to, though much less sustained than, the Northwest Ridge of Mount Sir Donald in the Selkirks.

The North Face, with its horizontal strata scored by sweeping buttresses, is one of the more popular face routes in the Rockies, with several classic hard lines that are nonetheless exposed to rock fall. Aside from one route's inclusion in *Fifty Classic Climbs of North America*, this popularity partly stems from the short access. Indeed, it may be the only such north face in the Rockies where tourists can wander virtually to its base, rising from the hanging Angel Glacier.

A prominent landmark for early travelers, the peak was known by natives as White Ghost and by early 19th-century fur trade voyageurs as La Montagne de la Grande Traverse. It was later called Duke, Fitzhugh and finally Geikie; the latter is now applied to a peak in The Ramparts to the west.

During World War I, Edith Cavell was a British nurse who treated wounded German troops in occupied Belgium but also surreptitiously helped Allied soldiers escape to Holland. On August 5, 1915—the day the peak was first ascended—Cavell was arrested by the Germans for treason and soon tried and executed. Five months after her death, the mountain was officially named in her honour. In further tribute to this famous martyr, a large wooden cross was later fastened to the summit.

History

Despite Mount Edith Cavell's prominence and easy West Ridge, the peak was not climbed until the relatively late date of 1915. The protagonists were A.J. Gilmour and Edward Holway, a University of Minnesota botanist who three years earlier was on the famed first ascent of Mount Sir Sandford in the Selkirks. Gilmour and Holway spent a leisurely 12 days exploring the Cavell area, turning around on one attempt of the West Ridge because of impending rain. On their summit day, they went directly up the narrow, corniced west arête, fearing a slip on easier but icier slopes to the south would send them hurtling over cliffs below.

"The conditions were perfect," wrote Holway. "The snow was frozen hard to the depth of an inch, so that it was nearly continuous step cutting, very steep in the upper part. Only for a short distance did we find any ice, but to avoid it we had to keep well out on the cornice. The Doctor (Gilmour), being in the rear and having plenty of time to look down the north face, made suggestions occasionally about getting farther away from the edge." By mid-morning they reached the summit, planting a jointed flagpole that Gilmour had carried strapped to his back.

In July 1924, L. Coolidge, G. Higginson, J.E. Johnson and guide A. Streich went partway up the East Ridge, avoiding its steep upper buttress by traversing south on a ledge to a couloir, which was ascended to regain the ridge higher up. The complete ridge was climbed a month later by Joseph Hickson and guide Conrad Kain. "This was a real nice climb, in parts rather hard rock work," Kain wrote in a letter to Monroe Thorington. "Of course, we had to spend the night out as we traversed the mountain." Some loose rock that early groups encountered on the East Ridge has subsequently been mostly cleared off.

The first winter ascent was made in February 1934 by Morris Taylor and Swiss guide Ernie Neiderer, who skied in via Maccarib Pass and the Tonquin Valley over three days in −35 Celsius temperatures. On their ascent day, they skied to the bottom of the West Ridge, then

Mt. Edith Cavell, E Ridge on left skyline.

kicked steps up the slippery rocks, climbing the steep shale band near the top with one pair of skis in tow, "determined to climb Edith Cavell *with* skis if not actually *on* skis." Reaching the frigid summit as the sun was setting, they raced back down the ridge and the scree gully on foot and then had to traverse back to the ridge in the dark to find the pair of skis they'd left behind. "I got my shoes full of snow as I repeatedly broke through the crust and sank to my waist. This snow in my boots melted and later froze," wrote Taylor. "What a time I had getting off my boots, frozen as they were to my socks!"

The compelling 1200-metre North Face taunted top American climbers like Yvon Chouinard. "For Dan Doody and me it stood as the symbol of our ideal, a technical climb in alpine conditions with objective dangers. Having discovered the wall independently, we had both fallen under its spell," Chouinard wrote. "We came with Ken Weeks in 1960 to climb it, but it rained and snowed every day. Also we made the mistake of looking at the wall too often. It is not a good thing to look at great walls for too long a time."

A year later, Chouinard and Doody were back, armed with emerging icon Fred Beckey, a movie camera and some new pitons Chouinard had fashioned for the stratified rocks. After ascending the Angel Glacier, they went up the steep rock rib that led straight to the summit (IV, 5.7), belaying from beneath overhangs to avoid steady rock fall from on high. Beckey led magnificently, often on loose, steep rock, for most of the day, which ended with a midnight bivouac high on the face. The next day, easier-angled rocks were offset by rain that turned to hail mixed with high wind and lightning. Above, the summit ice slope was granular and kept sliding, forcing Chouinard to chop 500 steps to reach the summit rocks.

"The next 300 feet took everything I had to lead," he wrote. "Each move was a desperate effort to keep from sliding down the wet slabs… The last pitch took me to 80 feet above Doody on extreme rocks with no protection. I got above a small band of dirt and there I was with my hands on the summit! I tried to pull myself up but could not. My feet slid continually and my fingers dug deeper into the dirt, but I could not move. I looked across 50 feet to the summit pole and then down 4,000 feet to the ground. O God, what a place to get it! I was afraid for the first time during that day. With frantic eyes I spotted a two-foot patch of hard snow ten feet to my right. I very cautiously eased over. It felt solid, so I pulled up, mantled and was up. Never have I felt so happy as that day on the summit with my friends." This was the first big north wall to be scaled in the Canadian Rockies.

Despite that experience, Chouinard returned in 1967 with Chris Jones and Joe Faint to put a new route up the North Face to Cavell's east summit (V, 5.8). The climbing was on much firmer rock and, higher, on a mix of snow arêtes, ice gullies, ice-plastered rocks and steep walls. "This was mixed climbing par excellence," wrote Jones. A decade later, two more lines were put up the North Face, one including *Into Thin Air* author Jon Krakauer.

Route

First Ascent August 5, 1915: A.J. Gilmour, Edward Holway – West Ridge
Route Described East Ridge (III, 5.3) *Recommended*
Gear Rope, ice axe, crampons, small rock rack
Map 83 D/9 Amethyst Lakes
Season mid-July to mid-September
Time 10-14 hours return

Access From the junction of Highways 93 and 16 at Jasper, drive 6.5 km south on 93 and then go 5 km along Highway 93A to the Edith Cavell turnoff. (It's about 20 km north on the rougher 93A from the Athabasca Falls turnoff if you're coming from the south.) Go 14 km up the steep, badly potholed Edith Cavell road to a parking lot at its end, below Cavell's North Face and the Angel Glacier. If you intend to descend the West Ridge and have a second vehicle, leave it 2 km farther down the road at the Cavell Lake/Tonquin Valley parking lot, across from the Youth Hostel.

Approach Follow the paved Cavell Meadows trail and where it bends left into the trees go right on a less distinct trail (forest on your left, moraine on your right), which wanders left and then up through a scree bowl and a small snowfield to a col at the base of the East Ridge. You can bivy here (packrats abound), especially if you plan to come back down the East Ridge, but a 5 a.m. start from the parking lot should get you to the col around 7 a.m.

East Ridge Note: Even if the ridge looks dry, it's worth carrying crampons and an ice axe for a short but usually icy and exposed crossing of a gully above the rock ridge.

From the col, scramble up easy rock to the right of a snow couloir and continue up the ridge, bypassing a knoll on the left, to reach a broad, relatively level shoulder. At the end of the shoulder, the ridge steepens on solid, blocky quartzite (5.3). The rock tends to be best along the ridge crest, which offers increasingly impressive views down the North Face. Above the rocks, a short, icy gully is crossed (some fixed protection may allow for a belay across the last, exposed bit). The angle eases off as the ridge goes over the east summit and up to the main summit.

Descent The most direct descent is back down the East Ridge, which involves several rappels and down climbing on the steep upper rock section. A longer, slightly more time-consuming but much easier way down is via the West Ridge, the "tourist" route up. Follow the ridge down, bypassing a steep shale step by briefly detouring left onto the Southwest Ridge. Regaining the West Ridge, continue easily down to the Cavell-Mount Sorrow col (GR 274362) and then go left down blocky scree into a large bowl with a lovely meadow at its base. Pick up a good trail descending along the right side of Verdant Creek and then turn right onto the highway-like Astoria River Trail, which is followed for about 4 km to the Cavell Lake parking lot. Unless you've left a second vehicle here, hike nearly 2 km up the Edith Cavell Road to the Angel Glacier parking lot.

E Ridge of Mt. Edith Cavell.

Mount Brazeau

3470 metres (11,384 feet)

Mount Brazeau is the highest peak in the front ranges of the Canadian Rockies and the loftiest between Mounts Alberta and Robson. It also overlooks the largest icefield east of the Icefields Parkway, feeding Maligne Lake and Brazeau River and Lake. Yet it's fairly anonymous, hidden from any road view and innocuous from distant summits along the Continental Divide.

Despite this isolation, Brazeau is a reasonably accessible peak in a wilderness setting, with spectacular views of the North Face of Mount Alberta, the north end of the Columbia Icefield and the nearby Sunwapta Peak. It offers a routine ascent up its South Face on foot or skis, the latter becoming an increasingly popular means of approach. Enterprising climbers can traverse Mount Henry Macleod, Valad Peak and Brazeau—along the high, western edge of the Brazeau Icefield—in a long but fairly straightforward day and perhaps also tackle the nearby Mount Warren.

While Warren is listed in *The Rocky Mountains of Canada-North* as 3300 metres, the new, metric map shows a 3350 contour, which if correct could elevate it into the 11,000er (3353-metre) club. Similarly, Brazeau has a 3500-metre contour and is listed in the *Atlas of Canada* as 3525 metres. Whether these are now more precise elevations or errors in converting from the old imperial map is hard to say.

Joseph Brazeau was an American-born Hudson's Bay Company employee. He used his proficiency in six Indian languages to help translate for the Palliser Expedition, whose geologist, James Hector, explored along the Brazeau River in the late 1850s. In 1902, Arthur Coleman extended the name to the mountain, which an earlier map had identified as Mount McGillivray, in honour of North West Company fur trader Duncan McGillivray, who passed through the area as early as 1800.

History

Like Mount Clemenceau, Brazeau had early alpine visitors, but its summit remained long untouched. Many of the same characters were involved in both mountaineering histories.

In 1902, a decade after his exploration of the Clemenceau area, Arthur Coleman again found himself staring at a compelling peak and headed off from the east to claim its summit. As with Mount Clemenceau, he was rebuffed

without ever setting foot on the mountain, this time hindered by soft snow and crevasses. "Halting on some projecting rocks at 10,550 feet, we held a council of war and decided that further climbing was too dangerous to risk," he wrote. "From clinometer readings made at our earlier halts, the top of Brazeau Mountain, as we named it, is about five hundred feet above our stopping point."

Other than this pioneering effort, there was little information about the area from either a mountaineering or geographical perspective. Thus, when Allen Carpe, Howard Palmer and outfitter William Harris set out in 1923, they were unsure of Brazeau's location. Attacking from the north, they commandeered a sheet iron boat with a mast and crude oars and muscled their way to the south end of Maligne Lake.

After a week of exploring from a camp in Coronet Creek to the west, they worked their way up the glacier and "were thrilled to behold a shining snowfield... extending for miles in every direction," wrote Palmer. Then, when they topped Mount Henry Macleod, at the southwest edge of the icefield, "an amazing apparition met our gaze... A splendid new peak cleft the clouds like an incandescent blade. Brilliant with fresh snow, its shapely crown reared itself over impregnable precipices on east and north. Our quarry at last... We had camped at its base for a week without ever suspecting its identity."

They then traversed over the intervening Valad Peak and ascended the powdery, deep snow and then sloping, wet rock of Brazeau's South Face to reach the summit. "We had 'scalped' one of the principal peaks of the Rockies east of the main axial range," Palmer said.

It must have been an especially triumphant moment for Carpe, denied on earlier attempts to be the first up both Clemenceau and King Edward. Amazingly, outfitter Harris, who was much more familiar with pack horses than climbing ropes, was also on the first ascent of Clemenceau exactly one month later.

Subsequent variations of the original route, plus traverses in both directions, were done during Alpine Club of Canada camps in 1930 and 1950, the former outing involving a party of 13 guided by Hans Fuhrer. In 1979, Harriet and Robert Kruszyna and Peter Vermeulen pioneered a "simple but elegant" snow and ice route up the North Face.

43

Mount Brazeau Approaches

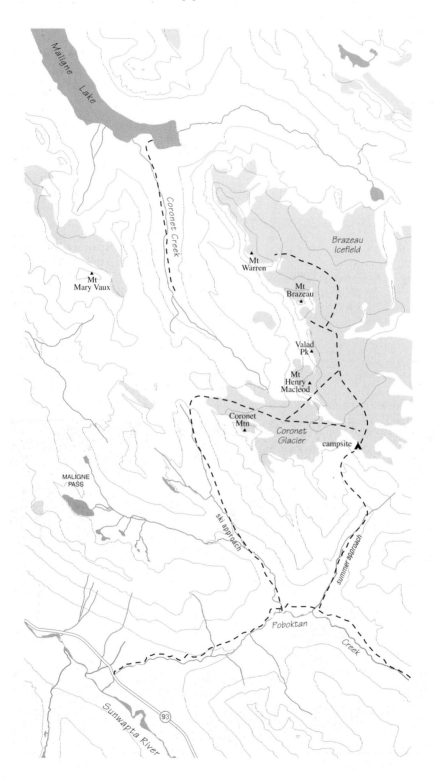

Route

First Ascent July 9, 1923: Howard Palmer, Allen Carpe, William Harris – South Face
Route Described South Face (I)
Gear Rope, glacier gear, ice axe, crampons
Maps 83 C/6 Sunwapta Peak,
83 C/11 Southesk Lake
Season mid-March to April on skis, July to September on foot
Time Trip – 2-3 days
Climb – 7-8 hours return from camp southeast of Mount Henry Macleod

Access and Approach Until fairly recently, most Mount Brazeau aspirants took a chartered boat the length of Maligne Lake to its south end and then followed a trail 7 km up Coronet Creek to a camp west of Brazeau. Though such charters are no longer available, it's still possible to paddle a boat 21 km down the frigid lake in a good four hours, trudge up to this low-elevation camp and then ascend nearly 1000 metres to the Brazeau-Valad Col. Paddling parties have also approached via Warren Creek, from the lake's southeast corner, but it's a half-day bash on foot with scant trails to reach a camp northeast of the icefield. Contact Maligne Tours in Jasper at 780 852-3370 for canoe or kayak rentals.

A simpler though somewhat taxing approach is to drive on Highway 93 to the Sunwapta Warden Station, 167 km north of Lake Louise or 70 km south of Jasper. Hike up the Poboktan Creek trail, passing the Maligne Pass trail turnoff at 6 km. Just over 1 km beyond, go northeast up a major side valley, following game trails along the right side of a stream and then angling up through a boulder field to reach a broad, open valley. Continue northeast through willowy flats, bypassing a small waterfall at the valley's end by briefly going up through woods right of the stream to gain an upper, rubble-filled basin – the start of 700 vertical metres of miserable scree and rock bashing.

It's best to initially stay fairly close to the stream's right side, skirting some low trees higher up and, just before the last island of trees, heading directly up towards some large gray boulders at the right edge of a low cliff band (around GR 776172 on map 83 C/11). Traverse left above this cliff band and, rounding the corner of a long headwall, go north up the middle of the upper basin until it's possible to angle more steeply right to a windswept campsite on a gravelly plateau below the southern edge of the Brazeau Icefield (GR 777179, elevation 2730 metres; 7-8 hours from the highway). The re-

Mt. Brazeau (l.) and a near 11,000er, Mt. Warren. Photo: Markus Kellerhals.

S Face of Mt. Brazeau. Mt. Warren to left.

ward for this bash is one of the most panoramic views in the Rockies, encompassing some dozen 11,000ers. Water is from nearby snowmelt or streams below the campsite.

Ski Approach Some parties have followed the summer approach above, though there is some avalanche risk. A better option is to turn earlier off the Poboktan Creek trail (6 km) and follow the Maligne Pass trail along Poligne Creek. This is the south end of the Six Pass ski route, and with luck there will be a broken track to follow. At about GR 739151 (83 C/6 map), go north up a side valley to gain the western edge of the Coronet Glacier (GR 729194 on map 83 C/11), which is ascended southeast (camp where the glacier flattens out) to its head, dropping down below the southern edge of the Brazeau Icefield, near the summer campsite. If avalanche conditions are moderate, a more direct approach from Coronet Glacier to the icefield can be taken by

tackling a steep couloir (GR 764191) over the southeast shoulder of Henry Macleod.

South Face From the edge of the Brazeau Icefield southeast of Henry Macleod, go up easy rock right of the broken edge of the icefield at GR 783187 (may be avalanche-prone in spring) and begin the long, rolling traverse north-northwest below Henry Macleod and Valad, taking care to avoid crevasses. Eventually, Brazeau's South Face comes into view and, from the Brazeau-Valad Col, is easily ascended on snow or scree. **Return** the way you came.

If time permits, a traverse over Valad and Henry Macleod is a lovely diversion, with particularly fine views from the latter. Warren can also be climbed in a longer day from the same camp by swinging well east of Brazeau in a descending half circle and then going up Warren's East-Southeast Ridge on snow and perhaps ice, at an initial angle of about 35 degrees, leveling off near the summit.

Mount Fryatt
3361 metres (11,027 feet)

Mount Fryatt is the dominant centre of a mass of peaks isolated by the diverging Athabasca and Whirlpool Rivers. The chiseled West Ridge on its summit block is a landmark for motorists driving south from Jasper on the Icefields Parkway. But the most spectacular view is looking south and west from the summit, unveiling a surprising and rarely-seen world of lakes and snowy peaks, most notably the nearby North Face of Mount Belanger.

The standard route up Fryatt is typical of Rockies south faces—a winding, scrambly line up broken ledges and loose shale—with a bit of intermediate rock climbing to gain the upper West Ridge. By contrast, the complete West Ridge is one of the better alpine rock climbs in the Rockies, with generally solid rock, good climbing on the upper ridge and excellent positions along the way. It's a long day either way.

In 1920, the Boundary Commission survey named the peak after Charles Fryatt, who captained the merchant ship Brussels, which was captured by German U-boats during World War I. Accused of trying to ram a submarine, Fryatt was shot by his captors. Globetrotting British climber Arnold Mumm had previously called the mountain Patricia.

History
Fryatt was easily spied from the Athabasca Valley but not easily climbed. Indeed, the first-ascent party in 1926 could find no sign of previous human presence as they pushed their way around the lesser peaks guarding this fortress. Theirs was a trying and circuitous approach, involving a ferry by raft across the raging Whirlpool River, a packhorse rolling over a cliff (and surviving) and incessant attacks by mosquitoes and "bulldog" flies.

But it was a determined team, comprising the guide Hans Fuhrer, Joseph Hickson and Howard Palmer, the latter having perfected the art of persevering after needing several expeditions to make the pioneering 1912 ascent of Mount Sir Sandford in the Selkirks, to the west. Palmer and Hickson—who at the time were the respective presidents of the American and Canadian Alpine Clubs—had in the previous two years scouted potential routes up Fryatt and even sent out a work party to hack a trail through dense jack pine to a lake above Divergence Creek, west of the objective.

From a higher, second lake, they launched their summit bid, taking a tortuous route to the South Ridge, where a deep notch forced them onto the Southwest Face. They easily made their way up through snow-covered rock bands, surmounted an icy chimney and skirted some precipitous summit cliffs, gaining the upper West Ridge via vertical cracks and overhanging rocks that required pitched climbing.

They were greeted at the summit by a brief thunderstorm that made ice axes and extended arms sizzle and were overtaken by darkness on the way down, forcing a bivouac. At dawn, they resumed their descent of the loose slopes, reaching camp 28 hours after setting out. "The litter of shale on Mount Fryatt is simply appalling," Palmer observed. "It crunches under foot like frozen grass."

To avoid the long approach and "scree slogging" of the standard route, Hartmut von Gaza and Athol Abrahams forged a rock route up the West Ridge in September 1972, two months after Abrahams had sprained his ankle in a fall on nearby Mount Olympus. The hardest climbing was at the bottom (5.6) and they primarily stuck to the ridge, traversing onto the Southwest Face route near the top. In 1985, Ken Wallator and P. Fehr added a direct finish to the route, the upper part providing the hardest (5.8) and best climbing.

Routes

First Ascent July 10, 1926: Joseph Hickson, Howard Palmer, *Hans Fuhrer* – Southwest Face

Routes Described Southwest Face (II 5.4), West Ridge (III, 5.6, 5.8 for direct finish) *Recommended*

Gear Southwest Face – Rope, ice axe, crampons, small rack. West Ridge – Rope, ice axe, crampons, rock rack, a few pitons

Map 83 C/12 Athabasca Falls

Season mid-July to mid-September

Time Trip – 3 days

Climb – Southwest Face: 12-14 hours return from camp below West Ridge; add a couple of hours if approaching from the hut

West Ridge : 14-plus hours return from camp below West Ridge

Access Drive 30 km south of Jasper, or 198 km north of Lake Louise, on Highway 93/Icefields Parkway to the Athabasca Falls turnoff. Go about 1 km up Highway 93A and turn onto the gravel Geraldine Lookout Fire Road. Park 2 km up this road for the Fryatt Valley trail and 5.5 km for the Geraldine Lakes trail (both marked).

Approach The convenience and comforting shelter of an Alpine Club of Canada hut lures many Mount Fryatt climbers up Fryatt Creek, the lower part of which can be mountain biked. But the climbing route from and back to the Sydney Vallance Hut is long and circuitous, making for a very long day. While less groomed, the approach via the Geraldine Lakes trail is shorter, more scenic, involves less elevation gain and lands climbers just below Fryatt's West Ridge in a sublime alpine camp that also provides a quicker approach to the standard Southwest Face route.

Geraldine Lakes Approach From the parking pullout, follow a good trail through woods to the first Geraldine Lake, beyond which the route climbs steeply along a waterfall, crosses a large boulder field and skirts a pond (cairns). More boulder hopping (slippery when wet) along the east side of the second lake leads to a campground at its south end and marks the end of the maintained trail (6 km). Just before a log creek crossing to the campground, pick up a rough trail and skirt left of a waterfall draining another lake, which is rounded on the right, as is a final, higher lake ringed with tremendous wildflowers in mid-summer. Continue up a grassy valley, heading left before its end and up steep slopes to reach a lovely bivy site (GR 361231) below the West Ridge (about 11 km and 5-7 hours from the trailhead).

Mt. Fryatt. A. SW Face. B. W Ridge. Photo: Peter Amann.

Ascending S Face of Mt. Fryatt.

To reach the Southwest Face route, climb over the low, flat end of the West Ridge and then make a descending, unpleasant sidehill traverse on grass and scree to a small gravelly area. Go just right of a waterfall, follow a ledge traversing back left and then scramble easily to a small lake (GR 376218) below the Southwest Face. Head up the left side of a basin and then pick your way up scree ledges (some cairns) to reach the lower face.

Fryatt Valley Approach The first 11 km of this trail, paralleling the Athabasca River, can be easily mountain biked. Beyond, a good foot trail follows Fryatt Creek for nearly 10 km to a campground, beyond which a final steep kilometre of switchbacks up a headwall leads to the Sydney Vallance Hut (6-7 hours with bike, 8-10 without). For hut bookings, contact the Alpine Club of Canada at 403-678-3200.

For the Southwest Face route, follow Fryatt Creek for a few hundred metres upstream and then head northwest up a watercourse to open meadows. The traditional route continues up to the 2680-metre col (GR 381209) and then goes up the south ridge of the 3020-metre peak, traversing west below the summit to gain a shoulder/col on its north side, from which the Southwest Face can be gained. This circuitous and somewhat tricky section can likely be avoided by instead going up the southeast ridge of the 3020 peak to its summit and then north to the aforementioned shoulder. From here, traverse left and slightly upwards on the Southwest Face.

Southwest Face Once on the Southwest Face, go up easy scree and ledges or the snow/ice couloirs between, depending on conditions and preferences. Higher, traverse left below steep cliff bands and across several couloirs (may be icy), looking for the easiest line through them— the rock climbing should be relatively short and no harder than 5.4—and aiming for a flat spot on the West Ridge, just below the summit block. Once on the ridge, a cairned ledge leads around right to a short, steep crack, which is climbed to regain the ridge. Traverse on exposed scree below the summit to reach the South Ridge, which is followed easily to the top.

West Ridge From the bivy site, gain the ridge, which is climbed in a series of steps. The first, steep step is climbed some 20 metres left of the ridge crest (5.6), and then easier climbing leads to a long scree slope. On the upper ridge, steep steps up to 5.8 are climbed on excellent, yellow limestone (though you may encounter some snowy or icy conditions, especially early or late in the season). The crux pitch is a steep, rising traverse on the left side of an overhanging prow, with tremendous exposure looking down the North Face. A slightly easier pitch then goes up and left, followed by more moderate ground to the summit. **Note:** The hardest but best climbing on this upper ridge can be avoided by traversing right on scree slopes to reach the South Ridge, as in the finish to the Southwest Face route.

Descent For all routes, descend the West Ridge to a rappel sling before, or east of, the top of the Southwest Face ascent route. Make three to four single-rope rappels (old slings and a few dubious pitons) down the Southwest Face to regain the lower scree ledges and easier ground.

Mount Woolley and Diadem Peak

Woolley and Diadem are twin peaks encircled by receding glaciers just north of the Columbia Icefield and west of the Sunwapta River. Visible from a lofty highway viewpoint just north of the Icefield Visitors Centre, their uplift blocks any roadside views of Mount Alberta, to the near west.

Given only a passing glance by most climbers groveling over Woolley Shoulder hell bent for Alberta, they are themselves worthy objectives, offering moderate alpine climbing in spectacular surroundings and the chance to bag two 11,000ers in one day. Those who grace their summits are treated to one of the grand spectacles in the Rockies—a bird's eye view of Alberta's grand East Face and the even more impressive north wall of Twins Tower, rising 1500 metres from the "Black Hole" of Habel Creek.

On their east side, these twins are split by a tremendous icefall that frequently calves serac chunks, which bound like bowling balls toward any climbers brazen enough to traverse below. From a safer distance, Woolley and Diadem are among the few big peaks in the Rockies where the entire climbing routes can be studied from below. Unless time is pressing, they are usually climbed together, since it's a straightforward ridge walk from either summit down to the intervening col and up the other peak. While both can be climbed in a long day from the road, they are usually tackled from a high camp below their east side.

Opposite: Mt. Woolley (l.) and Diadem Pk. A. Bivy site. B. Woolley's N Ridge.

Access From the Columbia Icefield Visitor Centre, drive 12 km north on the Icefields Parkway and park in a pullout on the east side of the road.

Approach From the parking area, cross the frigid Sunwapta River's braided channels (usually below the knee by mid-summer) and go a short distance downstream to where a major gorge empties Woolley Creek. Just left of the gorge, a good trail rises steeply through trees before leveling off and dropping down to the creek. A rough trail follows the left side of the main creek, angling right higher up to wander through the right side of a jumbled boulder field (cairns). Beyond, the trail climbs left of a small waterfall then levels out in an open, rubbly basin. Follow a fainter trail (cairns) left of the upper left branch of Woolley Creek to streamside gravel flats, with a couple of rock-walled tent sites, below a glacier descending from Mount Woolley (3-4 hours from the car).

The approach for climbing Woolley's South Slopes continues past these bivy sites by going southwest over a moraine into a rubble-filled valley, which is followed south to below the infamous Woolley Shoulder. It's usually easiest to struggle up descent paths, angling right at mid-height to round a small tower and then going back left to reach the shoulder's crest. Descend a short section of scree, contour around the glacier on the right and then swing back left to reach the Lloyd MacKay Hut at the end of the north ridge of Little Alberta at GR 701928 (6-8 hours from the highway). The hut sleeps six and can be booked through the Alpine Club of Canada (403-678-3200).

Diadem Peak
3371 metres (11,060 feet)

Diadem was the first 11,000er ascended north of the Columbia Icefield and one of only a handful scaled in the entire Canadian Rockies prior to 1900. It was nearly another 30 years before its higher companion, Mount Woolley, was finally climbed and decades more before any new routes were established on Diadem.

Today, there are two standard routes up the east side of Diadem. One skirts the icefield separating the two peaks and then, from an intervening col, goes up the easy South Ridge. A more direct line avoids the icefall altogether by following a right-trending snow couloir up the Southeast Face right to the summit. A much harder, 900-metre mixed route known as Humble Horse (IV, 5.7, W4) climbs a steep couloir that splits Diadem's precipitous and seldom-visited North Face.

Collie named the peak in 1898 for the curious 30-metre-high "diadem", or crown, of snow that capped the nearly flat summit rocks.

History
Just after their triumph on Mount Athabasca and subsequent failure on Mount Columbia, Collie's party wandered up Woolley Creek, bivouacking below the glacier on beds of heather and pine twigs. Despite an early-morning rain on their sleeping bags, they set out to climb the higher Mount Woolley, braving the formidable icefall between it and Diadem until a brief downpour forced them onto sheltering rocks.

"In five minutes it cleared, but the brief delay was possibly our salvation," they wrote. "We were just putting on the rope to ascend the icefall when, with a roar and a clatter, some tons of ice that had broken off near the summit came tumbling down, splintering into fragments in their descent. We took the friendly hint" and turned instead to scaling the face of Diadem.

They made their way up slopes of loose shale and ice, keeping close to an arête to avoid falling rock. "This involved us in a scramble up some rather diverting rock chimneys, after which a sort of miniature rock rib gave us safety from stones, and we followed it up to the summit. The rocks were very steep in places and, as usual, terribly insecure and splintered, and one had to be very careful." (Today's crampon-equipped climber avoids this rubbly rock by following a shallow snow gully all the way up the Southeast Face).

"It was bitterly cold on the top, but we stopped some time to enable Collie to make his plane-table survey and read the patent mercurial barometer, which gave the height as 11,500 feet" (later downgraded to 11,060). They descended the face in a series of thunderstorms, dodging lightning and hailstones and running to camp "like three drowned rats."

A route up the South Ridge from the Woolley-Diadem Col was ascended in 1962 by William Buckingham and Bill Hooker, who the same summer made the first ascent of Stutfield's East Peak. In July 1981, Jim Elzinga and a young Jeff Marshall (a.k.a. Humble Horse) pioneered a mixed climb up a long, steep ice couloir on Diadem's North Face. After climbing together up the lower 400 metres of the face to a five-star bivy, they ascended 10 steep pitches of ice, interspersed with some mixed sections.

"The last two pitches turn out to be the most exciting. Jim leads the second last pitch up a narrow ribbon of vertical ice that has a waterfall cascading over it," wrote Marshall. On the last pitch, "Jim gets up to the crack, decides the rock is too loose to climb, then traverses across a vertical wall of verglas up in some snow below a short rock wall that leads to the top. He starts up the wall, crampons scraping on rock, shouts down that he may fall off—which would result in the whole pitch pulling and having the force of the fall wang on a belay consisting of two melted-out screws." Elzinga, however, made it through this delicate passage and soon easy snow led to the summit.

Diadem Pk. A. SE Face. B. S Ridge. C. Woolley-Diadem Col.

Routes

First Ascent August 25, 1898: Norman Collie, Hugh Stutfield, Herman Woolley – Southeast Ridge

Routes Described Southeast Face (II), *Recommended, particularly when combined with an ascent of Mount Woolley,* South Ridge (II)

Gear Rope, glacier gear, crampons, ice axe, perhaps a few ice screws and second tool if icy

Map 83 C/6 Sunwapta Peak

Season mid-July to September

Time Trip – 1-2 days

Climbs – 6-8 hours return from high camp

Southeast Face From the bivy site, go up the right side of the glacier, to a long, right-trending snow gully that rises straight to Diadem's summit. Cross the bergschrund and simply follow this line, which steepens to more than 40 degrees higher up and can range from snow to ice to nearly bare and unpleasant rock late in dry years. Though it is possible, and tempting, to abandon this line higher up for similar gullies that lead more quickly to the upper South Ridge, gaining the ridge may require punching through a cornice.

South Ridge From the Woolley-Diadem bivy site, ascend the right side of a small glacier to the left-hand base of Diadem. Scramble up loose rock ledges to the right of the snow/ice couloir until it is safe, from ice fall, to move left into the couloir. Kick steps up the 40-degree slope, exiting left across rocks where the glacier levels off and is no longer fractured. Easily ascend the upper glacier to the Woolley-Diadem Col, turn right and follow the gentle South Ridge to Diadem's summit.

For both routes, **descend** the South Ridge route.

Mount Woolley

3405 metres (11,171 feet)

Mount Woolley is higher and more impressive than its twin, Diadem Peak, with an imposing, and as yet unclimbed, 600-metre East Face. The other side of the mountain is considerably less steep, offering a fine snow/ice route that follows the first ascent line. Most climbers, however, opt for the east side's standard route, which actually starts on Diadem to bypass a big icefall and then swings up Woolley's North Ridge.

This often-misspelled peak was named for Herman Woolley, a companion of Norman Collie and Hugh Stutfield on two British expeditions to the Columbia Icefield at the turn of the 20th century. A latecomer to mountaineering, he rose to the presidency of Great Britain's Alpine Club. His Rockies highlight was reaching, with Collie, the summit of Mount Athabasca and thus discovering the Columbia Icefield.

Jerry Skvarl on N Ridge of Mt. Woolley.

History

A few days after their Columbia Icefield exploration in 1898, Collie, Stutfield and Woolley set out to climb Mount Woolley, but bad weather and icefall dangers convinced them to settle for Diadem instead. Mount Woolley was left alone until 1925, when a nine-member Japanese team toasted their stunning first ascent of Mount Alberta with a decidedly easier jaunt up Woolley.

After a three-day rest to recuperate from their Alberta epic, this unwieldy group left their high camp above Habel Creek bound for Woolley's South Slopes. A third-person, one-paragraph entry in *Appalachia* provides a bare-bones, timekeeper's account of this first ascent—departed at 4 a.m., reached the summit in beautiful weather at 11 a.m., spent two-and-a-half hours enjoying the views and returned to camp at 5 p.m.

Today's standard route up the North Ridge was ascended in 1948, when members of a British-led expedition left Jasper to set up a camp along Diadem Creek and assess the climbing conditions on Alberta. While an international all-star team of Frank Smythe, Noel Odell and Henry Hall went to scout Alberta, David Wessel and John Ross headed up Woolley via a snow couloir right of the Woolley-Diadem icefall.

"To get into the couloir, we hurried nervously over a bridge choked with blue ice blocks dropped from over-hanging ice cliffs," Wessel wrote. "Then came about 2,000 feet of alternate step-kicking in hard snow and scrambling on the rotten rock so familiar to climbers in this region. The gradient was approximately 45 degrees, which would have afforded rapid ascent if it were not for the frequent necessity of detouring to the rocks to avoid undue exposure from threatening icefalls. At one place I slipped from my hand and foot holds. This mishap convinced us that falling ice was the lesser danger and we continued thereafter in the gully until we reached an easy snowfield stretching to the Diadem-Woolley col."

In deteriorating weather, they went up the North Ridge, cutting steps in a "steep wall of ice" near the summit. On the way down, Ross was nearly struck by a falling, basketball-sized rock.

S Slopes of Mt. Woolley. A. Lloyd MacKay Hut.

Routes

First Ascent July 26, 1925: Seiichi Hashimoto, Masanobu Hatano, Tanezo Hayakawa, Yuko Maki, Yukio Mita, Natagene Okabe, Jean Weber, *Heinrich Fuhrer, Hans Kohler* – South Face
Routes Described North Ridge (II), South Face (II)
Gear Rope, glacier gear, crampons, ice axe, (ice screws and a second tool may be needed for the South Face later in the summer)
Map 83 C/6 Sunwapta Peak
Season mid-July to September
Time Trip – 1-2 days
Climb - About 6-7 hours return from east glacier camp or Lloyd MacKay Hut

North Ridge From the bivy site at the head of Woolley Creek, ascend the right side of a small glacier to the left-hand base of Diadem. Avoid the temptation to immediately enter the narrow couloir on the left by dashing below the Woolley-Diadem Icefall, which cascades down ice blocks from collapsing seracs with frightening regularity. Instead, scramble up loose rock ledges right of the couloir until it is safe, from ice fall, to move left into the couloir. Kick steps up the 40-degree slope, exiting left across rocks where the glacier levels off and is no longer badly fractured. Easily ascend the upper glacier to the Woolley-Diadem Col and then go left up the North Ridge, which steepens just below the summit. **Note:** If you have first gone up the Southeast Face on Diadem, continue down its South Ridge to the col and then up Woolley's North Ridge.

Descend the same way.

South Face From the Lloyd MacKay Hut, ascend the glacier northeast to the obvious broad South Face, splitting two rock walls. Go straight up this 300-metre slope, which steepens to about 50 degrees higher up, before swinging right on an easier angle to intercept the North Ridge just below the summit.

In early summer, the South Face is usually covered in step-kicking snow, which because of the south-facing aspect can pose a risk of avalanche. It is thus advisable to start before first light and try to get back down before late morning. Later in the summer or in early fall, the slopes have usually turned to ice (like they do on Mount Lefroy), and a second tool and some ice screws could come in handy. Rock fall is also more likely under these conditions.

Descend the same way.

Mount Alberta

3619 metres (11,873 feet)

Mount Alberta is the hardest, loosest, scariest and most exhausting of all the 11,000ers, even by the so-called standard route. Yet in large part because of this notoriety, it's the one peak, other than perhaps Mount Robson, that serious Rockies' mountaineers most want on their climbing resumes. The other rewards are truly magnificent positions on the summit ridge and the stunning view of the magnificent north wall of Twins Tower rising from the "Black Hole" of Habel Creek and, lined up behind it, the North and South Twins and Mount Columbia.

Tucked into the angle between the Athabasca and Sunwapta Rivers, Mount Alberta is hidden from sight from a lofty viewpoint on the Icefields Parkway by the intervening bulk of Woolley and Diadem. What tourists and most mountaineers don't see is a rare Rockies' peak that has no easy way up it. Its three sheer faces have been so compressed into a tight triangle that there's scarcely a buttress or ridgeline providing angled access to the fortified summit.

The very sight of Alberta's brooding, black East Face from the top of Woolley Shoulder on the approach is sufficiently intimidating to turn some aspirants around. Even elite climbers intent on scaling the daunting North Face or Northeast Ridge routes are quite content, if those plans fall apart, to go up the normal Japanese route on the East Face.

Getting up Mount Alberta is all about experience and patience. Experience is the five-plus years of Rockies climbing to prepare for everything Alberta throws at you: an energy-sapping, scree-pounding approach with more than 1700 metres of total elevation gain, topped by 10 pitches of loose and hard-to-protect rock climbing, capped by one kilometre of narrow, often corniced ridge. And then, you have to turn around and go all the way back, knowing there's a good chance of a chilly bivouac above 3350 metres (when our party made one such bivy on the summit ridge in late August, I could hardly get into my frozen boots the next morning). More than anything, though, climbing Alberta is about having the equanimity to handle many tense hours of loose, exposed climbing, knowing you can't afford a slip.

Patience is waiting for Alberta to get in climbable shape. Often the East Face is snow covered or soaking wet, making the climbing nigh impossible, sometimes for a stretch of four or five years. But in sufficiently dry summers, the face climbing is easier, the rock fall much diminished and the ridge simpler to navigate.

Other than the first and last pitches, the belayed climbing up the East Face is mostly about 5.3 in grade, and thus most people wear boots rather than rock shoes. The problem is the holds are loose and gear placements are hard to find and largely untrustworthy. As well, it's easy to get off route onto some really chossy rock and/or unexpectedly hard climbing, all while lugging an alpine pack. Indeed, good route-finding skills are needed just to get to the bivy site and up to the upper ledge that leads to the start of the belayed climbing.

Like the province, the peak was named for Louise Caroline Alberta, the fourth daughter of Queen Victoria and wife of the Marquis of Lorne, Canada's governor general from 1878 to 1883; Lake Louise was also named after her. The mountain was first sighted in 1898 by Norman Collie, who upon reaching the summit of Mount Athabasca saw to the north this "high, flat-topped (peak) ringed around with sheer precipices, rearing its head into the sky above all its fellows." At first, he thought this might be the much sought after Mount Brown, which along with Mount Hooker had been erroneously estimated by 19th-century explorer David Douglas to be 16,000 feet high. Upon later learning these peaks were farther north, Collie applied the name Alberta to the mountain.

History

Days after his Mount Athabasca success, Collie ascended Mount Diadem and was suitably impressed by Alberta's nearby "overpowering mass (that) towered frowning many hundreds of feet above us. It is a superb peak, like a gigantic castle in shape, with terrific black cliffs falling sheer on three sides. A great wall of dark thunder-cloud loomed up over its summit; and there was a sublime aloofness, an air of grim inaccessibility, about it that was most impressive."

Such was this menacing aura that more than two decades passed before any serious designs were made on Alberta, as mountaineers contented themselves with claiming easier, more accessible big peaks. But there were few such unclimbed peaks left in 1921, when Howard Palmer's and Monroe Thorington's *A Climber's Guide to the Rocky Mountains of Canada* was published with a taunting frontpiece photo of

E Face of the hardest 11,000er, Mt. Alberta, from Stutfield Col.

Mount Alberta. Though he called it a "grim-visaged peak of terror," Palmer was keen to tackle Alberta, as was Conrad Kain, the finest alpine guide of his era, who had studied the peak and said he "could find a way up." In 1924, they and Joseph Hickson went up the Athabasca Valley and climbed King Edward. Bad weather prevented a subsequent attempt on nearby Alberta, though they did discover, and cut a trail up, the Habel Creek approach used a year later on the successful first ascent. Another accomplished Rockies climber, Val Fynn, led a bid in the early summer of 1925 but was turned back by area forest fires.

With these stalwarts stymied, the stage for the greatest climb in North America at the time was left to the unlikely first Japanese mountaineering expedition to Canada. Seasoned alpinist Yuko Maki, inspired by Palmer's guidebook photo, assembled a six-man team that, like early Himalayan expeditions, was chosen as much for expertise in geology, botany and photography as climbing skill. Arriving in Jasper with a mountain of equipment including movie cameras, 500 feet of silk rope and iron pitons, the Japanese joined forces with Swiss seasonal guides Heinrich Fuhrer and Hans Kohler—who had been invited to Jasper by the Canadian National Railway—and Swiss amateur Jean Weber. The expedition that thus left Jasper with 40 horses had swelled to nine climbers, attempting a huge, rotten, unclimbed peak none had seen; today, a party of four would be considered too slow and far too likely to dislodge rocks on each other to succeed on Alberta. About the only thing in their favour, besides blissful ignorance, was that the summer of 1925 was exceptionally dry.

From a high camp recommended by Palmer, this unwieldy team started up the lower southeast slopes of the mountain at 3:30 a.m. on July 21. It's hard to determine the exact route they followed up the East Face, though it was likely somewhat south of today's conventional gully line. Regardless, the face's horizontal strata were shattered, with scree piles over the ankles on some ledges and rock fall striking and cutting every climber and breaking two thermoses inside packs. As Weber noted, "every gripp (sic) had the tendency to remain in the hand." At one point, a four-metre, overhanging wall was overcome only by forming a human ladder, with Kohler standing unsteadily on Tanezo Hayakawa's shoulders and Fuhrer, in his felt rock shoes, perched precariously on Kohler's shoulders.

They reached the ridge at 4 p.m. and three-and-a-half hours later finally made the summit,

57

16 hours after setting out. "It was a most solemn moment for everybody," wrote Maki. "No exclamations of Bonsai. No cries of Bravo. We just shook hands voicelessly. I was simply moved to tears." Before turning around and spending a cold night halfway down the summit ridge, they marked this great achievement by leaving behind an extra ice axe and a Maki note, inside a tin can, that read: "We came from Japan so far called by this charming great mountain."

Over the next two decades, several attempts failed to reach the summit, though one group led by Rex Gibson discovered the Woolley Shoulder approach now universally used. It wasn't until 1948 that top American climbers Fred Ayres and John Oberlin, aided by the recent construction of the Jasper-Banff Highway, made the second ascent. The mountain was considerably snowier than in 1925 and the pair only got past a knife-edged, 20-metre-deep notch in the summit ridge by the "rather desperate procedure" of rappelling off an ice axe driven into the hard snow.

"I was delighted to have the security the fixed rope offered because, half way down, the veneer of snow over the ice was only four or five inches thick," Ayres wrote. "We hitched our way across the saddle horse-back fashion." At the summit, just beyond, they found that the Japanese ice axe, rumoured to be made of silver and donated by the Emperor, was instead of standard steel construction, rusted and frozen in the summit cairn. In their attempt to remove the axe for posterity, a broken piece of shaft was left frozen in place and the remainder taken to the American Alpine Club office in New York. Decades later, the two pieces were reunited in their new home in the Jasper-Yellowhead Museum.

The third ascent of Alberta, again by the East Face, was led in 1958 by Hans Gmoser, who went on to pioneer heli-skiing in Canada. A week later, locals Brian Greenwood and Dick Lofthouse made the first climb without a forced bivy, returning to their camp near today's hut well before nightfall. In 1990, Dane Waterman soloed and then down climbed the route, and in 1994 Shep Steiner and Richard Jagger did it in 33 hours, car to car", a time slashed to 18 hours a decade later by Raphael Slawinski, Dana Ruddy and Tim Haggerty. In February 2005, Slawinski, Scott Semple and Eamonn Walsh made the first winter ascent of Alberta, again by the Japanese Route.

In 1963, a four-man team led by Arthur Gran got within 60 vertical metres of the summit snow-cap via the West Face before being turned back by severe electrical storms and winter-like conditions. "All four of us suffered from leg and hand cramps, which hampered rappelling. Three had mildly frost-bitten fingers and toes," they wrote. When another party attempted the same side of the mountain seven years later, they found a note from the Gran group that read: "Go back. Go back to the pass. You will all be killed." In September 2007, Slawinski and Walsh finally made the first ascent of this steep, remote face.

Photos again inspired a route up Alberta, this time in 1972 after American legend George Lowe perused Ayre's shots of the stupendous North Face. Like Lowe's triumph on the nearby North Face of Twins Tower, Alberta's North Face (VI, 5.9, A2/A3) was one of the hardest and best big mixed routes in North America. Lowe and Jock Glidden made good time up the 600-metre ice wall and, after a first bivy and an intervening band of shattered yellow limestone, headed up 300 metres of solid rock interrupted by a smooth vertical section that required aid. Following a second bivy, they cruised up the remaining rock and summit ice fields to the top but needed one more night out while rappelling down the East Face.

In 1985, Kevin Swigert and S. Tenney climbed the Northeast Ridge (V, 5.10), a long, committing route with good rock on the steep upper headwall. More recently, Slawinski and Peter Smolik climbed this route in an amazing 14 hours, hut to hut. Slawinski calls this "an excellent and unjustly neglected route... much, much better than the Japanese route."

The "notch" on Mt. Alberta's upper S Ridge, Twins in rear.

Descending Mt. Alberta's corniced summit ridge. The Twins behind. Photo: Nancy Hansen.

Route

First Ascent July 21, 1925: Seiichi Hashimoto, Masanobu Hatano, Tanezo Hayakawa, Yuko Maki, Yukio Mita, Natagene Okabe, Jean Weber, *Heinrich Fuhrer, Hans Kohler* – East Face

Route Described East Face (V, 5.6/5.7)

Gear Two 60-metre ropes, crampons, ice axe, alpine rock rack, a few pitons and ice screws, rappel slings, bivy gear

Map 83 C/6 Sunwapta Peak

Season Late July to early September

Time Trip – 3-4 days

Climb – 12-14-plus hours return from a high camp, and often a forced bivouac

Access From the Columbia Icefield Visitor Centre, drive 12 km north on the Icefields Parkway and park in a pullout on the east side of the road.

Approach From the parking area, cross the Sunwapta River's braided channels (usually below the knee by mid-summer) and go a short distance downstream to where a major gorge empties Woolley Creek. Just left of the gorge, a good trail rises steeply through trees before leveling off and dropping down to the creek.

A rough trail follows the left side of the main creek, angling right higher up to wander through the right side of a jumbled boulder field (cairns). Beyond, the trail climbs left of a small waterfall then levels out in an open basin. Follow cairns along a fainter trail left of the upper left branch of Woolley Creek.

Near bivy corrals below the east side of Woolley and Diadem, work your way southwest over a moraine into a rubble-filled valley, which is followed south to below the dreaded Woolley Shoulder, a steep slope of teetering, backsliding rock. It's usually easiest to struggle up descent paths, angling right at mid-height to round a small tower and then going back left to reach the shoulder's crest, where stunning views of the North Face of Twins Tower provide an opportunity to catch your breath.

The Lloyd MacKay, or Alberta, Hut is visible some 250 vertical metres below, perched at the end of the north ridge of Little Alberta at GR 701928. After directly descending a short section of scree, contour around the glacier on the right and then swing back left to reach the hut (6-8 hours from the highway). This cozy hut sleeps six and has Coleman stoves and lanterns, cooking equipment and sleeping mattresses. The window in the nearby composting toilet

Mt. Alberta. A. N Face. B. NE Ridge. C. E Face. Photo: Markus Kellerhals.

provides a wonderful, seated view of Alberta's summit ridge. Phone the Alpine Club of Canada at 403-678-3200 for reservations.

The hut provides a good stopping point if you're planning a two-day approach to the high bivy site but is a very long way from which to mount a summit bid. Before leaving the hut, take the time to study the approach route to the bivy ledge and to the higher, broad ledge that leads to the start of the belayed climbing up the East Face; it's easy to get lost on both. The route up the face follows a prominent gully that rises on a right-trending angle to the second major notch from the south end of the summit ridge.

From the hut, another 200-plus, hard-earned metres must be lost dropping onto and crossing, in a southwest direction, the toe of the glacier below Alberta's East Face. Now make a rising traverse left on loose scree left of the glacier's edge to gain a bit of a trail at the base of a cliff band, towards the south end of the East Face. Traverse left under the band (some exposure) until a break near its end allows you to turn a corner right into a large scree basin. Take a rising traverse left up this wearisome scree and then, before getting too close to the edge of the West Face, work back right beneath the steep end of the South Ridge, scrambling up through a small gully on the right that should easily pierce a short cliff band. Just beyond and slightly to the right is a wide ledge, at the far left end of the East Face, with several good tent sites (4-6 hours from the hut).

Alternatively, the tent sites can also be reached via a more direct, albeit more difficult, route by scrambling upward directly left of the glacier to gain the base of the second cliff band. A steep diagonal ramp breaks the cliff band here and tops out just to the right of the bivy sites. For those comfortable on steep terrain while carrying heavy packs, or attempting a lighter, one-day climb from the hut, the latter approach promises a significant time saving.

East Face From the bivy site, go about 100 metres north along the ledge to the bottom of a large gully, marked by a large cairn; a perhaps easier alternative is to get onto ledges closer to the bivy site and angle upwards to the left of the gully. Either grovel up loose and perhaps snow-covered rock in the gully or stay on rock to the left. The gully steepens as it angles left, requiring a few fifth-class moves to reach the top of a small tower, looped with rappel slings.

From here, angle right, up a small scree bowl, to gain the indistinct start of the upper ledge (bivy corral). Despite appearances, it should be fairly easy though exposed walking north on this ledge (if you're on more difficult terrain, you're probably too high). Follow the ledge until you're beneath several prominent gray "elephants' asses." Just before the ledge crosses a gully, scramble up loose rock along a left-facing corner, where the belayed climbing begins from a sling on a chockstone. If conditions are dry and rock fall is low, an easier alternative is to begin, from about 100 metres south on the ledge, a rising traverse right that intercepts the normal route near the top of the second pitch.

Otherwise, work your way up the left-facing corner to the bottom of a steep, compact wall (poor protection, 5.6/5.7) that leads to a wide belay ledge. (Note: The belay stations all the way up the face double as rappel stations and the slings can often be used as anchors, with the odd fixed piton for added security.) The second pitch, a full 60 metres, goes straight up and slightly right, while the third works its way right to the edge of the prominent gully leading to the second notch on the summit ridge. The route now meanders up ribs to the left of the gully, though with good snow or ice considerable time can be saved by kicking steps up the upper gully. Beware, though, that any rock fall will be funneled down this gully, and it could be troublesome getting back onto the rock ribs if conditions in the gully deteriorate.

About three-quarters of the way up the face (7-8 pitches), cross to the right side of the gully where two rappel/belay stations are close together, one on each side. Climb the face on more solid, compact rock and then swing left to gain the top of the gully where it meets the summit ridge, which suddenly reveals a 2000-metre drop down the west side to the Athabasca River.

While fairly level, the South Ridge is long, reasonably narrow and broken, with many small steps that must be gone over or around, the difficulty being determined by the amount of snow cover. About one-third of the way along the ridge, a steeper step may require belaying if it can't be circumvented. Not far from the summit, an intimidating, 20-metre-deep gap in the ridge is encountered. Depending on conditions, bang in a couple of pitons or ice screws, attach a rappel rope and then carefully make your way down the knife edge of snow or rock, leaving the rope in place for the return and taking care to secure its loose ends. With the remaining rope, continue along the final bit of ridge, which can be tricky, unnerving and time-consuming if corniced.

Descend the same way. About 10 double-rope rappels are needed to get down the East Face, closely following the ascent route. You can save considerable time and frustration if, instead of tossing the ropes down into an inevitable series of snarls, you carry it with you in a rope bag or coiled and attached to your harness, paying it out as you go down. There's a good chance you won't make it all the way back to your high camp, so be prepared to bivy. If you are benighted on the ridge, there are a couple of good bivy corrals, one at the notch at the top of the East Face and another about one-quarter of the way along the ridge at a relatively wide spot.

E Face of Mt. Alberta. A. Bivy site. B. S Ridge. C. Summit ridge "notch".

Columbia Icefield

The Columbia Icefield, perched atop a broad, high plateau, is the largest continuous uplift in the Canadian Rockies. It contains 11 of the range's 11,000ers, with another half dozen a few kilometres beyond its glacial reach. Indeed, every peak in a counterclockwise ring from Athabasca to Columbia is over 3,353 metres/11,000 feet. Have a good climbing week up here, and you might start thinking, "There are only 40 to go."

At 325 square kilometres, the Columbia is also the biggest icefield in the Rockies, though it has shrunk by some 20 per cent over the past 130 years. Indeed the Athabasca Glacier, one of the icefield's six major outlet glaciers, has receded nearly 1.5 kilometres and lost two-thirds of its volume during that time. But the icefield's lure to mountaineers remains as strong as when it was discovered in 1898.

"We stood on the edge of an immense icefield, bigger than the biggest in Switzerland, which stretched mile upon mile before us like a rolling snow-covered prairie," Norman Collie and Hugh Stutfield wrote of that 1898 view from the top of the Athabasca Glacier. "The peaks, we noticed, were all a long way off, and sparser and fewer in number than in the Alps, rising only here and there like rocky islets from a frozen sea."

By far the best means of transport on this glacial highway is by alpine touring or telemark skis, something climbers have been using on the Columbia Icefield since around 1930. In late winter and spring, the icefield crevasses are mostly filled in and skiers can skim across the long flat stretches and, most importantly, descend back to civilization in rapid time. Climbers can even ski to the summit of five of the 11 peaks. Some of the first winter ascents of these peaks were by Allied troops in training during World War II.

Facilities The Columbia Icefield Centre has a restaurant and cafeteria and a Parks Canada office (780-852-6288), where you can register your icefield trips and obtain overnight camping permits. The Sunwapta Warden Station is 30 km to the north (780-852-5383). There are two campgrounds, Wilcox and Columbia Icefield, just south of the centre, and the Beauty Creek Hostel 17 km north (403-670-7580, or check www.hihostels.ca for online bookings). Pricier lodgings are available at the Columbia Icefield Chalet (1-877-423-7433). The nearest gas station (closed in winter) is 52 km south at Saskatchewan River Crossing.

Access The Columbia Icefield is reached via the Icefields Parkway (Highway 93), 127 km north of Lake Louise or 101 km south of Jasper. The side road descending to the Athabasca Glacier parking lot is closed until late spring, adding about a half-kilometre walk to the glacier's toe.

Approach For Mounts Athabasca and Andromeda (Skyladder route), cross the highway from the Columbia Icefield Centre and go up the Snocoach Road for less than 2 km to a small car pullover right of a stream. From May through October, the gate at the bottom of this road is usually open to general traffic from evening until about 9 a.m., allowing early starters to drive to the pullover, though on the way out you'll have to wait for a passing bus to open the gate (check with the Brewster Snocoach dispatcher at the Icefield Centre the day before your climb for exact times). In 2004, there were plans to relocate the climbers' parking lot about a 15-minute walk lower down the road.

For all other 11,000ers on the Columbia Icefield, including the South Ridge route on Andromeda, the initial approach involves a 6-km roped ascent of the Athabasca Glacier to reach the main ice sheet, though continued glacial recession may one day make this approach impractical. **Note:** Beyond the Athabasca Glacier, the various approaches are described separately for each peak or cluster of peaks.

Athabasca Glacier approach to Columbia Icefield. A. Mt. Andromeda.

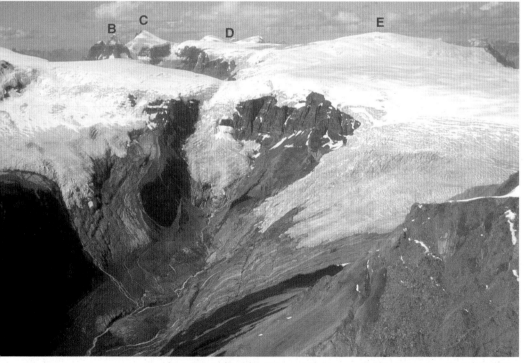

Columbia Icefield from Mt. Bryce. A. Mt. Columbia. B. South Twin.
C. North Twin. D. The Stutfields. E. Snow Dome.

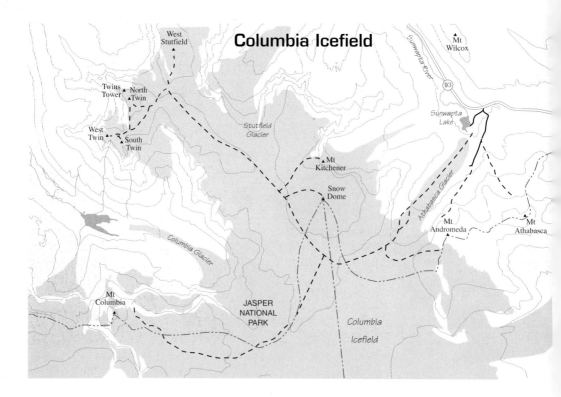

Columbia Icefield

In late spring, one can usually ski right from the toe of the Athabasca Glacier. By early summer, skis may have to be carried for the first few kilometres (another option is to walk up the Snocoach road and then drop onto the glacier). The route generally heads up the middle right of the glacier, aiming for ascending snow benches to the right of some icefalls, a few kilometres up the valley. Just below these benches, parties must choose one of two poisons.

The quickest option is to head up these right-hand snow slopes, which traverse above two icefalls. But this route exposes parties to serac fall from the heights of Snow Dome, on the right, and these ice avalanches can come crashing down at any time. While the exposure is relatively short-lived, the debris from avalanches past is a constant reminder to scurry through this shooting gallery.

The second option is to angle left up snow ramps through the middle of these icefalls. Although the odds of poking into a crevasse are considerably higher here, careful probing and a tight rope should mean any misadventures are less catastrophic than braving the serac fall. In dry years, some parties go all the way to the left edge of the glacier to bypass these icefalls. If none of these options appeals to you, the Saskatchewan Glacier, to the southeast, offers a safer approach, though it adds nearly a day to your travels.

The various routes join at the base of a long, steep snow ramp at the head of the Athabasca Glacier. Switchback up the centre of this exit ramp, taking care not to stray into crevasses, along its edges. The top of the ramp, where the angle eases, also conceals some large crevasses and caution is needed if the snow bridges are at all thin. While the icefield beyond is less crevassed, remaining roped up is strongly advised, regardless of the route taken.

Whiteouts are also common on this great ice sheet, making travel difficult and potentially dangerous. The need to carry great masses of wands to mark one's route has been lessened by the advent of GPS receivers, which can be used to easily mark waypoints, changes in direction and camps. Failure to do so has left a number of parties wandering blindly for a camp that might be less than a few hundred metres away.

Descent A number of people have fallen into crevasses skiing unroped down the Athabasca Glacier. Staying roped up is strongly advised, particularly near the top of the glacier and just below the steep exit ramp, where crevasses are more numerous than many skiers realize. Most parties choose to quickly traverse below the Snow Dome seracs, on the skier's left, rather than pick a line down the middle of the icefalls.

The Twins from Mt. Alberta. A. North Twin. B. Twins Tower. C. South Twin. D. West Twin. E. Mt. Columbia.

The Twins

The four 11,000er Twins comprise an island of towering white peaks, guarded by icefalls and spectacular drop-offs, particularly on the west. Skiing along the narrow bench of snow that connects them to the northwest end of the Columbia Icefield feels a bit like crossing a drawbridge to a well-fortified castle.

The Twins were named by climber Norman Collie in 1898 as he stared far across the Columbia Icefield at the bookends-appearance of the North and South peaks, joined by a snow col. As one gets closer, the South Twin is decidedly more impressive, with its steep snow and rock faces.

The North Twin is an easy ascent on ski or foot and the West Twin a steep but short bit of step kicking. The two signature climbs here are the South Twin and Twins Tower, with their short but stunning snow ridges that overlook a 2100-plus-metre plunge to the silvery threads of the upper Athabasca River.

Given the long approach to the Twins, it's well worth waiting for a three- or four-day window of clear weather, an infrequent occurrence especially in late spring. If there are any storm clouds on the Columbia Icefield, they'll undoubtedly be draped over the Twins. Nonetheless, a spring ski trip is much preferred to a long summer's march on foot.

Approach It is possible to climb the North or the South Twin in a day from a camp between Snow Dome and Mount Kitchener. But if you're planning on climbing two or more of the Twins, plus perhaps the two Stutfield 11,000ers, it's well worth making a high camp near Stutfield Col. Admittedly, this is a very long day from the car with big packs, exacerbated by 1600 metres of elevation gain and a last long trudge at an energy-sapping altitude of more than 3200 metres.

From the top of the Athabasca Glacier, go west-southwest up a gentle snow draw below the flanks of Snow Dome till you are almost south of the peak at a GR of about 790794. Angle right up steeper snow slopes and traverse northwest along the lower western slopes of Snow Dome to around GR 770818 (due west of the summit), taking care to avoid a large open crevasse just below this point. Drop down onto a flatter plateau and continue northwest, aiming to the right of the North Twin. The objective looks tantalizingly near, but it's nearly 6 km of tedious, rolling terrain—passing on the right below a 3300-metre bump—to reach camp near Stutfield Col (GR 722863), a little hollow between the Stutfields and the entrance to the Twins.

North Twin from Twins Tower.

North Twin
3730 metres (12,237 feet)

The North Twin's primary attraction is its lofty elevation. It's the third highest peak in the Canadian Rockies, the highest entirely in Alberta and one of the range's four 12,000ers.

Aesthetically, it's a big snow hump, enlivened by an arresting icefall that plunges east from its summit. Likewise, the two standard routes, while crevassed, are fairly pedestrian ascents of either snow slopes or a moderate ridge. Indeed, one can often ski to within a few vertical metres of the top, which rewards summiteers with a dazzling panorama of the region's high peaks.

History

If you think the approach to the Twins' high base camp is long, consider what the North Twin's first-ascent party endured in 1923. With no Icefields Parkway to whisk them to the toe of the Athabasca Glacier, they traveled from Lake Louise for a week on horseback, fording several rivers en route, to reach their base camp at Thompson Pass. That left them with the entire length of the Columbia Icefield to cross on foot, a distance of nearly 27 kilometres from camp to summit.

Leaving their treed camp at 3:20 a.m. and passing Castleguard Mountain, guide Conrad Kain and his two medical clients—Monroe Thorington, a Philadelphia ophthalmologist, and William Ladd, a New York diabetes specialist—trudged for hours across the white expanse, stopping once for a late lunch near the base of North Twin. A final 450 vertical metres up the snow and ice of the southeast slopes put them on top in 13 hours. After 20 minutes on the misty summit, they headed back.

"Someone, following in our track, may one day realize the efforts of this journey; it will afford to the analytical mind some insight of the psychology of fatigue," Thorington wrote. "The immensity of the field, the little blizzard obscuring our track and exhausting us… burning thirst until the glacier tongue was reached… and the long pull through the bush to the campfire embers, with morning light on the hills. Twenty-three hours; enough of a walk!"

In 1924, Fred Field, Osgood Field, Lem Harris and guides Joseph Biner and Edward Feuz, Jr. ascended the South Ridge after making the first ascent of the South Twin, though an unwilling Fred Field had to be almost pulled up the ridge. The distant return to their camp off the icefield ended a 24-hour day.

In 1937, a party led by Rex Gibson and Sterling Hendricks discovered skis were ideal, even in early July, for covering the long, low-angled distances to and from the icefield's peaks. Still, they fully stretched the daylight on a wandering day trip from a camp atop the Athabasca Glacier. Abandoning their initial objective of Mount Columbia when thick cloud descended, they turned around and instead groped their way up Snow Dome. When the weather suddenly cleared, they then made a dash for the North Twin, summiting at 7 p.m. and limping back to camp after 11 p.m. Like the first-ascent party, they tackled the final snow slopes on foot. In 1961, Donald Lyon, Bernie Schiesser and others claimed the first complete ascent of North Twin on skis.

Below summit of North Twin.

Routes

First Ascent July 10, 1923: William Ladd, Monroe Thorington, *Conrad Kain* – Southeast Slopes
Routes Described Southeast Slopes (II),
South Ridge (II)
Gear Rope, glacier gear, ice axe, crampons
Map 83 C/3 Columbia Icefield
Season April to early July on skis, mid-July to September on foot
Time Southeast Slopes: 4-5 hours return
South Ridge: 5-6 hours return, both from Stutfield Col

Southeast Slopes From the Stutfield Col, traverse south-southwest on a broad snow bench above a slope that drops off gradually and then abruptly over cliffs to the left. Swing back right and switchback (skis) or kick steps (foot) up the North Twin's southeast slopes (watch for crevasses), intercepting the South Ridge shortly before the summit. Changes to the upper ridge in recent years means you'll likely have to go on foot the last bit, traversing left below the corniced ridge.

Descend the same way. With good snow, this is a lovely, fast descent on skis, though you may want to keep the rope on to avoid any crevasse surprises.

South Ridge This route is usually taken when traversing the North and South Twins. Start as for the Southeast Slopes route but continue traversing around the North Twin's southern slopes to reach the South Ridge. You can keep skiing up the moderately-angled ridge but may find it easier at some point to go on foot, especially if the ridge has been wind blasted. **Descend** the same way or go down the Southeast Slopes.

Kelly Adams approaching South (I) and North Twin
A. N Ridge on South Twin. B. South-North Twin
Col. C. S Ridge on North Twin. D. SE Slopes.

Twins Tower

3640 metres (11,942 feet)

The sudden view of Twins Tower from the summit of North Twin is one of the most striking and sphincter-tightening in the Canadian Rockies. Its sharply etched South Ridge is a rising sliver of snow, with precipitous drops to the Athabasca Valley on the left and the Habel Creek drainage on the right.

Fortunately, the ridge is neither as steep nor as knife-edged as it appears and under good snow conditions it is a relatively straightforward, albeit exposed, climb. But the considerable exposure will be more keenly felt if one is unable to kick good snow steps or securely protect the climb with pickets or ice screws. The greater challenge in lean snow years may be safely navigating crevasses on the descent from the North Twin to its connecting col with Twins Tower. Indeed, continuing glacial recession could one day make this route all but impassable.

Although unknown to many mountaineers, Twins Tower is the fifth-highest peak in the Canadian Rockies, falling just shy of the magic 12,000-foot club. It is most often approached in late spring on skis, which are left below the summit of North Twin.

In summer, a handful of top alpinists have ventured into the "Black Hole" in Habel Creek and tried their hand at the 1500-metre North Face, one of the greatest and hardest big walls in North America. While this face is often considered part of the North Twin, it actually rises to the summit of Twins Tower.

History

The leader of the first-ascent party, Fritz Wiessner, was arguably the most accomplished international alpinist to visit the Rockies in its first four decades of climbing history. The German-born American climber's resume included first ascents of B.C.'s Mount Waddington and Snowpatch Spire and Wyoming's Devil's Tower. In 1939, he nearly summited K2 on a controversial American expedition that cost one climber his life and Wiessner his American Alpine Club membership for 25 years.

On the more pedestrian 1938 trip up Twins Tower, Wiessner and Chappell Cranmer reached the col at the base of the South Ridge by traversing the east side of North Twin on a snow terrace between the upper summit slopes and lower ice walls. They then climbed the tower over ice and snow just to the left of the corniced ridge. This direct, elevation-saving approach to the col appears no longer feasible, as the terrace now ends in a jumble of seracs. Instead, today's approach goes over the summit of North Twin.

In 1965, Henry Abrons, Richard Millikan and Peter Carman ventured into the "Black Hole" beneath the great North Face of Twins Tower. "In one of the more remote valleys of that sub-arctic rain forest called the Canadian Rockies, there is a mountain wall which acts like a strong drug on the mind of the observer," wrote Abrons. "So dark, sheer, and gloomy is the North Face of North Twin, like a bad dream, that I shall say very little about it. However, (we) approached the north side of North Twin last summer on the theory that where there is a face, there is a ridge."

The 1300-metre Northwest Ridge (IV, 5.7), on the right edge of the North Face, was reached via a lower glacier, an icy couloir and then an icefall. After Abrons dislocated his shoulder on a strenuous move, his companions led up the loose rock ridge to a bivouac. "Occasionally there were steep pitches or tricky moves, and a few pitons were placed for irony. But for the most part, it was as easy as climbing a rickety staircase." The next day's adventures included a deep notch that was "steep and loose and held together by verglas" and a lightning and hail storm that struck shortly before they struggled to the summit.

Abrons considered the North Face a great face problem for the next generation. But only nine years later, in August 1974, two of America's finest alpinists, George Lowe and Chris Jones conquered perhaps the biggest, hardest and scariest wall on the continent. Mind you, it took them seven days to do it. Guidebook author Robert Kruszyna condensed their challenges into a sentence: "Overhanging cracks, hard blue ice, heavy, wet snow falling continually, determination, hanging belays and bivouacs, tied-off pitons, pendulum traverses, dropped or otherwise irretrievable hardware, no possibility of retreat, fatalism, lack of food, leader's falls, rocks ricocheting down the face, cuts and bruises. Less a mountaineering feat than a gratuitous test of endurance and courage. The last great wall had yielded."

The local hard-core contemporaries of Lowe and Jones were Barry Blanchard and David

Nancy Stefani near summit of Twins Tower. Photo: Dennis Stefani.

Cheesmond. In 1986, they put up a six-day route on the North Pillar (VI, 5.10d, A2), which involved continuously hard, and sometimes gymnastic, climbing up steep and unusually solid limestone cracks, often threatened by rock fall. Bivouacking on a narrow ledge below a nearly blank wall high on the face, "we both knew how difficult, dangerous, expensive and perhaps impossible retreat would be from here," Cheesmond wrote.

"We both awoke from our troubled dreams at one point, when a huge slide of rock poured down the face to our left, with sparks lighting up the night and a terrible crashing and rumbling as tons of limestone tumbled past, following gravity to the glacier. We were shocked and stunned by our smallness in such a vast and powerful environment." Fortunately the next morning,

a perfect finger crack led up a small flake on the wall. With a storm brewing, they raced up the last, easy ground to the summit of Twins Tower, though it took them two more days on the descent to reach the highway.

In April 2004, Steve House and Marko Prezelj made just the third ascent of this intimidating north wall, putting up a new ice and rock line between the two earlier routes. During their third bivouac high on the face, House dropped the plastic shell of one boot and—after shredding one rope in a big swing when a piece of protection pulled out—had to follow his partner up the remaining steep wall for more than a day with an inner boot lashed to a crampon. Unable to return to their skis, they then had to posthole all the way across the Columbia Icefield and down the Athabasca Glacier.

Route

First Ascent July 29, 1938: Fritz Wiessner, Chappell Cranmer – South Ridge

Route Described South Ridge (II) *Recommended*

Gear Rope, glacier gear, crampons, 1-2 ice tools, couple of snow pickets and ice screws

Map 83 C/3 Columbia Icefield

Season April to early July on skis, mid-July to September on foot

Time 8-10 hours return from Stutfield Col camp

South Ridge From the Stutfield Col, ascend North Twin by the Southeast Slopes, intersecting its South Ridge shortly before the top. In spring, you can ski nearly to the summit, from where it's a steep 200-metre descent on cramponed foot to the Twins Tower col. Conditions on the descent can range from good, step-kicking snow to ice. Be prepared to navigate around some significant crevasses, which may be hidden by thin snow cover.

From the col, Twins Tower's South Ridge rises at a moderate angle but with considerable exposure, particularly at the bottom. On a warm day, snowballs bound down hundreds of metres before hurtling into the void. Under good snow conditions, it's three-plus pitches of step kicking, secured by t-slot protection with pickets and/or ice axes. The small snow summit offers superb views looking south past North Twin to South and West Twins and Mount Columbia.

Descend the same way.

Twins Tower from North Twin. Mt. Alberta in background. The route follows the obvious ridge.
Photo: Nancy Hansen.

South Twin

3580 metres (11,745 feet)

The North Ridge of South Twin is mostly a slog up a broad snow shoulder, with a sting in the tail. The narrow, last stretch of ridge is only a couple of hundred metres long, pretty much level and usually not technically demanding. But it is one of the Rockies' most attention-riveting summit snow ridges, especially as one traverses right of its crest on slopes that drop precipitously for 2100 metres to the twinkling green waters of Lake Columbia, adorned with chunks of floating ice. Once you have tiptoed past this exposed section, it's just a few more upward steps to the small summit, which offers a superb perch for admiring the steep north ridge of Mount Columbia and looking back past one's tracks to the North Twin and, in the near distance, Mount Alberta.

History

Like the North Twin's first ascent party in 1923, the South Twin's initial climbers were camped, a year later, south of the Columbia Icefield, facing a marathon march to and from their objective. Rather than leave at dawn and flail back in the dark, like their predecessors, they departed Castleguard Meadows at 8 p.m. and trekked across the icefield under a bright night sky, reaching the North Twin's base at 4:30 a.m. Shortly thereafter, they were kicking and cutting steps up the steep, hard snow of South Twin's north flank to reach the summit ridge, where things literally slowed to a crawl.

"The wind was blowing in furious gusts up here and, perched on a narrow ridge with appalling precipices on both sides, our insignificance in this particular part of the world was all too apparent," wrote Osgood Field. Thirty vertical metres from the summit, "an hour was spent cutting steps down to the edge of the rock cliff on the right, only to find that route to the summit impractical. Regaining the ridge, we started along its crest. Our progress was slow, due to the need of exercising great care, for on both sides the drop was terrifically steep and the wind was doing its best to dislodge us. We crawled along on hands and knees, the three of us in the middle of the rope moving, while the guides were anchored, and then anchoring ourselves while they in turn crawled forward."

After reaching the summit at 8 a.m. and carefully descending the ridge, they headed north and made the first ascent of the South Ridge of North Twin, reaching the top at noon. Then came the interminable trudge home, the first half into a stiff wind, the second in soft snow.

"The monotony of this work was really painful. Landmarks ahead never seemed to get any nearer. After hours of this, one's mind becomes a complete blank," said Field. "Several of us fell into a daze while walking… and mirages began to appear before us (of) bushes and trees." This delirium was not surprising, considering they'd been 24 hours on the go, covering nearly 60 kilometres on foot and climbing two peaks with an average height of 12,000 feet.

Though Fred Field and Lem Harris planted an American flag on the virgin summit of the South Twin, neither was a typical patriot. Fred later turned his back on the family (Vanderbilt) fortune, supported the Communist Party and, after spending nine months in jail for refusing to name sympathizers, spent 30 years in exile in Mexico. Harris, too, rejected family fortune to work for land ownership changes for mid-west Depression-era farmers.

Icy summit ridge of South Twin.
Photo: Mike Mokievsky-Zubok.

Skiing towards South Twin's N Ridge.

Route

First Ascent July 8, 1924: Fred Field, Osgood Field, Lem Harris, *Joseph Biner, Edward Feuz, Jr.* – North Ridge

Route Described North Ridge (II) *Recommended*

Gear Rope, glacier gear, ice axe, crampons, snow pickets and ice screws

Map 83 C/3 Columbia Icefield

Season April to early July on skis, mid-July to September on foot

Time 7-8 hours return from Stutfield Col

North Ridge From the Stutfield Col, follow a snow bench south-southwest towards the South Ridge of the North Twin. Shortly before the ridge, one can take a slightly descending traverse to reach a rocky bit of the ridge, from where steps can be kicked down to the South-North Twin Col (GR 703845). Alternatively, a more direct descent can be taken, sometimes on skis, angling down steep slopes just before the ridge. Caution: There is a long run-out here, with a cliff band below the left side of the slope.

From the col, traverse right up a short slope to reach the base of the North Ridge. Kick steps up its broad shoulder for about 250 vertical metres till the ridge levels out. The final stretch of ridge is often a snowy knife edge, with the sheer East Face on the left and the impressive plunge to the Athabasca Valley on the right. It may be possible to tightrope this ridge crest, but more likely you'll be traversing just below it on slopes to the right.

If it's hard snow or icy, you can crampon across these final slopes. If it's soft snow, you'll be facing in and kicking bucket steps. In either case, it's a good idea to belay each other across these two rope lengths of considerable exposure. **Descend** the same way.

West Twin
3360 metres (11,023 feet)

Is the West Twin truly a peak or just an extension of South Twin? At just seven metres over the magic mark, is it even an 11,000er, given the imprecision of mountain measurement?

The Rocky Mountains of Canada-North gives a qualified yes, listing it as a peak, albeit an unnamed one. To further muddy the waters, the West Twin wasn't part of the original 51-peak list of 11,000ers, though it's now considered a member of the updated club of 54.

In any event, it's a pleasant, one-hour diversion on the way to or from South Twin. From the bottom of its steep East Face, it's scarcely more than 100 metres of elevation gain to the summit, which offers a fine perspective of the other three Twins as well as Mount Alberta.

History

The first ascent belongs to Dane Waterman in 1975, making the West Twin the second last 11,000er to be climbed, if you include Centre Goodsir (1979) on the list. It's also one of only two 11,000ers boasting a solo first ascent, joining guide Conrad Kain's subversive climb of Whitehorn Mountain in 1911.

In the mid-1970s and again in the late 1980s, Waterman, with little fanfare, made some amazing solo ascents on and around the Columbia Icefield. These included first ascents of the Northwest Ridges of Mount Clemenceau and King Edward as well as the West Face of Mount Columbia, most of the North Face of Mount Bryce and the standard East Face of Mount Alberta, which he descended by down climbing unroped.

In typical fashion, Waterman's first ascent of the West Twin was not via the standard Columbia Icefield approach but from the depths of the upper Athabasca Valley, to the west. As part of an 18-day expedition in the area, he traversed a wide ledge along the base of the Twins, at 2285 metres, and then climbed a long couloir that offered "the choice of steep, slushy snow or rotten rock." This couloir led to what he called the false west summit of South Twin, which was actually the top of the West Twin.

E Face, West Twin. Tracks indicate route.

A. N Ridge, South Twin. B. Mt. Columbia,. C. West Twin. D. Mt. King Edward.

Route

First Ascent July 1975: Dane Waterman, alone - West Face

Route Described East Face (II)

Gear Rope, glacier gear, ice axe, crampons

Map 83 C/3 Columbia Icefield

Season April to early July on skis, mid-July to September on foot

Time 5-6 hours return from Stutfield Col

Approach From Stutfield Col, follow a snow bench south-southwest towards the South Ridge of the North Twin. Shortly before the ridge, one can take a slightly descending traverse to reach a rocky bit of the ridge, from where steps can be kicked down to the South-North Twin Col (GR 703845). Alternatively, a more direct descent can be taken, sometimes on skis, down steep slopes just before the ridge (Caution: There is a

long run-out here, with a cliff band below the left side of the slope). From the col, traverse right up a short slope, pass beneath the South Twin's North Ridge and continue a few hundred metres to the base of West Twin's East Face.

East Face Note: The East Face gets early morning sun, so if you're concerned about heat-provoked avalanches, you may want to leave the climb till later in the day. The face's right side has the least amount of exposure and usually offers a reasonable crossing of the bergschrund. The left side, if not corniced at the top, is also feasible, though it is briefly exposed to a terrific drop to the Athabasca Valley. Whichever way you choose, it's about 100 vertical metres of step kicking or frontpointing up the 40-degree face and then a brief walk along the North Ridge to the top. **Descend** the same way.

Stutfield – West Peak

3450 metres (11,319 feet)

The two Stutfields are the 11,000er orphans of the Columbia Icefield. Passing mountaineers en route to the nearby Twins could be forgiven for thinking this is a mere double-humped snow bump at the northwest end of the icefield, not two full-fledged, named peaks.

For what it's worth, the West Peak can claim supremacy over its eastern twin for two reasons. It's 50 metres higher and was climbed 35 years earlier, simply because no one figured the East Peak was a distinct summit. Thus for several decades, the West Peak was considered the one and only Stutfield Peak; it's still named as such on the 1:50,000 topo map.

Both West and East Stutfields are easy ski- or walk-ups, providing fine views of the nearby Twins. Like the Twins, they are much better done as a spring ski trip than as an interminable summer trudge. The two are usually ascended together as a half-day outing from Stutfield Col or as a full day that includes one of the Twins or perhaps Mount Kitchener. At the end of a Twins' expedition, the Stutfields can also be ascended early in the morning, before heading out.

The peak is named for Hugh Stutfield, who accompanied Norman Collie and Herman Woolley on their famous exploratory expedition to the Columbia Icefield area in 1898. A co-author with Collie of the classic *Climbs and Explorations in the Canadian Rockies*, Stutfield did not join the historic ascent of Mount Athabasca, as he was hunting bighorn sheep that day to replenish their diminishing larder. He seemed to enjoy stalking game as much as big peaks.

History

In 1925, Yuko Maki's large Japanese party that made the first ascent of Mount Alberta, also attempted Stutfield. From their camp at the head of Habel Creek, they went up the glacier north of the Stutfields but were forced by time to turn around below the summit, though it's not clear which of the two peaks they were on.

The first ascent of Stutfield's West Peak was part of the most memorable 36 hours of peak bagging in Rockies history. It started at 1 a.m. on July 2, 1927, when 19-year-old Harvard student Alfred Ostheimer III and guide Hans Fuhrer left their camp in the depths of the upper Athabasca Valley, armed with three days' food. They first ascended the Columbia Glacier—bypassing an icefall by going up a steep, loose rock couloir —to reach the main icefield. After waiting out a blizzard, they got soaked ascending the deep snow of the North Twin's Southeast Slopes and, upon summiting, retreated to the Stutfield Col for food and brandy. At 8 p.m., they cached their rucksacks and headed up Stutfield's West Peak.

"With frozen rope, we ascended the southwestern snow slopes of the mountain and snatched a moment's rest on a shale outcrop," wrote Ostheimer. "At 8:55 p.m. we gained the extreme northern crest and returned immediately afterward to (our packs). We then headed toward Mt. Kitchener, singing as we went. We were on the 'Roof of the Continent', yet our thoughts were far distant."

Ostheimer and Fuhrer then made the first ascent of Kitchener, summiting after midnight, continued south to make the first traverse of Snow Dome (summit 4:10 a.m.) and were headed for Mount Columbia when deteriorating weather finally sent them homeward down the Columbia Glacier, where they forced a passage down the icefall. "We jumped, roped off, slid, fell—anything—but always with towering seracs and seemingly cracks on all sides of us," said Ostheimer of the final hours of this 61-kilometre epic.

Approaching Mt. Stutfield. W Peak left. Photo: Glen Boles.

Route

First Ascent July 2, 1927: Alfred Ostheimer III, *Hans Fuhrer* – South Slopes
Route Described South Slopes (II)
Gear Rope, glacier gear, ice axe, crampons
Map 83 C/3 Columbia Icefield
Season April to early July on skis, mid-July to September on foot
Time 2-3 hours return from near Stutfield Col

Approach As for the Twins (see page 65).

South Slopes From just east of the Stutfield Col, swing left around a small rock band and contour right to gain the broad South Slopes that lead gently to the summit. **Descend** the same way.

Stutfield Col, Mt. Kitchener behind.

West (l.) and East Peaks of Mt. Stutfield. A. North Twin. B. Twins Tower. C. Stutfield Col.

Stutfield – East Peak

3390 metres (11,122 feet)

Like its western summit, the East Peak of Stutfield is a snow hump, easily ascended on skis or foot from the north end of the Columbia Icefield, usually as part of a traverse of the two peaks. What climbers don't realize from these moderate slopes is the impressive drop-off on the east to the Sunwapta Valley. These steep walls are much better appreciated from the Tangle Creek viewpoint on the Icefields Parkway. If you're interested in bagging a near-11,000er while you're at it, the summit of Mount Cromwell lies two kilometres north of the East Peak, via a connecting col.

History

With the ascent of the Centre Peak of Mount Bryce in 1961, it was assumed the last of the Canadian Rockies' 11,000ers had been climbed (Harrison, West Twin, Centre Goodsir and Tusk were later added to the list). Bill Hooker and William Buckingham were thus surprised shortly thereafter to discover the virgin East Peak of Stutfield shown as a distinct 11,000-foot summit on a new Boundary Commission map.

While most people now climb the Stutfields via the Columbia Icefield, Hooker and Buckingham took a much more direct, albeit steeper approach in 1962. Fording the Sunwapta River below Tangle Creek before dawn in mid-August, they followed a stream from the Stutfield Glacier and then a north lateral moraine towards a small, stone-covered glacier.

"Direct passage from here to the col between the East Stutfield and an unnamed 10,900-foot peak (Cromwell) was blocked by three formidable cliff bands," they wrote. "A few hundred yards to the right, we went up a steep snow gully, followed by several hundred feet of scrambling to an unstable scree band along which we traversed left to the col. The peak was then ascended by moderate ice and crusted snow on its northwest ridge." After traversing over the West Peak, the pair descended via the Columbia Icefield and Athabasca Glacier.

The Southwest Slopes, today's standard route was first ascended in August 1973 by Frank Campbell, Glen Boles, Don Forest and Mike Simpson. The latter three were members of a loose collection of Calgary climbers known as the Grizzly Group. Like Forest, the unassuming Campbell was a late bloomer, pioneering hard rock and ice routes, particularly in the Ghost River Valley, well into his 60s.

Route

First Ascent August 15, 1962: William Buckingham, Bill Hooker – Northwest Ridge
Route Described Southwest Slopes (II)
Gear Rope, glacier gear, ice axe, crampons
Maps 83 C/3 Columbia Icefield, 83 C/6 Sunwapta Peak
Season April to early July on skis, mid-July to September on foot
Time About 4 hours return from Stutfield Col

Approach As for the Twins (see page 65).

Southwest Slopes From just east of Stutfield Col, ascend the West Peak of Stutfield via its South Slopes. From the summit, descend about 250 vertical metres northeast to the col with the East Peak. Ascend the latter's easy Southwest Slopes for about 215 vertical metres to the rounded summit. **Return** the same way.

Mount Kitchener

3480 metres (11,417 feet)

Mount Kitchener is perhaps the easiest of all the 11,000ers to ascend. The only real challenge is navigating the crevasses and icefalls on the Athabasca Glacier approach. Its Southwest Slopes are so mellow, it's sometimes hard to generate enough speed to make decent ski turns on the descent. It can be climbed on skis in a long day from the car, but most parties set up a nearby camp, which also allows ascents of the Twins, Stutfields or Snow Dome.

A much more aesthetic line is the East Ridge, rising almost directly from the highway and offering fine views over the Sunwapta Valley. This pleasant snow route is abruptly interrupted near the top by a short but loose and exposed notch, adding considerable excitement to the day. It's often best to save this route for later in the summer, when the notch is more likely dry and the river crossing easier.

Like the neighbouring peaks lining the eastern escarpment of the Columbia Icefield, Kitchener is most impressively viewed from the Icefields Parkway, with its glacial cap draped over the steep North Face. In sharp contrast to the gentle icefield side, this face harbours two of the hardest alpine ice and rock climbs in the Rockies, both often requiring a bivouac.

In 1898, Columbia Icefield discoverer Norman Collie named this Peak Douglas for the Scottish botanist David Douglas, whose wildly inflated estimate of the elevations of Mounts Hooker and Brown, to the north, fuelled early alpine exploration in the Rockies. In 1916, it was renamed to honour Lord Horatio Herbert Kitchener, the famed British field marshal, killed by an exploding mine in World War I.

E Ridge of Mt. Kitchener. A. Notch. (Clive Cordery)

History

The grand scale of the Columbia Icefield seems to attract epic sieges. The midnight first ascent of Mount Kitchener was part of the ultimate icefield endurance test, in which four far-flung peaks were bagged in a 36-hour push. From a camp in the depths of the Athabasca Valley, Alfred Ostheimer III and guide Hans Fuhrer had already climbed the North Twin and the West Peak of Stutfield when they headed for Kitchener in the dark, guided by a tiny candle lantern.

"At 10:55, we stopped for ten minutes, trying to melt water in a jam tin over 'meta' flames (they had been without water for a full day). But during ten minutes, the bottom of the can did not even warm!" wrote Ostheimer. "I honestly believe we slept as we walked, at least must have dozed. Suddenly, I was rudely startled as my feet walked upon empty space and I dropped to my shoulders in a concealed crevasse. As the rope snapped tight, I felt Hans gently pulling, and with his aid I crawled back to safety." They reached the summit at 12:10 a.m. and, after peering down into the dark Sunwapta Valley, continued on to do the first traverse of Snow Dome.

The East Ridge of Kitchener proved a much more direct route to the top, via a long trudge up the Dome Glacier from the Icefields Parkway. The 1955 first-ascent party found the snow ridge straightforward until they reached an unexpected notch near the summit, which they thought was a "poor joke on the part of the mountain. The cleft was of distinctly inferior design, with both sides composed of loose, vertical shale and the bottom, 75 feet below, a steep ice chute covered by an unstable cornice. Fortunately the mists were now thick enough to prevent our seeing the total exposure," Dick Irvin and Don Claunch wrote of this exposed crux.

"Dick, belayed, moved down the rocks to an icy patch, chipped tiny holds for fingers and spikes, then crossed to more rocks and let himself carefully down onto the snow of the cornice, crossed the gap and sunk in his ice axe for a belay... it went right through the cornice." The other party member, Fred Ayres, who had been on the second ascent of Mount Alberta, slipped descending into the notch but was held by Claunch, who had made the pioneering ascent of Mount Robson's Wishbone Arête the same year. The ascent of the far side of the notch was uneventful, and they soon stood on the summit.

The true Kitchener epics were reserved for the later ascents of its North Face, which featured steep ice and loose rock. In July 1971, Chris Jones and Graham Thompson tackled this "awesome pile of rock and ice" via an ice field and then a difficult rock buttress, the latter forcing a retreat on the second day. A month later, fortified by Jeff Lowe, they avoided the rock by staying on ice and, after a miserable bivouac, finished late the next day with mixed climbing over the summit cornice. It was "one of the best climbs we had ever made," wrote Jones of what is now known as the Ramp Route, rated V, 5.8, A1.

Four years later, Lowe returned with Mike Weis to make the first ascent of the slightly harder route to the left, the Grand Central Couloir (V, 5.9, A2, WI5), named for frequent rockfall that sounded like the busy train station. "I doubt if anywhere else in the Rockies there is a couloir of equal size that is at once so beautiful and steep and singularly imposing," wrote Lowe after the intense, 26-hour climb of the couloir, which had repelled several earlier attempts.

A. Mt. Kitchener B. Snow Dome from North Twin. Photo: Thomas Choquette.

Routes

First Ascent July 3, 1927: Alfred Ostheimer III, *Hans Fuhrer* – Southwest Slopes

Route Described Southwest Slopes (II), East Ridge (II, 5.2)

Gear Rope, glacier gear, perhaps ice axe and crampons in summer, add a bit of rock gear and a few pitons for East Ridge

Map 83 C/3 Columbia Icefield

Season April to early July on skis, mid-July to September on foot for Southwest Slopes, July to September for East Ridge

Time Southwest Slopes – 2-3 hours return from nearby camp, a long day from the road
East Ridge – About 12 hours return

Southwest Slopes From the top of the Athabasca Glacier, contour around the south and then west slopes of Snow Dome at an elevation of about 3200 metres. The flats to the northwest of Snow Dome make a good central camp (around GR 760830) for ascending both Kitchener and Snow Dome. Ascend the broad, gentle Southwest Slopes for 300 vertical metres, easily skiing or walking to the summit. **Return** the same way.

East Ridge Caution: While the crossing of the Sunwapta River is usually straightforward early in the morning, it can be precariously high from glacial melt water on the return, especially on a hot day. From the Icefields Parkway about 2 km northwest of the Columbia Icefield Centre, cross the Sunwapta River and ascend the rocky ridge right of the Dome Glacier. Follow this ridge over a subsidiary peak known as K2, drop down to a saddle and then continue easily up the East Ridge on snow. Just shy of the summit, there's an unexpected notch, which is loose and exposed. Rappel or carefully down climb into the notch and then climb up the other side (about 5.2, with some fixed pitons), carrying on easily to the summit.

On the **descent**, a rappel may be needed to get down into the notch. From the saddle between Kitchener and K2, go south down a big scree slope to reach the Dome Glacier, which is followed down towards the river crossing. If the river is high, it may be better to traverse from the lower Dome Glacier across a shoulder to the toe of the Athabasca Glacier.

Snow Dome

3451 metres (11,322 feet)

As its first-ascent party noted, Snow Dome is the hydrographic apex of North America. Its melting snows descend into three great river systems that empty into three oceans—to the Pacific by the Columbia River, the Atlantic via the North Saskatchewan River and the Arctic via the Athabasca River.

In 1931, Snow Dome became the second Rockies 11,000er to be ascended in winter and on skis; a year earlier, Mount Resplendent had fallen to a solo skier. And though Snow Dome hasn't lived up to the early prediction that its descent would become one of the world's finest ski runs, it remains a popular destination on skis from spring until early summer. From almost any aspect on the Columbia Icefield, it's an easy ski ascent, though crevasses and seracs can pose a problem, particularly in a whiteout. Indeed, more than one ill-equipped party has been benighted on these seemingly benign slopes. The easy icefield approaches are in sharp contrast to Snow Dome's steep, 1000-metre East Face, which harbours the classic alpine ice route Slipstream.

This aptly-named peak was called The Dome by the Collie party, the "Snow" being added later. During the recent controversy over renaming Canada's highest peak, Mount Logan, in honour of former prime minister Pierre Trudeau, the Alpine Club of Canada briefly suggested Snow Dome instead sacrifice its long-standing name. While that idea, too, was shot down, it almost seemed fitting, considering Snow Dome is often bagged as a consolation when grander Columbia Icefield objectives are abandoned. A final bit of controversy: *The Rocky Mountains of Canada-North* lists Snow Dome as 3,451 metres/11,322 feet, the Imperial topo map gives it an 11,500-foot contour and the *Atlas of Canada* weighs in at 3,520 metres/11,545 feet.

History

Like many subsequent parties, the first-ascent team of Collie, Stutfield and Woolley turned to Snow Dome when it became clear they wouldn't make it up Mount Columbia. "After a hot and very tiring climb through snow that broke under our feet at every step, we finally reached the summit at 3:15 p.m.," they wrote of their August 1898 ascent. "The thunder clouds were now gathering, so we ran down the snow, as fast as the hidden crevasses permitted, to the head of the Athabasca icefall. The storm burst before we got off the glacier, and we reached camp at nightfall drenched to the skin."

On March 19, 1931, Clifford White, Joe Weiss and Russell Bennett culminated an 11-day ski approach from Jasper by skiing up Snow Dome via the Athabasca Glacier. They then swooshed and stem-christied down 1600 vertical metres in a continuous, hour-long run over 10 kilometres to the toe of the glacier.

"I believe that it can be classed among the few great ski runs of the world," gushed Bennett. "In spite of its present location, it is one, we believe, that all ski enthusiasts will want to include in their experience." While modern mountaineers on fat skis might find the glacial angle a tad mellow for exhilarating turns, they must admit it sure beats walking.

Much more excitement was found by intrepid alpinists along Snow Dome's steep northeast escarpment. In 1967, Don Vockeroth and Charles Raymond scaled the Northeast Buttress (IV, 5.7 A2) in one-and-a-half days, climbing mostly on rotten rock, with a 50-metre ice cliff near the top. In late December 1979, John Lauchlan and Jim Elzinga put up the nearby Slipstream (Grade IV, WI 4), named for the constant light spindrift avalanches on their first, three-day ascent.

"The next two days were spent climbing a route that is by far the best quality, classiest ice climb I have ever done," wrote Lauchlan, a leader of modern Canadian alpinism, who died soloing the nearby ice climb Polar Circus two years later. "This gully is filled by a beautiful blue stream of ice flowing from the serac at the top to the glacier 2,000 feet below." Nonetheless, at least half a dozen climbers have died climbing or descending this hazardous route since the mid-1980s.

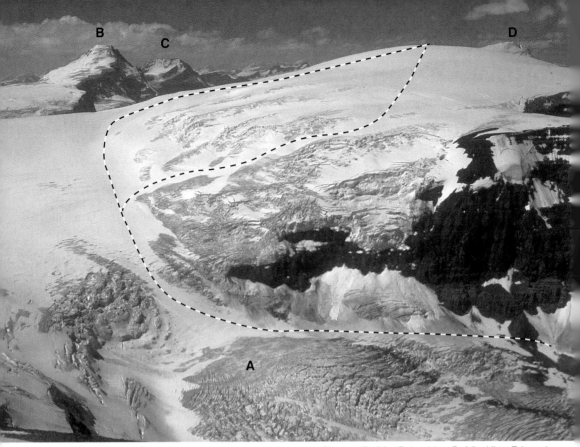

Snow Dome from Mt. Andromeda. A. Upper Athabasca Glacier. B. Mt. Columbia. C. Mt. King Edward D. North Twin. Photo: Clive Cordery.

Route

First Ascent August 20, 1898: Norman Collie, Hugh Stutfield, Herman Woolley – South Slopes

Route described South or West Slopes (II)

Gear Rope, glacier gear, plus ice axe and crampons in summer

Map 83 C/3 Columbia Icefield

Season March to early July on skis, mid-July to September on foot

Time About 7-8 hours round trip from toe of Athabasca Glacier, or 2-3 hours return from an icefield camp at base of peak

South or West Slopes From the top of the Athabasca Glacier, follow a gentle snow draw to the southwest until nearly due south of the summit (GR about 785796). From here all the way around to the west, the peak can be easily ascended via moderate slopes; watch for crevasses and seracs. The summit is the rounded top of the glacier, which provides fine views of the west flank of Mount Andromeda.

Descend the same way.

Opposite: Long approach to Mt. Columbia.
A. Trench. B. The Twins.
C. Mt. Alberta. D. the Stutfields.

Mount Columbia
3747 metres (12,293 feet)

Mount Columbia is the second-loftiest peak in the Canadian Rockies and the highest one straddling the Alberta-B.C. border. It is a magnificent, wedge-shaped mountain with a long, gradual snow ramp on its southeast side and stunning ice and rock precipices on its north and seldom-seen west aspects.

Columbia is one of the Rockies' prize ski ascents, with the final 400 or so vertical metres on foot. While not a difficult climb by the standard East Face route, poor snow conditions, notoriously fickle icefield weather and the long approach conspire to repel many an attempt. One hard-luck but persistent mountaineer needed 14 tries to reach the summit.

As its name suggests, Mount Columbia's massive southern glacial flank feeds its namesake river to the south, via the Bush River. Its northern icefields drain into the headwaters of the Athabasca River. The peak was first seen from this side in 1901 by German explorer Jean Habel, who called it Gamma.

History

Norman Collie may well have deserved the first ascent of Mount Columbia, but James Outram snatched it from his grasp in a classic case of mountaineering opportunism. When Collie and Herman Woolley made their historic ascent of Mount Athabasca in 1898, they discovered both the Columbia Icefield and its biggest peak. "Chisel-shaped at the head, covered with glaciers and ice, it also stood alone, and I at once recognized the great peak I was in search of," wrote Collie of Mount Columbia, which he mistook for the exaggeratedly high Mount Brown, in reality some distance to the north. A couple of days later, they and Hugh Stutfield set out for Columbia via the Athabasca Glacier, the latter taking five hours of navigating around crevasses and seracs to surmount. While Columbia appeared an easy "snow grind," it was still a long ways off so, in deteriorating weather, they turned back and bagged Snow Dome as a consolation.

Descending from Mt. Columbia. Photo: Markus Kellerhals.

Two years later, Collie and Stutfield tried to reach Columbia and its neighbouring giants from the south, via the Bush River Valley. But after several energy-sapping weeks of hacking their way through dense, swampy forest, they admitted defeat, still some 20 kilometres from their objective.

In 1902, Collie and his companions returned to the Rockies for another crack at Columbia and other area peaks. But their departure from England was delayed, and by the time they reached an arranged Glacier Lake rendezvous with Outram, they discovered the ambitious pastor and his guide, Christian Kaufmann, had just scooped Columbia on them. Though in the gentlemanly British tradition of the time, nothing was written about this disappointment, it's interesting to note the only description they applied to Outram—who spent the next week climbing with them—was "indefatigable".

Outfitter Jimmy Simpson might have chosen a different word to describe Outram, who apparently refused his request to accompany the pair up Columbia. Simpson soon got his revenge, turning down Outram's request to

climb Lyell 2 and help carry surveying and camera equipment.

Outram and Kaufmann certainly needed stamina to climb Columbia in a 22-hour day from a camp at Thompson Pass, south of the icefield. "Thus far it had been a long, monotonous tramp, over a dozen miles in length, through soft snow, with an almost continuous easy rise," Outram wrote of the approach. "Now a steep snow arête rose before us, somewhat ladder-like, in which we sunk to our knees or deeper, although at almost every step our feet reached a glassy surface of ice, necessitating caution against both slipping and avalanching." But they soon reached the summit, thus claiming the first ascent of a 12,000er in the Canadian Rockies.

This East Face was the intended route of a 1924 party, which included three packers who "had never had any experience in mountain climbing, other than that which is necessary for hunting sheep and goat," wrote trip leader Osgood Field. But a "gaping bergschrund and huge snow cliffs" forced them to do a first ascent of the South Ridge, where a rotten cliff band required three hours to gain 100 vertical metres. At the end of the 23-hour, 45-kilometre return trip, Field said of novices Ernie Stenton, Cecil Smith and Max Brooks: "As far as they were concerned, mountain climbing was now a thing of the past."

The first attempt on skis was a two-and-a-half week epic, covering 360 kilometres to and from Jasper in March 1932. Peter Withers, Joe Weiss, C.V. Jeffery and A.D. Jeffery skied up the upper Athabasca River Valley and then weaved through the huge ice blocks of the Columbia Glacier. After camping in a snow hole, they crossed the icefield and descended all the way down the Athabasca Glacier to a food cache. After two days of storms and gale-force winds, they broke trail in fresh snow for 32 kilometres to the foot of Columbia, where recurring storms and dwindling daylight forced them to turn around 100 vertical metres from the summit and ski all the way back. It took another week to ski back to Jasper, via Brazeau and Maligne Lakes. In 1937, Rex Gibson, Sterling Hendricks and Ken Boucher climbed Columbia after a July ski approach, Gibson and Hendricks thus becoming the first to climb all four of the Rockies' 12,000-foot peaks.

Columbia's snow and rock West Face was climbed in 1951 by George Bell and David Michael in half a day. The nearly 2000-metre North Face/North Ridge (V, 5.7), one of the Rockies' finest mixed climbs, was ascended by Chris Jones and Graham Thompson in August 1970 after an approach via the Athabasca Valley. They went up two icefields connected by a ramp, mostly on hard, steep ice that required substantial step cutting. After nearly two days with crampons on, they reached the North Ridge, where a number of hard rock pitches led to a second bivouac, in a blowing snowstorm that left their feet numbed. Finally, on the third day, they reached the summit in poor visibility, then stumbled down the Columbia Icefield.

"The climb did not take eight hours, as we had thought, but two-and-a-half days of intense effort, perhaps the finest alpine climb we had ever done," wrote Jones. "We had a lot to be thankful for."

Mt. Columbia from the Twins.
A. E Face. B. N Ridge.

Mt. Columbia camp. A. S Ridge. B. E Face. Photo: Roman Pachovsky.

Routes

First Ascent July 19, 1902: James Outram, *Christian Kaufmann* – East Face

Routes Described East Face (II) *Recommended,* South Ridge (II)

Gear Rope, glacier gear, crampons, ice axe, perhaps a couple of ice screws and pickets

Map 83 C/3 Columbia Icefield

Season April to early July on skis, mid-July to September on foot

Time 6-8 hours return from camp near the trench

Approach From the top of the Athabasca Glacier, head southwest, taking an almost straight bearing for a prominent trench (GR 757760), almost 7 km away (6-7 hours from the road). Camp in or on either side of this trench, a low spot where the glacier flows south, its melt waters emptying into the Bush River.

East Face From the trench, ascend a long, gradual snow slope west-northwest to the base of the peak, taking care to avoid crevasses. Cross the bergschrund (may be problematic) and kick steps for about 400 vertical metres up the snow face, to the south of some seracs. Beware of avalanche conditions on this face, especially on warm spring days.

South Ridge This is a slightly longer but more aesthetic line than the East Face. Traverse left to the base of the South Ridge, which is climbed directly, other than for two loose cliff bands, which are avoided on steep snow to the right of the ridge crest.

The **descent** for both routes is usually the East Face, unless avalanche or bergschrund conditions dictate a safer route down the South Ridge.

Opposite: Nancy Hansen skiing below Mt. Andromeda. A. AA Col. B. NE summit. C. SW summit.

Mount Andromeda

3450 metres (11,319 feet)

Mount Andromeda sits on the Continental Divide at the east end of the Columbia Icefield, overlooking the Athabasca Glacier to the north and the Saskatchewan Glacier to the south. It boasts two summits, listed as being of equal height, though the northeast one appears slightly higher.

Despite the proximity to its famous neighbour, Mount Athabasca, Andromeda was long consigned to obscurity. Perhaps because it was nameless, no one bothered climbing it until 1930, making it the last of the significant Columbia Icefield peaks to be scaled. The latest edition of the official guidebook, *The Rocky Mountains of Canada–North,* still lists it as "Unnamed (Andromeda)".

But Andromeda has made up for lost time in recent decades, with more than a dozen named routes, many of them steep alpine climbs crowded into the North Bowl and Northeast Face. For intermediate climbers, Skyladder—with its elegant, sweeping rise above the Athabasca Glacier—is one of the most popular snow-and-ice ascents in the Rockies. For hardcore alpinists,

Andromeda Strain is among the range's hardest mixed routes. And for ski mountaineers seeking new challenges, the overlooked South Ridge offers a superb spring ascent, with an exhilarating run back down the Athabasca Glacier.

In 1938, climber Rex Gibson named Andromeda for the mythological wife of Perseus, who rescued her from a sea monster. It is also the name of a constellation, containing the nearest galaxy to our Milky Way, a mere two million light years away.

History

Andromeda was finally climbed in 1930 by four Americans, who called it Mount Cirque for the prominent amphitheatre on its Northeast Face. They obviously didn't think much of their accomplishment, submitting only a cursory account of their ascent to the *Canadian Alpine Journal.* Following today's standard ski route, they marched up the Athabasca Glacier to its head and cramponed over hard, steep snow to the base of the South Ridge.

Descending S Ridge, Mt. Andromeda. A. unnamed 3330-metre peak. B. Mt. Bryce.

"The shaly and snow ridge was then followed over Peak 11,200 to Peak 11,300," they wrote. "An attempt to traverse to Mount Athabaska (sic) was frustrated by rock-swept perpendicular cliffs." They instead returned the way they came, ending the round trip in just over 11 hours.

It was a hectic summer of mountaineering in the Canadian Rockies for this climbing team. It ended suddenly, and tragically, for Newman Waffl, a New Jersey teacher and musician, who disappeared, likely in an avalanche while soloing the West Face and Northwest Arête of Mount Robson. "Mount Robson is not so much difficult as dangerous. It is no mountain to trifle with," he had prophetically said following an earlier attempt on the mountain that summer. A peak close to Robson is named for him.

Andromeda's Skyladder route was first climbed in 1961 by John Fairley and Bert Parke, who were working at a geophysics camp on the Athabasca Glacier. They had no difficulties with this 50-degree route, other than sore ankles from cramponing up hard snow in obviously soft boots. On the descent towards the Athabasca-Andromeda Col, avalanche danger from a metre of snow atop ice forced them instead to walk all the way down the Saskatchewan Glacier. Unable to hitch a ride back, they slept beside the road and trudged back to their camp the next morning, late for work but very satisfied.

On the northeast side of the mountain, Andromeda Strain (5.9, A2, WI4) follows a narrow, 650-metre couloir system split at mid-height by a steep, 100-metre rock band. In the early 1980s, it repelled the repeated efforts of two premier Rockies alpine climbers, Barry Blanchard and David Cheesmond. Finally in April 1983, on the fourth attempt for each and with Tim Friesen in tow, they finally got up the route in two nerve-wracking days.

"After two hours in the chimney, I've gained 70 feet," wrote Blanchard of a crux section near the end of the first day. "The climbing is an intense mixture of free moves, aid moves, mixed climbing and the constant clearing of snow mushrooms." Though the technical difficulty eased on the second day, the gear placements were thin and delicate tool hooking was required on scant ice patches and small rock ledges.

Opposite: Clive Cordery near top of Skyladder.
Photo: John Shaw.

Routes

First Ascent July 21, 1930: William Hainsworth, John Lehman, Max Strumia, Newman Waffl – South Ridge

Routes Described South Ridge (II) *Recommended as a ski route,* Skyladder (III) *Recommended*

Gear Rope, glacier gear, crampons and ice axe. For Skyladder, add a second ice tool and ice screws and for the AA Col descent, add rappel gear

Map 83 C/3 Columbia Icefield

Season March to June (South Ridge, on skis), late May to September (Skyladder)

Time South Ridge – About 10 hours return
Skyladder – About 12 hours return

South Ridge Though this route can be tackled on foot in summer, it is recommended primarily as a ski ascent. In spring, the Athabasca Glacier's crevasses are largely filled in and the ski run down is usually fast and fun, in sharp contrast to the tedious trudge out on foot.

Approach Ascend the Athabasca Glacier (see page 62). Once safely beyond the biggest cracks at its top, swing left, aiming roughly for the bottom of the South Ridge. To avoid some large, obvious holes, take a high, traversing line on slopes to the right, curving around the shoulder of an unnamed subsidiary snow peak, just shy of being an 11,000er itself. Placing some

wands from the top of the Athabasca Glacier to the toe of the ridge might prove a godsend, should a sudden whiteout obscure the route on the return.

Route From the col just beyond this subsidiary bump, follow the South Ridge, skiing as far as you can before going on foot up the ever-narrowing ridge. After passing the top of the Skyladder route (a number of alpinists have *skied* down this "don't-fall" route), head east up a broad slope to the rounded southwest summit, staying well clear of cornices on the left. It's about 30 minutes farther to the northeast summit via a narrow, corniced ridge. On a clear day, the summit provides stellar views of the Columbia Icefield, Mount Columbia and, in the distance, the edge of the Twins.

Descend the same way if on skis, taking care to avoid crevasses above and on the Athabasca Glacier. If on foot in summer, a shorter but more complex option is to descend to the Andromeda-Athabasca (AA) Col (see below).

Skyladder Because of its accessibility and popularity as a "moderate" snow/ice route, Skyladder attracts a fair number of inexperienced mountaineers—witness the high number of misadventures and rescues over the past two decades. The problem is usually underestimating either the length of the day or the AA Col descent, which is longer and often more challenging than going up. The typical scenario is a descending party, often in poor visibility, mistakenly wanders down the Southeast Ridge instead of down the East Ridge towards the AA Col and, if lucky, suffers no more than a night out high on the mountain. All groups should properly research the descent route, carry a map and a compass or a GPS and sufficient clothing, food and water.

Skyladder can range from kicking steps in good snow early in the season (May-June) to bashing one's way up ice and even some exposed gravel later in the season. With continued glacial recession, this route may one day disappear altogether.

Approach Across the highway from the Columbia Icefield Centre, either park at the bottom of the Snocoach Road and go on foot or, if the gate is open, drive less than 2 km to the climbers' parking area, right of a stream and just before

Skyladder route, Mt. Andromeda.

a second gate. Continue walking up the road for about 20 minutes, departing left onto an indistinct trail near the Snocoach parking lot. Traverse right on moraines below the Northeast Face amphitheatre and then take a rising line to gain the fractured lower glacier, staying on the left edge past seracs and crevasses (could be problematic when dry) to gain a more level bench. Traverse across this to the bottom of the Skyladder route.

Route Cross the bergschrund where feasible (challenging later in the season), picking a line up the right side of the face between exposed rocks. There is often considerable danger from rockfall here, which may be lessened by hugging the right side of the snow/ice. This bottom section is the steepest, 45-to-50 degrees, backing off to 35 degrees or less as the route swings back left towards its top at the shoulder. It's still a fair plod, along the South Ridge, if you choose to go to the summit. Beware of cornices on the left and also of avalanche hazard after recent snowfalls coupled with wind.

Take your pick of evils on the **descent**. Going down the South Ridge and Athabasca Glacier is gentler but a long trudge, often in soft snow, and exposed to big crevasses in the summer and early fall. The standard descent follows the East Ridge, with a couple of rappels (backed up with some pitons) needed to get down a steeper, loose and shallow gully on the lower ridge. To find the first rappel station, follow a bend in the ridge left until almost directly above AA Col and then scramble down the shallow gully a short distance (some avalanche hazard if snow conditions are unstable). There is another line of rappel stations farther to the left, going down the arête in a more direct line to the col.

From the AA Col, take care descending the steeper snow/ice slopes to the AA Glacier. A rappel station on rocks to the right (east) can be used to get over the bergschrund, though those with a single rope may need to build a second, ice station farther down before rapping over the bergschrund. Rope up for the glacier and head to its lower right corner, where a well-beaten trail descends to the Snocoach Road.

Mount Athabasca

3491 metres (11,453 feet)

Overlooking the crowded Columbia Icefield Centre, Mount Athabasca is one of the most photographed and climbed of all the 11,000ers. It's the first glaciated peak ascended by many budding mountaineers—often on an introductory snow-and-ice course—and it also attracts many guided and foreign alpinists. On a sunny summer's day, spectators in the Icefield Centre parking lot can watch black dots of climbers marching up a well-beaten snow track on the North Glacier towards the mountain's north flanks.

Athabasca's popularity arises from its shining visibility, short approach and diversity of routes. The glaciated northern aspect harbours three classic lines for alpinists of all ambitions—moving from right to left, the trudge up the North Glacier route, the 45-degree snow-and-ice route on Silverhorn and the up-to-55-degree North Face, topped by an often icy and challenging rock exit. The reward for all summiteers on a clear day is to discover the Columbia Icefield's wondrous expanse and majestic peaks.

Many parties get a pre-dawn start for all three routes to beat the crowds, bypass the seracs on Silverhorn early, and get up and down the mountain before the North Glacier's snow turns to mush. All three are exposed to considerable crevasses and to avalanches, even in summer, though the steeper North Face and Silverhorn routes get icier as the season progresses. For that reason, the AA Col route, following the basin between Athabasca and Andromeda, offers a moderate alternative to the North Glacier route for unseasoned mountaineers, though it can be icier. It can also be an easier and safer descent line, particularly if the snow on the North Glacier route has softened or visibility is poor.

Athabasca is believed to be from a Cree word meaning "where there are reeds or grasses." In the late 1700s, fur traders used this word—or variations ranging from Great Arabuska to Athapaskow—to describe the swampy, willowy delta where the Athabasca River empties into Lake Athabasca in northeast Alberta. The name, often spelled "Athabaska" in early years, found its way to the river's source in 1898, when the first-ascent party christened the mountain Athabasca Peak.

History

The first ascent of Mount Athabasca was a seminal event in Canadian mountaineering history, resulting in the discovery of the Columbia Icefield. Norman Collie had seen the peak from Mount Freshfield, some 50 kilometres to the southeast, in 1897 and, thinking it might be Mount Brown or Hooker (reputed to be more than 16,000 feet high), launched another Rockies expedition a year later.

After an 18-day, 240-kilometre approach by horseback led by outfitter Bill Peyto, Collie's party reached the base of this "noble, snow-crowned peak, about 12,000 feet in height, with splendid rock precipices and hanging glaciers; and on its right the tongue of a fine glacier descending in serpentine sinuosities to the bottom of the valley." Leaving Hugh Stutfield behind to hunt for bighorn sheep, Collie and Woolley ascended Athabasca's Northeast Arête, a mixture of rotten limestone and steep ice, the latter requiring Woolley to cut steps for two hours. After squeezing up a loose chimney and surmounting an overhanging rock step, they reached the summit at 5:15 p.m. and were astonished at what they saw.

"The view that lay before us in the evening light was one that does not often fall to the lot of modern mountaineers," wrote Collie in perhaps the most famous passage in Canadian mountaineering. "A new world was spread at our feet; to the westward stretched a vast icefield probably never before seen by human eye, and surrounded by entirely unknown, unnamed and unclimbed peaks."

The much easier North Glacier route was climbed in 1920 by Joseph Hickson, E.L. Reford and guide Edward Feuz, Jr. The nearby Silverhorn route fell in 1947 to a party that included Rockies stalwart Rex Gibson and two famous British climbers—Frank Smythe and Noel Odell, the last man to see George Mallory and Andrew Irvine alive on Mount Everest in 1924.

Duane Soper's and Dean Rau's 1971 ascent of Athabasca's North Face—involving five-and-a-half, 200-foot pitches of ice up to 55 degrees—was one of the early bigger ice face routes in the Canadian Rockies. Today, this compelling line remains a popular test for climbers graduating to steep alpine snow/ice climbs.

Routes

First Ascent August 17, 1898: Norman Collie, Herman Woolley – North Ridge

Routes Described North Glacier (II), Silverhorn (II) *Recommended*, North Face (III, 5.4/5.5) *Recommended*, AA Col (II)

Gear Rope, glacier gear, ice axe and crampons on all four routes. A second tool and ice screws are needed on the North Face (and on Silverhorn if it is icy), plus a small rock rack. Ice screws may also be needed on the AA Col route

Map 83 C/3 Columbia Icefield

Season Mid-May to early October

Time 8-12 hours return for the North Glacier, Silverhorn and AA Col routes; add a couple of hours for the North Face

Access Across the highway from the Columbia Icefield Centre, either park at the bottom of the Snocoach Road and go on foot or, if the gate is open, drive less than 2 km to the climbers' parking area, right of a stream and just before a second gate.

Approach For all three described routes that start up the North Glacier, head left from the climbers' parking lot on a trail up the ridge of a moraine. Where the moraine reaches a headwall, either go up a steep, loose gully if there is good snow or descend slightly off the moraine (cairn) and pick up a switch-backing trail that finishes with an ascending traverse left under cliffs. Continue up the moraine to near its end, dropping down easily onto the glacier at an elevation of about 2600 metres. Take a rising traverse left across the glacier, aiming roughly to the right of a prominent rock and ice bulge below the main, dish-shaped face. Move as quickly as possible beneath an upper icefield section exposed to

Mt. Athabasca. A. N Face. B. Silverhorn. C. North Glacier.

serac fall, staying in the flats and avoiding the temptation to traverse too high, which runs into a series of parallel crevasses.

North Glacier Beyond the left end of the seracs and just before a steeper slope leading to the Silverhorn Col, head straight up underneath the top of the Silverhorn route (beware of crevasses), then traverse right on a rising snow ramp. Take care here as the ramp has become considerably steeper over the years and is exposed to avalanches and to potential falls over the seracs below. From the top of the ramp, watch for crevasses as you head up more open slopes leading to an often windblown saddle. Follow the usually hard-packed and sometimes snow-free West Ridge easily to the top of the Silverhorn route and continue on the near-level ridge to the summit.

Silverhorn From where the North Glacier route swings right, continue left up the glacier to reach a col at the base of a steep, right-trending shoulder. Cross a bergschrund and head straight up the shoulder on 40- to 45-degree snow and/or ice for about 300 vertical metres, using running protection or pitching out if necessary. Upon reaching the false summit, follow the West Ridge briefly left to the summit.

North Face From the base of Silverhorn, traverse left into a bowl under the main face until below an obvious weakness near the left (east) end of the rock band far above. (A similar, slightly harder, route known as The Hourglass, starts below the right-hand end of this upper rock band where it meets a serac). Cross the bergschrund and head straight up the face toward the weakness for some 300 vertical metres on slopes that steadily steepen to upwards of 50 degrees. Be prepared for both ice and snow or, if you're unlucky, thin snow over brittle ice (the view from the highway should provide a general idea of what shape the face is in). Depending on conditions and climber expertise, the lower sections can range from running belays to pitched-out climbing.

Near the top of the face, the route angles right through a steeper pitch of loose rock, which is the crux, particularly if covered in verglas or tool placements are poor, in which case the 5.4/5.5 grade will seem low (a couple of fixed pitons may provide some security). A final 100 metres of easier ground leads to the summit.

Approaching crux on Athabasca's N Face.
Photo: Doug Fulford.

AA Col From the climbers' parking lot, continue on foot up the Snocoach Road, departing left onto an indistinct trail near the Snocoach parking lot. As the trail traverses right on moraines below the Northeast Face amphitheatre, take a well-beaten track that goes more directly up toward the left side of this amphitheatre. Round a rock corner and ascend the left side of the AA Glacier, or stay on scree to the left, to the head of the basin. Cross the bergschrund and go up steeper slopes of snow, ice and/or scree to the AA Col and then follow the West Ridge easily to the summit.

Descent For the first three routes, the usual descent is down the North Glacier route. In soft snow conditions, an alternative is to follow the West Ridge all the way down to the AA Col. From here, descend a short section of steeper ice or snow to a glacier, which is followed down (or on scree slopes to the right) to a rock corner on the right, where a well-beaten trail descends to the Snocoach Road.

Clemenceau Icefield

The Clemenceau Icefield is one of the most remote and spectacularly rugged mountaineering destinations in the Canadian Rockies. Located on the B.C. side of the Continental Divide, just west of the popular Columbia Icefield, it seems another world away. Unless you fly, the shortest approach into the heart of the icefield is at least three hard days on foot, making it the longest self-propelled access of any area described in this book.

But it's definitely worth the effort. The Clemenceau contains three stunning peaks over 11,000 feet—Mount Clemenceau, Tsar Mountain and Tusk Peak—and 20 others over 10,000 feet, the majority along the icefield's western rim and overlooking perhaps the most tortuous mass of ice in the entire range. "In 25 years of photographic surveying in the Canadian Rockies, I have not seen a more wonderful and panoramic (view) of glaciers and their tributaries," wrote A.O. Wheeler, head of the Alberta/B.C. Boundary Commission, which mapped the area around 1920.

While the icefield's size (313 square kilometres) falls just shy of the Columbia's 325 square kilometres, its 10 officially-named glaciers outrank its neighbour in number and complexity. And the various approaches from the Icefields Parkway are among the grandest marches in the Rockies, crossing numerous glaciers, fording various rivers and streams and passing beneath soaring summits. Indeed, the actual climbs are just highlights of a magnificent wilderness expedition, where you might roam for a week without seeing another party.

As one of only four 12,000-foot peaks in the Rockies, the massive, wedge-shaped Mount Clemenceau is the primary objective of climbers and ski mountaineers on the icefield. But the splendid pyramid of Tsar is another fine objective and Tusk, a late entry to the 11,000er club, boasts one of the Rockies' premier summit views.

History

Despite its remoteness, the area had early mountaineering visitors. In 1892, while searching for the supposed giants Mounts Hooker and Brown, Arthur Coleman made an aborted effort to reach what he called Pyramid Mountain (now known as Clemenceau). Four years later, Walter Wilcox and Robert Barrett stared at this impressive peak from Fortress Mountain. In 1920, the icefield was reached via the Wood River and Clemenceau Creek by the Alberta/B.C. Boundary Commission, which couldn't establish a complete line of survey stations and thus failed to identify a couple of glaciers on the resulting topographical map of the area.

The first ascents of the icefield's big peaks in the mid-1920s involved extended expeditions from Jasper supported by outfitters, packers, cooks and long horse trains. Four years after Mount Clemenceau was finally scaled in 1923, Alfred Ostheimer III and guide Hans Fuhrer knocked off more than a dozen first ascents during their amazing, whirlwind tour of 1927. Other than a mid-1930s visit by Rex Gibson, Bob Hind, Sterling Hendricks and J. Southard, the area was subsequently all but forgotten until a group led by George Bell added a few first ascents in 1951. Most of the remaining virgin summits fell to groups from the Alpine Club of Canada's 1972 General Mountaineering Camp.

Approaches For a long time, the normal approach to the Clemenceau Icefield was a four- or five-day slog from the Icefields Parkway, complete with a few sizable river crossings. Today, the painless way for most parties is to simply fly in, either by helicopter (phone Alpine Helicopters in Golden at 250-344-7444) or by fixed-wing airplane in winter or spring (phone Alpenglow Aviation in Golden at 250-344-7117). But for those interested in earning their peaks the old-fashioned way, there are several three-to-five-day walking approaches from the Icefields Parkway, all through spectacular, glaciated wilderness.

The Sullivan River Road is no longer a viable access route to the Clemenceau Icefield from the south, which used to cut two to three days off the approach. The upper section of the logging road was decommissioned and a critical bridge removed in the summer of 2005. The options now are to fly in or to walk in the old way, from the Icefields Parkway – a three-to-five-day approach, albeit through spectacular terrain.

Icefields Parkway Approaches
Maps: 83 C/12 Athabasca Falls, 83 C/5 Fortress Lake, 83 C/6 Sunwapta Peak, 83 C/4 Clemenceau Icefield.

Several routes have been used to access the Clemenceau Icefield from the Icefields Parkway,

Access for Clemenceau Icefield
and Bush River 11,000ers

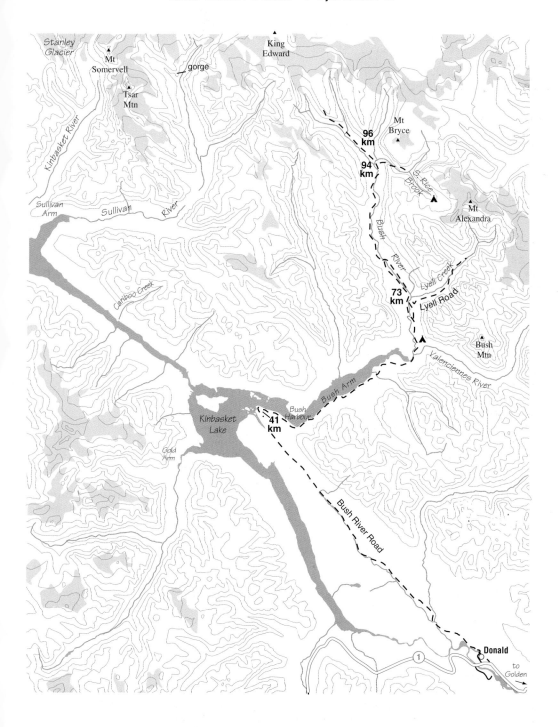

Mt. Clemenceau from below Lawrence Grassi Hut.

north of the Columbia Icefield. All require three to five days of walking, or skiing, considerable route finding and numerous river and stream crossings. These crossings can be dangerous or impassable early in the season or at other times of high water, such as on hot summer days with considerable glacial runoff. Continued rapid glacial recession also means many of the area's glaciers are considerably reduced from their depiction on topo maps, often resulting in unmarked meltwater lakes at their toes and rock-hard moraines to traverse.

All the following routes lead to the northern end of the Clemenceau Icefield and reasonably close to two 11,000ers – Mount Clemenceau and Tusk Peak. Reaching the third, Tsar Mountain, requires nearly another day's walk south across several glaciers (see detailed description on page 108).

Perhaps the most direct approach, especially for accessing Mount Clemenceau and Tusk Peak, is the Chisel Pass route. From the Sunwapta Falls parking lot on the Icefields Parkway, head south on a good, level trail along the east side

of the Athabasca River, which is crossed on a bridge at about 15 km. Further along, you ford the Chaba River (usually reasonable in mid-summer), shortly before reaching Fortress Pass and the east end of Fortress Lake (campground) at about 24 km. Next, bash your way around the south end of the lake (sloshing through the water in running shoes helps avoid the fallen timber) for about 5 km to a fishing camp and then follow a good trail southwest through woods along Chisel Creek. From gravel flats beyond, bypass a narrow canyon by scrambling up a short wall to the right of a small waterfall above the right side of the creek. After traversing rubbly slopes above the same side of the creek and skirting right of a receding glacier, round a rocky hump on its right to reach Chisel Pass (GR 401933).

From the pass, descend south on barren slopes, gradually working your way left, crossing the outlet stream of a small lake (good campsite, with waterfall above, GR 401905). Ascend a short treed ridge to the northwest and then descend south-southwest through jumbled boulders, eventually angling left through thin bush to gain a large moraine, which is ascended on a goat track for about half a kilometre. Traverse right to reach a narrow canyon, with a huge slab on the left, and ascend it to a large lake, carefully crossing its outlet stream and then angling left up a rubble slope to reach broad meadows above the lower Clemenceau Glacier (GR 397867, good campsites).

Another fairly direct route has a similar start as the Chisel Pass approach, heading south from Sunwapta Falls along the Athabasca River. But instead of turning west near Fortress Pass to reach Fortress Lake, continue south along the Chaba River and follow its west fork to the foot of the West Chaba Glacier. Go west up the glacier, crossing the divide at a pass (GR 429923) 1.5 km southwest of Mount Franklin and then swing west to cross a higher col less than 1 km southeast of Mount Brouillard. Go south along the col's ridge for several hundred metres until a broad snow couloir leads down onto the Peary Glacier. Contour southwest across the glacier and then go up through a gap left of a small knob on the west end of Mount Peary. Drop down scree on the other side to reach the Younghusband Glacier, which is crossed to gain the Clemenceau Glacier.

A more circuitous but spectacularly scenic approach starts by going over Woolley Shoulder as if approaching Mount Alberta (see page 59 for details). From Woolley Shoulder, go around the east side of Little Alberta (3 km southeast of Alberta; superb meadow campsites in the shadow of the North Face of Twins Tower), descend a dry streambed right of cliff bands, cross to the left side of Habel Creek, at its outlet from a little glacial lake, and follow it down to the broad, upper Athabasca River Valley. Go south up the valley, sloshing across numerous braided channels, and take the river's west fork, north of Mount King Edward, to the toe of the Toronto Glacier, which has receded considerably and requires skirting a sizable meltwater lake, below the glacier toe, along its right shore. Go south along the west edge of the glacier to around 2200 metres and swing west and then north up the Wales Glacier. Cross the Chaba-Wales Peaks Col (GR 549829) at its lowest, northern, point (loose, fifth-class rock that may require a few pitons) and drop onto the Apex Glacier, which is followed northwest and exited just south of Apex Mountain to reach the Clemenceau Glacier.

In spring, some ski parties have crossed Fortress Lake to its west end and followed Wood River west and then Clemenceau Creek south to gain the lower Clemenceau Glacier. This route, too, is a multi-day thrash.

For all of the Icefield Parkway approaches, the Clemenceau Glacier is crossed and the Tusk Glacier ascended on its left side to reach both Mount Clemenceau and Tusk Peak.

Base Camps The flat top of the Tusk Glacier provides a good campsite for accessing Tusk and Clemenceau, with superb glacial surroundings and views of the two peaks. If you prefer a drier tent site, go a little farther west onto the lower rocks of Reconnaissance Ridge.

The Alpine Club of Canada maintains the Lawrence Grassi Hut (GR 322815) some 4 km away on the end of Cummins Ridge, above the southwest corner of Cummins Glacier. Phone 403-678-3200 for reservations. Besides dry, comfortable lodgings for up to 18, the hut offers superb views of Mount Clemenceau, Pic Tordu and two all but inaccessible lakes, a sheer drop below to the southwest. But staying in the hut adds about two hours of walking to and from the base of the two big peaks; the 150-metre ascent of blocky scree to the hut is particularly grueling at day's end. The hut is probably best saved for ski mountaineering trips, though its entrance may have to be dug out.

Note: Some ski mountaineering parties fly into the Grassi Hut area, climb Clemenceau and then ski out via the Chaba and Columbia Icefields, the crux being the access to the latter via ramps southwest of Mount Columbia.

Mount Clemenceau

3658 metres (12,001 feet)

Mount Clemenceau is a massive, imposing mountain, with big rock and ice faces, hanging glaciers and sharp, steep arêtes that rise to fluted and heavily corniced summit ridges. All aspects are steep and seldom, if ever, climbed, save for the West Face, which offers a fine, moderate route to the summit for both alpine climbers and ski mountaineers.

Clemenceau is one of only four 12,000-foot peaks in the Canadian Rockies—maybe. The 1920 Alberta/B.C. Boundary Commission survey listed the peak at 12,001 feet, though I'm curious to know how it arrived at that exact number. Modern cartographers have knocked the magical 12,000-foot contour off the latest imperial topo map (the highest contour on the new metric map is 3600 metres), maybe because of glacial recession over the intervening decades. Perhaps technology will someday provide a precise answer, or perhaps this will remain a delightful mystery.

The climb via the standard West Face is a fairly routine glacier ascent, with a few steeper rolls for interest. Indeed, some parties ski almost to the summit in the spring. The crux is often the zigzagging route finding, particularly through the lower seracs and around crevasses that may be difficult to cross in dry years. Wanding the route is recommended, as it's easy to get lost on the return if the weather rolls in or your footprints have disappeared.

Arthur Coleman named the peak Pyramid during his 1892 exploration of the area. The Boundary Commission changed the name to honour Georges Clemenceau, a journalist who rose to twice become prime minister of France, most notably near the end of World War I. His nickname was "the Tiger," hence the name of the glacier draining the peak's southwest flank.

Mt. Clemenceau's massive, fractured SE Face.

History

The Clemenceau area was visited by early mountaineering explorers, but the mountain's isolation and uncharted slopes kept summiteers at bay for several decades. Coleman spied this "white pyramid" from Fortress Mountain, to the northeast, in 1892, but his hopes of climbing it ended when he reached the summit of Brouillard Mountain and realized it did not connect to his Pyramid Mountain. "Its top was probably two thousand feet above us and three or four miles away, and it seemed very isolated, so we had to forgo any attempt at climbing it, since our supplies were low," he wrote.

While Walter Wilcox also sighted the peak from near Fortress Lake in 1896, no one set foot on the Clemenceau Glacier until the Boundary Commission survey set up several camera stations above Clemenceau Creek in 1920. The same summer, Allen Carpe saw Clemenceau from a distant peak and two years later mounted the first serious climbing expedition from Jasper, in company with Henry Hall, Jr. and Henry DeVilliers-Schwab, several outfitters and 13 packhorses.

After reaching the icefield via Fortress Lake and Wood River, the group spent most of their time in gloomy weather exploring the mountain's great walls in search of a practical route. "Close at hand, the west face of Mt. Clemenceau supported a large, steep mass of ice, much crevassed, which disappeared into the clouds above 10,000 feet. The lower part looked difficult but feasible under favourable conditions," wrote Carpe, who had discovered the key but too late to mount a summit attempt.

In 1923, DeVilliers-Schwab and Hall returned with an unguided expedition of 11 men and 27 horses, convinced that Clemenceau "was the greatest prize awaiting conquest in all the Canadian Rockies." Three weeks after leaving Jasper, three American climbers set off from a bivouac southeast of the peak, taking along outfitter William Harris as added insurance against the Tiger Glacier's crevasses. Slowly, the party wound its way up the mountain's fractured west flank, gaining a terrace that led to the corniced west summit ridge. Upon reaching the top, they shook hands, exclaimed "Vive Clemenceau!", melted snow on a stove for a drink and soaked up the panoramic view.

Alfred Ostheimer III and guide Hans Fuhrer made the second ascent of Clemenceau during their whirlwind tour of the area in 1927. Other than a South Ridge finish to the original line, no new routes were added until 1980, testifying to the remoteness and difficulty of all other lines of ascent. In February 1976, Gary Bruce and Doug James made the first winter ascent, in nine days return from Sunwapta Falls on wooden skis, launching their summit bid from a snow cave in a crevasse.

The 2100-metre, heavily-corniced Northeast Ridge (V) is comparable in length and difficulty to Mount Robson's Emperor Ridge. But because of its isolation and difficulty of access, it remained untouched, other than a 1951 attempt by a group led by George Bell. Later, it became the fixation of American Graham Thompson, who led multi-day approaches in 1974 and 1978. On the former, it took nearly two days just to ferry loads across the swollen Athabasca River. The first attempt was defeated by perilous snow conditions, the second by bad weather. Finally in 1980, he and Dennis Eberl, Paul Jensen, Tobin Kelley and Jim Wilson succeeded in an 11-day expedition from off the Icefields Parkway. Bivouacking high on the ridge, they made it to the top the second day after surmounting a knife-edged snow ridge with a vertical step on the edge of a cornice.

"The climb of Clemenceau's northeast arête demonstrates that a climb of substantial difficulty in a remote place can be done nicely in traditional manner without artificial aids (i.e. helicopters) on the approach," Thompson wrote. "The approach becomes an integral and pleasant part of the entire trip. Climbing is essentially a matter of human rather than mechanical effort and achievement. This observation should apply to approaches as well as to the ascent itself."

Subsequent parties pushed that credo a step further on new routes. In 1987, Dane Waterman soloed the Northwest Ridge. "The route is not technically difficult," he wrote, "but it is very big, a lonely place to be by oneself." Then in 1989, Jasper's Ken Wallator along with T. Thomas and G. McCormick undertook a 16-day expedition in February, pushing an elegant snow and ice route up the centre of the North Face after following the lower Northeast Ridge. In the late 1970s the face, framed by nearly symmetrical ridges that rise to form a pyramid, lost much of its glacial cover in a huge slide that may have been caused by an earthquake.

Mt. Clemenceau W Face in 2005. Routes shown are approximate, the line varying considerably depending on crevasses.

Red line: summer route.
Briefly diverging blue line: winter route.

Route

First Ascent August 9, 1923: Dana Durand, Henry Hall, Jr., William Harris, Henry DeVilliers-Schwab – West Face

Route Described West Face (II) *Recommended*

Gear Rope, glacier gear, ice axe, crampons, wands, perhaps some ice screws

Map 83 C/4 Clemenceau Icefield

Season March-May on skis, July to September on foot

Time 8-11 hours return from Tiger Glacier

West Face From just above the toe of the Tiger Glacier, southwest of the peak, ascend a steep, hanging bit of glacier ice or easy rocks to the right. Make a rising traverse left below seracs to gain a broad basin. Angle right until you can go straight up between crevasses and then work your way back left up a short, steep slope to reach the West Ridge just to the right of a small bump. Ascend this ridge to reach a broad snow bench below the impressive, fractured South Ridge. Traverse left along the bench to the corniced Northwest Ridge and follow it more steeply to the summit, staying well clear of cornices. Skiers will likely have to go on foot the last 100 vertical metres.

Descend the same way.

Tusk Pk.

Tusk Peak

3360 metres (11,023 feet)

Although not on the original list of 51 peaks topping 11,000 feet, Tusk Peak shows an 11,000-foot contour on the 1:50,000 Imperial topo map and is listed in the *Rocky Mountains of Canada–North* as seven metres, or 23 feet, above the magic mark. Despite this belated admission to the club, Tusk is well worth climbing for its spectacular surroundings and a front-row view of arguably the most beautiful peak in the Canadian Rockies—Mount Shackleton, with its cascading, heavily fractured north glacier (see page 10). On a clear day, summiteers can also see all four of the Rockies' 12,000-foot peaks, highlighted by the sheer Southeast Face of Mount Clemenceau next door. Sir Sandford and the Bugaboos stand out on the western horizon.

The climb up the standard South Ridge is a mix of snow and rock, featuring a steep, often icy section below the col, a bit of rotten rock, a couple of technical rock moves on the South Ridge and a narrowing summit ridge. In other words, a typical mixed alpine outing in the Rockies. While the Northwest Ridge is only slightly harder and a more aesthetic line, the rock is reportedly poor on its lower sections. Because of the long approach, most parties climb Tusk from a central camp that

also allows an ascent of their primary objective, Mount Clemenceau.

The pyramid-shaped Tusk was so named by the Alberta/B.C. Boundary Commission because it is a "sharp cone of rock."

History

Tusk was one of a string of Clemenceau Icefield peaks that fell in rapid succession to the Ostheimer and Fuhrer party in 1927. From a nearby camp, they ascended the Tusk-Duplicate Icefall, which Ostheimer described as dangerous and as difficult as any ice they climbed all summer (two climbers were killed here by falling seracs during the 1972 Alpine Club of Canada camp, and it has since been avoided by prudent climbers). The climbers reached the Shackleton-Irvine Col, scampered up Mount Irvine and then headed north for Tusk, ascending the rock and snow of the South Ridge.

While the young Ostheimer was terse as a descriptive writer, he was a stickler for recording times, as the following passage shows. "The summit was reached without difficulty (1-¼ hours), and we discovered with joy that the view was excellent. After enjoying a prolonged rest, we descended to the rucksacks (½ hour) and continued to the Tusk-Irvine Col, from which we continued via steep, loose couloirs to the glacier below, rounded the Tusk and sped into camp before dark (6 hours). We thus completely circled Tusk Peak during the day's climbing. While descending the western couloirs, a tremendous boulder crashed upon us, passing between two of the party."

In 1951, George Bell and John Rousson climbed the long Northwest Ridge (5.4) during an expedition to the area. "The bottom of the ridge had some abominable rock, but the top 1,000 feet were fairly interesting, with a high degree of exposure," wrote Bell. Recalling the energy and ambition of the Ostheimer party, Helmut Microys and Michael Rosenberger in 1972 climbed the Northwest Ridge, descended the South Ridge and then carried on over Irvine, Chettan and Shipton—a horseshoe traverse completed in 16 hours. During the same camp, the pair traversed Pic Tordu, Cowl Mountain and all three peaks of Shackleton in another long day.

Hopping glacial stream below Duplicate-Tusk Icefall. A. Mt. Shackleton.

S Ridge route on Tusk Pk. A. NW Ridge. B. Tusk-Irvine Col. C. Irvine. Photo: Alan Kane.

Route

First Ascent July 31, 1927: Alfred Ostheimer III, John de Laittre, W.R. Maclaurin, *Hans Fuhrer* – South Ridge

Route Described South Ridge (II, 5.4)

Gear Rope, glacier gear, ice axe, crampons, a couple of small to mid-sized cams, perhaps a second tool and a few ice screws later in the season

Map 83 C/4 Clemenceau Icefield

Season July to September

Time 8-10 hours return from near head of Tusk Glacier

South Ridge From the top of the main Tusk Glacier, northwest of the peak, make a zig-zagging traverse southeast up a glacial bowl, aiming for the Tusk-Irvine Col at its upper left end. A final couloir leading to the col is about 35 degrees, exposed to a large crevasse below and sometimes icy, with loose rock at the top. The reward, upon reaching the col, is the sudden view of Shackleton's sublimely glaciated North Face.

From the col, follow the ledgy rock of the South Ridge, skirting right onto snow occasionally. After a longer traverse right, the ridge is regained by climbing a loose, down-sloping gully. Just beyond is the crux, a delicate move over a smooth, bulging rock with loose holds above (one pin, gear placements). It is apparently possible to bypass this crux by, from just below, going diagonally right and up on shale. Above, it's easier scrambling on loose rock and snow as the summit ridge narrows above the precipitous West Face and the steepening East Face.

Return the same way, rappelling the crux (or going around it) and either rapping or carefully down climbing the loose gully just below.

Note: From the Tusk-Irvine col, it appears possible to also reach the summit by traversing well right on snow to gain the Southeast Slopes, which steepen below the top.

Tsar Mountain

3424 metres (11,233 feet)

Tsar Mountain is a splendid pyramid that would see far more ascents if it were closer to civilization. Because of its isolation at the south end of the Clemenceau Icefield, it is often bypassed by those intent on climbing the higher Mount Clemenceau, a day's tramp away. Indeed, it is likely to see even less traffic, other than helicopter-assisted parties, with the closure of the upper Sullivan River approach road. But those willing to make the effort are rewarded with spectacular glacial surroundings, lakeside camping and a decided scarcity of human company. Most impressive is the peak itself, with sharp, steep lines carved by glaciers that now lie much fractured around its base.

The climb along the standard route is mostly fourth-class scrambling—with superb positions along the North Ridge—topped by a short bit of steep glacier. Because it takes at least four days to approach Tsar on foot (and the same number to exit), self-propelled parties may want to spend a few extra days in the area and attempt Clemenceau, Tusk and perhaps other icefield peaks, if they can shoulder the extra weight in food and fuel.

"When I saw it, so strikingly dominating its surroundings in isolated majesty, I named it Czar," wrote Alberta/B.C. Boundary Commission and Alpine Club of Canada czar Arthur Wheeler. "But later, when recording it, the spelling with 'Ts' seemed more appropriate."

History

The first ascent of Tsar was the culmination of an incredible 1927 expedition headed by 19-year-old Harvard student Alfred Ostheimer III and guide Hans Fuhrer, in which they ascended some 30 peaks in 63 days on the Clemenceau, Chaba and Columbia Icefields. The two, along with Swiss amateur Jean Weber (who helped guide the first ascent of Mount Alberta two years earlier), were in top shape by the time they skimmed south toward Tusk, encountering a mother grizzly and cub at their bivy site north of the peak.

Equipped with two days' food, gasoline, stove and 1,000 feet of motion picture film, the three ascended the Tsar Glacier to the pass between Mount Somervell and their objective. Gaining the western rock ridge, they were surprised to discover it was separated from the main peak by a small, glacier-filled valley. Caching their excess gear, they descended to the secondary glacier and then tackled the icy Northwest Face, with Fuhrer cutting some 500 steps to reach a broad snow saddle. An avalanche crashed below them as they reached the final, steep west arête, which was followed via rock and ice to the top, where they were impressed by airy drops on three sides. Subsequent glacial recession made much of this face route impassable to later parties.

It was a quarter century before Tsar was climbed again. In 1951, George Bell, Graham Matthews and David Michael followed the North Ridge, bypassing the summit glacier on the right via the West Ridge. Two decades later, Glen Boles and Don Forest led an Alpine Club of Canada party up onto the subsidiary west spur (as in the first ascent), which was then followed to the North Ridge.

Opposite: Fractured NW Face of Mt. Tsar.
Photo: Dan Doll.

Route

First Ascent August 8, 1927: Alfred Ostheimer III, Jean Weber, *Hans Fuhrer* – Northwest Face
Route Described West Spur/North Ridge (II)
Gear Rope, glacier gear, ice axe, crampons, ice screws later in season
Map 83 C/4 Clemenceau Icefield
Season mid-July to September
Time Trip – 3 days return
Climb – About 9-10 hours return from camp

Approach See pages 96-99 for fly-in options and descriptions of several initial approaches to the Clemenceau Icefield from the Icefields Parkway, north of the Columbia Icefield. Nearly all the self-propelled approaches will land you somewhere along the northeastern edge of the Clemenceau Glacier. Work your way to the top of the glacier (roughly GR 435830) and ascend another glacier southeast to a broad col (GR 454810). Descend southeast to around 2,560-metres, contouring west and then south on the upper Tsar Glacier, bypassing Mount Ellis 1 km. to its east. Continue south past Mount Somervell, bypassing seracs on the left and descending easy rock to a low spot, where a stream has cut an easy path through cliff bands. Cross the glacier and swing around on a moraine to gain a short, steep snow slope that leads to lovely campsites along a winding stream or, a little further along, beside one of two lakes. This route is reversed if heading from Tsar to the Clemenceau/Tusk area.

West Spur/North Ridge Just beyond the second, smaller lake, head south up snow slopes and traverse left on easy rock and then scree. Kick steps up a steep snow slope above (often a great glissade on the descent) to reach the broad, flat subsidiary West Spur. Follow this spur easily left—with a couple of short steps and a bit of rotten, dinner-plate rock—to its intersection with the North Ridge, which offers superb views over the eastern glacier far below and the icefall above and to the right. The ridge is mostly followed (with some detours available on the right) until it's feasible to descend onto the upper glacier. Traverse to the right beneath a serac roof, cross the bergschrund (may be open and challenging) and then climb a couple of short, steep sections on snow or ice to gain the summit. Take care not to stray too close to the corniced top. **Descend** the same way.

W Spur/N Ridge route on Mt. Tsar.

Mt. King Edward from the Twins.

Mount King Edward
3490 metres (11,450 feet)

Mount King Edward is the forgotten 11,000er of the Columbia Icefield area. Perched on the Continental Divide above the icefield's western edge, it is overshadowed by the towering masses of Mount Columbia and the Twins to the east. It is also isolated by access. Though King Edward is only a few kilometres by air from Mount Columbia, an intervening icefall means the usual approach is via a long logging road and some B.C. bushwhacking. As a result, it is climbed infrequently.

Yet viewed from the northwest end of the Columbia Icefield, King Edward is an impressive peak—its steep east and north aspects tumbling 2000 fractured metres to the headwaters of the Athabasca River. It also boasts wild, lovely glacial surroundings and offers alpinists a rare glimpse of the spectacular western walls of Mount Columbia and the Twins.

The climb, by the standard South Slopes route, is a fairly routine snow and scree ascent, enlivened by a final detour onto the upper East Face, with a few thousand feet of exhilarating exposure beneath one's feet. When the sum-mit is reached soon thereafter, it's comforting to know that the rise at the far, north end of a long, connecting ridge, is slightly lower. **Note:** In low snow years, the lower South Slopes can be reduced to disagreeable, loose and even difficult slabs and may require some fifth-class climbing.

Perhaps appropriately, Northern Rockies' explorer Mary Schaeffer named this overlooked peak for King Edward VII, whose brief rule at the outset of the 20th century followed the 64-year reign of his mother, Queen Victoria. It was earlier called Mount Manitoba by Jean Habel of Berlin, who explored the Athabasca Valley in 1901.

History
While few mountaineers today venture into the rugged upper reaches of the Athabasca Valley, it was the preferred summer means of accessing peaks like Alberta, Columbia and the Twins in the 1920s, when horseback approaches made the river crossings more feasible. In 1920, Howard Palmer and Allen Carpe made the first serious

mountaineering journey up the Athbasca, intent on bagging King Edward.

From the forks at the head of the Athabasca River, they followed a tributary stream to the Ontario Glacier below the West Face, which was ascended to within a few hundred feet of the summit, when the dwindling afternoon forced a turnaround. "The climbing was of a peculiarly laborious and disagreeable nature, the rock being rotten and slippery, interspersed with a mushy and unstable scree and swept by water and falling stones from the melting snow above. The view was completely obscured by smoke," wrote Carpe, whose dismal day was punctuated by a spill while recrossing the swollen Athabasca River.

Four years later, Palmer returned to the valley with Joseph Hickson and guide Conrad Kain. After a four-day approach with 14 horses and three packers, they set up a higher camp on the west side of the mountain. Palmer noted the King Edward massif "fills almost four miles of skyline, rising 6,400 feet above the valley (with a) graceful symmetry beguiling to the eye." He wasn't as impressed with the South Face's scree-covered slabs, which he called "laborious in the extreme." This monotonous route, however, led the climbers to the upper East Face, which was ascended to the summit via a 30-metre chimney.

Palmer considered King Edward a training climb for Mount Alberta. After discovering an approach from the Athabasca Valley up Habel Creek to below Alberta's East Face, his attempt was rained out. A year later, a large, guided Japanese party bagged Alberta using Palmer's reconnaissance information.

In the 1970s, soloists put up two new routes on King Edward from valley camps. H. Michel ascended the Northeast Ledges in 1973, and two years later the shattered Northwest Ridge fell to Dane Waterman, who called the climb "another crumbling classic."

Dry S Slopes/E Face route on King Edward.
Photo: Alan Kane.

Opposite: Ascending through cliff band on Mt. King Edward's S Slopes.

Route

First Ascent August 11, 1924: Joseph Hickson, Howard Palmer, *Conrad Kain* – South Slopes/East Face

Route Described South Slopes/East Face (II, 5.2)

Gear Rope, glacier gear, ice axe, crampons, a few ice screws, a small rock rack and perhaps a few pitons

Maps 83 C/3 Columbia Icefield, 83 C/4 Clemenceau Icefield

Season mid-July to September

Time Trip – 2-3 days

Climb – About 10 hours return from a high camp

Access The easiest but most expensive way is to fly in, either directly from Golden or from the Bush Road. Phone Alpine Helicopters in Golden at 250-344-7444.

While it is still feasible to approach King Edward from the Athabasca Valley, for those who don't mind a few river crossings, most parties now arrive from the south via logging roads up the Bush River. From Golden, drive 22 km northwest on the Trans-Canada Highway, turning right onto a paved road just before the old Donald sawmill and the bridged crossing of the Columbia River. The Bush River Road beyond is an excellent gravel road, with new kilometre signs, as of 2003, that begin at 0 at the start of this road. It is followed northwest along the Bush Arm of Kinbasket Lake and then north along the Bush River; stay on the main road at all junctions. Phone Louisiana Pacific in Golden at 250-344-8800 for current road conditions. The radio frequency for checking truck traffic on the Bush Road is 153.230. The logging trucks refer to it as the B Road for the first 61.5 km (to the Sullivan Road turnoff) and as Bush North thereafter. See map on page 97.

Near the 96-km sign, take the left fork, which follows the upper Bush River (the right fork briefly goes up Bryce Creek). No longer maintained, this logging spur road is becoming rougher and grassed over – a high-clearance vehicle is suggested. About 5 km beyond the fork, a bridge across a stream has been removed, necessitating a short, cold ford and a longer approach on foot than in the past, starting at the lowly elevation of 1100 metres. Be sure to wrap your vehicle in porcupine-proof chicken wire. The driving time from Golden is about 3 hours.

Approach Walk up the remaining logging road – which includes some steep switchbacks – for several kilometres and follow a faint trail up the middle of the final, overgrown cut block to its upper end. Take a well-maintained, flagged all-terrain vehicle track up through the bush to treeline. Once above the trees, traverse right below a ridge, gaining the glacier south of King Edward and camping below large downward sloping gray limestone outcrops, right of the glacier, at 2150 metres (5-plus hours).

South Slopes/East Face Cross the glacier, heading for King Edward's southeast corner – the glacier becomes more fractured closer to the peak's base. Cross the bergschrund and head up the South Slopes left of the corner, with conditions ranging from snow to slabs to tedious scree. Later in the season, the initial snow ramp off the glacier may have melted back, exposing a tricky section of rock climbing to access the higher South Slopes. Scramble up through a small cliff band at mid-height (belay may be necessary) and then continue up more toilsome scree, aiming for the upper right corner of the face, which abuts cliffs.

Turn the corner below these cliffs and take a rising traverse right on a broad ledge, bypassing one loose gully to reach a second gully high on the East Face, with the glacier now visible far below. Half a rope-length up this gully leads to a large block, followed by a long rope-length up rock and/or ice (5.0 to 5.2 when dry) to a chimney, which is ascended to gain the South Ridge, just below the summit. Under good snow conditions, it may be possible to bypass the chimney by, from below the chimney, taking a rising traverse right to intercept the South Ridge.

Descend the same way.

Mount Bryce

From the broad expanse of the Columbia Ice-field, the most compelling sight is not the lofty Mount Columbia or the gleaming Twins. Instead, it is the massive northwest wall of the nearby Mount Bryce, rising nearly 2300 sheer metres from the depths of Bryce Creek to three linked summits, two of them over 11,000 feet. Bryce is one of the jewels of the Canadian Rockies, boasting a couple of big, gorgeous routes in a remote setting.

"It is really a minor range, jutting out laterally from the (southern edge of the) Columbia névé," wrote Howard Palmer in the early 1920s. This massif is built like a fortress, well guarded by high walls on all sides, save the south, which offers a steep glacial approach.

An external layer of protection, on the west, is the worst bush in the Canadian Rockies. Until fairly recently, it took eight hours of thrashing, log hopping and cursing to crawl three kilometres over a ridge just to get within sight of Bryce's southern flanks. Mercifully, the completion of a logging road up Rice Brook in the mid-1990s all but eliminated this hellish approach, making the standard routes pleasantly accessible. In 2004, however, this road was decommissioned and the bridge across Rice Brook removed, adding fresh challenges.

There are still plenty of climbing challenges left, particularly the classic Northeast Ridge route, which despite modern technology is scarcely easier today than when James Outram and Christian Kaufmann made their amazing and bold first ascent in 1902. The South Glacier route is a much more straightforward means of reaching the main, Southwest Peak and the easy Centre Peak. The 2000-metre North Face remains one of the biggest and best test pieces in the Rockies for expert ice climbers.

In 1898, Norman Collie named this peak for Lord James Bryce, president of the Alpine Club, historian and later Great Britain's ambassador to the United States.

Access For current conditions on the Bush River Road, phone forestry company Louisiana-Pacific in Golden at 250-344-8800. The radio frequency for checking truck traffic on the Bush Road is 153.230. The logging trucks refer to it as the B Road for the first 61.5 km (to the Sullivan Road turnoff) and as Bush North thereafter. See map on page 97.

From Golden, drive 22 km northwest on the Trans-Canada Highway, turning right onto a paved road at the old Donald logging mill, just before the bridge crossing of the Columbia River. This soon becomes the Bush River Road, an excellent gravel logging road (fine for two-wheel drive vehicles) that follows the Bush Arm of Kinbasket Lake before heading north along the upper Bush River; stay on the main road at all junctions. The old mileage signs have been replaced with ones that begin at 0 kilometres at the start of the Bush Road and are much simpler to follow.

Immediately after recrossing the Bush River to its right side at the 94-km sign, turn right onto a small side road, which makes two sweeping switchbacks up the steep, logged hillside before rounding a ridge and gradually dropping into the Rice Brook valley. With the decommissioning of this road, you may have to walk or cycle up much of the roadbed - about 5 km. to where the bridge used to cross Rice Brook. It is now a more formidable crossing perhaps best, if riskily, accomplished on fallen logs. A good alternative may be to ford this "brook" just upstream of the old bridge site, where the channel is more braided and the roadbed can be quickly regained without much bushwhacking.

Mt. Bryce from Columbia Icefield. A. NE Peak. B. Centre Peak. C. SW Peak. Photo: Markus Kellerhals.

Approaches *For South Glacier/Southeast Face* Once safely across Rice Brook, walk about 30 minutes farther up the road and then go left (cairn in 2004) up a watercourse in an avalanche slope to get above tree line without bushwhacking. A couple of hundred metres up the watercourse, traverse left and go up another creek bed. Traverse left below steep walls and cross the stream that forms a waterfall, now far below. Continue hiking up through meadows to reach the toe of the South Glacier and a few bivy sites on bedrock (3-4 hours).

For Northeast Ridge Once across Rice Brook, walk about 6 km up the road to where it ends in a cutblock. From the upper left side of the cutblock, head north through fairly open woods and a little drainage, angling right higher up to reach a lovely pond-side bivy site below the 2800-metre col (GR 796677) at the base of the Northeast Ridge (6-7 hours from the bridge).

Opposite: Southwest Peak of Mt. Bryce from Centre Peak.

Mount Bryce – Southwest Peak

3507 metres (11,506 feet)

Bryce's stunning Southwest Peak boasts two of the Rockies' finest hard alpine routes. The Northeast Ridge is a demanding, exhilarating climb up and then back down a narrow crest. It requires at least one very long day on the mountain and involves a mix of snow, rock and ice. The route traverses the three, successively higher, summits of Bryce, though many time-pressed parties bypass the Centre Peak, despite it being an 11,000er. For hard-core alpine ice climbers, the North Face is one of the biggest routes of its kind in the Rockies.

A considerably easier way to the summit is via the South Glacier, an approach that also provides access to the Centre Peak. Most of the elevation is gained on a 600-metre pound up a gully of snow (if you're lucky) or ice, leading to a glacial plateau. The sting is in the summit ridge—a spectacular and intimidating fin of snow, usually sporting a double cornice, which ends with a short, tightrope walk above the plunging North Face.

History

The first ascent of the Northeast Ridge of Mount Bryce in 1902 was a daring mixed alpine climb years ahead of its time; indeed, the route was not repeated for more than six decades. It illustrated the superb skill of guide Christian Kaufmann—climbing in hobnailed boots, without crampons or rock protection—and his and client James Outram's willingness to push the limits to reach a summit.

Like Mount Columbia, Bryce was a climbing prize first identified by Norman Collie and partners, who made a futile attempt to reach both mountains via the jungle-like Bush River Valley in 1900. Instead, both peaks were quickly claimed by Outram and Kaufmann, though Collie's team was invited to join them on Bryce after the two groups had made the first ascent of Mount Forbes. Collie declined and the intrepid duo, after a failed attempt at Mount Alexandra en route, launched their Bryce bid from a base camp at Thompson Pass.

Their ascent was fuelled by ambition, not food, as they were without matches at their bivy site and thus made do with a supper of cold water the night before and mostly with rationed chocolate the day of their 20-plus-hour climb. The chief obstacle, low on the narrow, ridge, was a 20-metre, 5.6 buttress that was "nearly perpendicular, with few excrescences to grip or place even the corner of a boot upon and of a consistency so rotten that only a small percentage of the existing few would probably be reliable," wrote Outram.

Upon reaching the first, northeast, summit at noon, "a prospect of a night out on the mountain seemed inevitable, unless we gave up the prospect of finishing the climb. This neither of us was prepared to consider for a moment." To save time, they traversed on a glacial bench under the southeast side of the Centre Peak and then delicately worked their way up the narrow snow ridge to the summit of the higher Southwest Peak by mid-afternoon.

But they now had to retrace their challenging steps, particularly the lower rock step, which they down climbed in the dark. For an hour, they inched their way down this cliff, Outram stopping to stand precariously whenever the rope ran out and anxiously waiting for Kaufmann to join him, keenly aware any slip would mean the end for them both.

"The remembrance is still vivid of the blind feeling for the scanty holds with chilly fingers, the wild helpless waving of the feet in the dim depths for something on which to rest for the next search, the agonizing hopes and fears as to their stability when found, the sickening 'emptiness' that seemed to come with the 'give' of the treasured footing and the sound of its fall reverberating as it leapt into the blackness of 7,000 feet of night."

In 1929, the esteemed British climber Colonel L.S. Amery and guide Edward Feuz, Jr. descended upper Rice Brook from Thompson Pass in search of a shorter route from the south. "Mount Bryce from the south is a truly imposing spectacle," wrote Amery. "A tremendous triangle, almost a steeple, of sheer rock face, facing approximately southwest, soars into the sky. From it to right and left descend two curving curtain ridges, enfolding a glacier between them." They went up the left-hand, or south, ridge and after surmounting much rotten rock traversed rightward onto the glacial bench below the summit block. An unstable layer of snow atop ice on the Southeast Face, however, demanded much step cutting and ultimately thwarted their bid less than 100 vertical metres from the summit.

Feuz was back in 1937 with fellow guide Christian Hasler, Jr. and their energetic clients, the American Lillian Gest and the Briton Kate Gardiner (the latter put up 33 first ascents in the Rockies and Selkirks). After many rain delays, they went up the right side of the South Glacier, filming the ascent of the corniced snow ridge to the summit.

The complete traverse of the Northeast Ridge route wasn't accomplished until 1971. Arriving via the Saskatchewan Glacier, the Calgary juggernaut of Glen Boles, Don Forest and Murray Toft traversed all three peaks and made it back down in just over 16 hours, despite a couple of lengthy breaks and some dozen crampon changes.

American icon Fred Beckey, among others, had long coveted a first ascent of Bryce's North Face. But Jim Jones and Eckhard Grassman beat him to it in 1972, exactly seven decades after Outram beat Collie up Bryce and Columbia. In rain, snow and then just bitter cold, the pair hammered their way with primitive ice gear up the immense face, which reared up to 55 degrees on the higher pitches. The prospect of this steep finish prompted Grassman to remark: "We probably shit our pants up there."

"No place to make a mistake. Some of the ice is brittle. Just get to the top. We're miles from nowhere," wrote Jones, in a terser style than Bryce's early climbers. "How far to the top now? We can see it above but we have lost all feeling for distance. The sun is setting. Is it twenty feet more or two hundred? Suddenly Eckhard disappears from view. He is over the top."

After a frosty bivouac between the Southwest and Centre Peaks, the two stumbled down the Northeast Ridge to their small tent. "The night brings torrents of driving rain," said Jones. "The tent proves itself by leaking like a sieve, soaking us to the skin. After penance comes the baptism." Grassman later died on the North Face of Mount Edith Cavell.

Mt. Bryce from Whiterose Mtn. A. S Glacier approach. B. SW Peak. C. NE Ridge route. D. 2800-metre col. E. Mt. Columbia.

Routes

First Ascent August 20, 1902: James Outram, *Christian Kaufmann* – Northeast Ridge
Routes Described Northeast Ridge (IV, 5.6), South Glacier/Southeast Face (II) *Recommended*

Gear	Rope, glacier gear, ice axe, crampons, a few pickets and ice screws (plus small rock rack and pitons for Northeast Ridge)
Map	83 C/3 Columbia Icefield
Season	mid-July to mid-September
Time	Trip – 3 days return for both routes
	Climb – South Glacier/Southeast Face: About 12 hours return from South Glacier bivy
	Northeast Ridge: 16 or more hours return from bivy below col

South Glacier/Southeast Face From the bivy site below the South Glacier, ascend scree on the left until feasible to traverse rightward onto the glacier. Go straight up a long gully (nearly 40 degrees at its steepest) that can range from good snow to ice embedded with fallen rock. Climbers need to watch for wet snow slides or rockfall from above, particularly while descending this route on a hot afternoon. Go past a prominent gendarme at the top of the gully to reach a glacial plateau below the summit block.

From here, either go straight up the Southeast Face on snow or ice or take a shallower, shorter slope to the right to intersect the Northeast Ridge below its prominent fin. If either of these slopes looks unstable, traverse farther right to the col between the Southwest and Centre Peaks and then go up the Northeast Ridge, which involves fourth-class rock and a narrow snow ridge.

The spectacular snow fin below the summit is not as bad as it looks, though considerable care is required, particularly if it is double corniced. If snow conditions permit, you can belay this stretch, using pickets and/or buried ice axes as protection. If the cornice looks nasty, you may want to kick steps or front point across the Southeast Face below the fin.

Descend along the Northeast Ridge, either to the col or down the shallower snow on the Southeast Face, and then go back down the gully to the South Glacier.

Northeast Ridge From the 2800-metre col, go over a small tower to gain the base of the Northeast Ridge. The ridge begins as a loose, triangular face (fourth class) that gives way to scrambling on the ridge crest. Shortly beyond is the crux, a 20-metre, 5.6 step on a gray band of rock, tackled directly from a two-piton belay. Placements for protection are scanty but the rock is generally good, with a piton at mid-height and a four-piton rap station atop the pitch. Though the angle then eases off, the ridge crest leading to the summit of the Northeast Peak is often narrow, alternating between short rock steps and ice or snow ridges.

If time and conditions permit a complete traverse of the Northeast Ridge, follow the ridge down from the summit over broken rock to the col. Beyond, the often icy and corniced ridge, interrupted by a couple of rock sections, steepens closer to the summit of the Centre Peak. From this second summit, continue down the ridge on easier rock to the col and then scramble up more rock to reach the knife-edged, corniced snow fin, which is delicately followed to the summit of the main, Southwest Peak. If cornices unduly threaten this ridge, kick steps or front point below it on the Southeast Face.

If you wish to bypass the Centre Peak, carefully down climb south from the Northeast Peak on snow or ice to the glacier. Traverse easily below the Centre Peak and regain the ridge either at the ensuing col or via snow slopes to its left on the Southeast Face.

Though parties carrying all their camping gear can **descend** the South Glacier, most parties go back down the Northeast Ridge, bypassing the Centre Peak. Below the Northeast Peak, a number of rappel stations ease the descent of steeper or looser rock steps.

Opposite: Doug Fulford climbing NE Ridge of Mt. Bryce. Photo: Nancy Hansen.

Mount Bryce – Centre Peak

3370 metres (11,056 feet)

From the top of Bryce's South Glacier, the Centre Peak appears as little more than a bump on the ridge en route to the main attraction, the higher Southwest Peak. Still, it is an 11,000er and an easy bonus of less than an hour of scrambling if one has already climbed the main peak from the standard southern approach.

It is much more impressive when its fluted Northeast Ridge is tackled as part of the complete traverse of Bryce, a much longer and more challenging climb. The summit of the Centre Peak provides a superb reward—a full view of the knife-edged snow fin rising to the apex of the Southwest Peak.

History

The Centre Peak of Bryce was bypassed on the 1902 ascent and overlooked as a distinct peak for decades after. By 1960, however, it was identified as the only unclimbed summit over 11,000 feet in the Canadian Rockies (Mount Harrison, the West Twin and the Centre Peak of the Goodsirs were first ascended some years later, though some would still argue the latter two are not distinct peaks).

In 1960, Jo Kato, Robi Fierz and three others hoped to climb it as part of the first complete traverse of Bryce's Northeast Ridge, but they were forced to turn around in a snowstorm early on. A year later, they and two others focused on the Centre Peak, this time via the South Glacier. On the approach, they drove up an old fire road towards the Saskatchewan Glacier Hut, chewed-up pieces of which can still be seen in summer on the glacier. They continued over Castleguard Meadows and descended to the rushing Castleguard River, crossed by felling a tree. From Thompson Pass, they went down the north branch of Rice Brook and traversed across "abominable alder slides with our bulky packboards" to reach the snout of the South Glacier.

Leaving camp at 4 a.m., they cramponed up the icy glacier, reaching the upper névé in a snowstorm. Even under these conditions, they were able to ascend the Southwest Ridge of the Centre Peak. "It rises 700 feet with rather rotten rock in the lower portion, but the rock improves as one ascends," wrote Kato. "The only difficulty was an icy couloir of about 20 feet that had to be crossed, and it lay at an angle of about 60 degrees. I had an ice piton in my pack which was used to cut steps and handholds, and after some fairly interesting scrambling the summit was attained by 7:55 a.m."

With the weather further deteriorating, they abandoned plans to climb the Southwest Peak and headed back down. Thirty-one years later, our party found the metal film canister containing their summit record. In 1971, Don Forest, Glen Boles and Murray Toft crossed the summit of the Centre Peak as part of the first complete traverse of Bryce's Northeast Ridge.

Scrambling up SW Ridge of Mt. Bryce's Centre Peak. Photo: Roman Pachovsky.

SW Ridge of Centre Peak, Mt. Bryce.

Routes

First Ascent July 27, 1961: Jo Kato, Siegfried Bucher, Robi Fierz – Southwest Ridge

Routes Described Southwest Ridge (II), Northeast Ridge (IV, 5.6)

Gear Rope, glacier gear, crampons, ice axe, ice screws, alpine rack if via NE Ridge

Map 83 C/3 Columbia Icefield

Season mid-July to mid-September

Time Trip – 3 days return
Climb – About 8 hours return, from South Glacier camp, 16-plus hours return as part of the Northeast Ridge traverse

Southwest Ridge From the toe of the South Glacier, gain the glacier's left side where feasible and ascend the long, 40-degree couloir on snow and/or ice, watching for rock fall and snow slides from above (more likely on hot days, particularly on the descent). Pass a gendarme at the top of the couloir and cross the glacier to the col between the Centre and Southwest Peaks. Ascend snow and fairly good rock to the Southwest Ridge, which is followed easily on rock and then snow to the summit (about 1 hour from the col). **Descend** the same way.

Northeast Ridge See the description of the Northeast Ridge traverse of Mount Bryce on page 119.

Descend the same way or come down the South Glacier (see Southwest Ridge description above).

Ascending upper SW Slopes of Mt. Alexandra, Whiterose Mtn. in rear.

Mount Alexandra

3388 metres (11,115 feet)

Mount Alexandra boasts the nastiest bush approach of any 11,000er in the Canadian Rockies. After a few hours of dodging alders and devil's club, hopping fallen logs and getting face and shins whacked by assorted shrubbery, you might wish you had arranged a helicopter ride.

An old logging road up Lyell Creek shortens the misery to about a day—a mere walk in the park compared with the four or five days the Calgary-based Grizzly Group spent bushwhacking up the same valley in the 1970s. There is another, higher-level approach up the South Rice Brook valley that promises less bush, at the expense of much circuitous sidehill gouging. Whichever ground route you choose, you might need a day to recover before tackling the peak, which everyone seems to climb by the fastest, most direct route possible, up the steep snow and fourth-class rock of the Southwest Slopes.

When you add the relative isolation of the Bush River Valley and the greater fame and aesthetics of nearby Mount Bryce (which now has a simpler logging road approach), it's easy to see why few parties make the effort to climb Alexandra. These days, visitors tend to chopper in, setting up base at a site used by recent Alpine Club of Canada camps.

A cheaper way to avoid the bushwhacking, in spring, is to ski all the way up the Lyell Creek roadbed (exposed to avalanche) and then go up the filled-in creek bed. The bush higher up is also mostly covered by snow, though you'll likely have to carry your skis once or twice closer to the mountain.

Alexandra's obscurity is a shame. It sits high on the divide, between the Lyells and Bryce, and offers splendid views and fine camping on an ancient coral reef with surrounding flowery meadows, hanging glaciers and cascading waterfalls. There are several other worthy mountaineering objectives in the area, including a sublime snow/ice traverse of Whiterose Mountain and a rare ascent of Queens Peak, a "bump" on Alexandra's North Ridge.

Climbed only a couple of times, the latter is allegedly only three metres shy of being an 11,000er, though it appears considerably lower than the attached Alexandra, which is only 35 metres above the magic mark (a recent GPS reading on Alexandra's summit added 13 metres to the official height). The reason for the discrepancy may be that the 1918 boundary survey map listed Alexandra as 11,214 feet and Queens as 10,990. Alexandra's height was later lowered to 11,115, and while Queens was also dropped to 10,900 in a 1960s version of the official guidebook, its elevation reverted to 3350 metres (10,990) in the latest edition. To further muddy the waters, the latest topo map only offers Queens a 10,700-foot contour.

Norman Collie named Alexandra for the bejeweled Danish princess who married King Edward VII (reign: 1901-1910) and later founded a nursing corps. It's a good thing Collie didn't use her full name: Alexandra Carolina Maria Charlotte Louise Julia.

History

James Outram and Christian Kaufmann needed two attempts to scale Alexandra, the only blip in their amazing summer of 1902, when they knocked off five 11,000ers. Their first attempt was on August 19 from the same "Camp Content" in the Alexandra River Valley they used to climb Lyell 2 earlier that summer. Traveling southwest, they reached the west arm of the Alexandra Glacier, which was ascended through a fractured icefall to a glacial pass west of Oppy Mountain. From here, a long arête was followed west until steep cliffs turned them back.

Four days later, after their amazing triumph on Mount Bryce, they took care of some unfinished business. This time, they crossed the high glacial pass and traversed west, below the divide and around Douai Mountain, and then easily went up Alexandra's southwest snow slopes. Reaching the summit in early afternoon, they gazed at all the first ascents they had made along the Continental Divide, from Mounts Freshfield to Columbia, over the past hectic few weeks. "By 2:30," Outram wrote, "we were glissading gaily down delightful slopes of admirable snow," returning to camp 12 hours after departing.

In 1937, Lillian Gest, Kate Gardiner and guides Edward Feuz, Jr. and Christian Hasler, Jr. climbed the same route from South Rice Brook, up which their packers had hacked a crude trail. After sitting out a day of rain, they ascended the upper valley to the Whiterose Glacier and traversed left to reach the Alexandra Glacier and then the base of the route. They reached the summit in a fog and returned in a downpour that soaked them to the skin.

Route

First Ascent August 23, 1902: James Outram, *Christian Kaufmann* – Southwest Slopes

Route Described Southwest Slopes (II, 5.2 step on the approach from South Rice Brook)

Gear Rope, glacier gear, ice axe, crampons, ice screws, a bit of rock gear

Maps 82 N/14 Rostrum Peak, also 83 C/3 Columbia Icefield if approaching via South Rice Brook

Season July to September on foot, April to early May on skis

Time Trip – 3-4 days
Climb – 10-12 hours return from a high camp

Access If you value your flesh, clothing and time, simply call Alpine Helicopters in Golden (250-344-7444) and arrange for a quick flight from the Bush Road near Mount Bryce into the Alexandra environs. If you prefer a purist, skinflint approach, there are two self-propelled choices, equally heinous. Both start on abandoned logging roads off the main Bush Road and initially promise painless access, a promise soon betrayed in an endless thicket of prickly greenery. Phone forestry company Louisiana-Pacific (250-344-8800 in Golden) for current road conditions; the radio frequency for checking truck traffic on the Bush Road is 153.230. The logging trucks refer to it as the B Road for the first 61.5 km (to the Sullivan Road turnoff) and as Bush North thereafter.

Drive 22 km northwest of Golden on the Trans-Canada Highway to the old Donald logging mill and then follow the main Bush River road north. If you're taking the South Rice Brook approach, drive 94 km up the Bush Road and then go right on a small, rough side road on foot or in a high-clearance vehicle. This abandoned logging road, decommissioned and the upper bridge removed in 2004, makes two sweeping switchbacks up the steep, logged hillside before rounding a ridge and gradually dropping into the Rice Brook valley.

If you're taking the Lyell Creek approach, drive up the Bush Road and just before the 73-km sign, go right on the Lyell Main road, a now-abandoned logging road. Though steep, this is a good gravel road for 4 km before suddenly deteriorating into a rough, grassed-over track. A high-clearance vehicle and some persistence may allow you to drive a few kilometres farther (a mountain bike would hasten the rest of the approach along the remaining roadbed). The roadbed stays high on the right side of the valley (in spring, some avalanche chutes must be crossed) before dropping down to cross Lyell Creek on a bridge (about 14 km from the Bush Road). The road continues up the left side of the creek for a few more kilometres, with a couple of side streams crossed on foot.

Approaches

From Lyell Creek From the end of the roadbed, fight your way up truly nasty bush along the now narrower, steeper Lyell Creek Valley. After a few kilometres of bushwhacking that can consume hours, a clearing where three branches of the creek come together (GR 875540) provides a good campsite, with views up to Alexandra and the Lyells. While Alexandra can be climbed in a long day from here, it involves 2100 metres of elevation gain and another section of miserable bush. It may be worth placing a second, high camp on the glacier.

From this first campsite, follow the left stream branch and, about 1 km farther, take the right fork. Shortly beyond, follow the middle of three stream branches, staying to its right to go up through a bushy cliff band and then angling right up a slight ridge to get above tree line (GR about 872563). Take a rising traverse left across broken moraines and the lower Alexandra Glacier and then kick steps up steeper slopes to reach the Alexandra-Whiterose Col (GR 854581).

From South Rice Brook It is possible to simply follow South Rice Brook, from its junction with Rice Brook, all the way to the head of the valley, but the bushwhacking is sustained and ugly. A more circuitous alternative is to walk or drive up the steep switchbacks of the side road that leaves the Rice Brook road at about 4 km, shortly before the latter drops down to the creek. From the top of this side road, bushwhack to the top left corner of a steep cut block and continue up a long boulder/scree slope to a broad pass with a little lake. Descend to some larger lakes and then contour the best you can, dropping into and climbing out of some side valleys, staying above treeline and avoiding the temptation to take a shortcut by dropping into the thick bush above South Rice Brook. Eventually, the side-hill gouging ends and one descends to a lovely alpine campsite near three small lakes and between two streams (GR 834586). This is also the preferred campsite for a fly-in trip.

South Rice Brook approach and SW Slopes route on Mt. Alexandra.
A. Mt. Coral. B. Fresnoy Mtn. C. Queens Peak.

From this camp, go north across an upper branch of South Rice Brook and ascend weaknesses in a headwall (cairns) to the right of a major waterfall, starting just right of an island of scrub trees. A loose scree slope above leads to a short slab on the right (perhaps 5.2 and topped by a bolt anchor/rappel). Beyond, traverse right on an exposed but broad scree ledge that passes below a prominent red block of rock on the South Face of Mount Coral (GR 843596). This long traverse leads to the left edge of the heavily crevassed West Alexandra Glacier, which is perhaps best ascended left of its centre to reach the Alexandra-Whiterose Col.

Southwest Slopes From the Alexandra-Whiterose Col, go up a snow/ice gully, or loose rocks to the left, to a bench. Either tackle the face above directly on snow or ice (upwards of 35 degrees) or ascend firm, easy rock to the left to reach gentler snow slopes, which are followed right and then back left to the summit, staying clear of any cornices.

Descend the way you came up, the upper rocks offering the easiest passage if the face is icy. If you're returning to the South Rice Brook camp, rappel or down climb the lower 5.2 step.

Foreshortened view of SW Slopes of Mt. Alexandra from Whiterose Mtn.

Alder bashing along Rice Brook. Photo: Nancy Stefani.

The Lyells

Mount Lyell is a single massif with five distinct 11,000er peaks, each rising about 100 metres from intervening cols. Straddling the Continental Divide – and overlooking the Bush River drainage to the west and feeder rivers of the North Saskatchewan to the east – it commands the northwest end of the long, gradually rising Lyell Icefield, which is 50 square kilometres in size, and shrinking. Mount Lyell boasts spectacular icefalls on its north and west aspects and steep rock faces on the east sides of all but Peak 2.

"Like five fingers, the peaks of Lyell jut from the ice field," wrote Alfred Ostheimer III following his 1926 expedition to the area. "Number one stands out to the east in a great block; number two is a tremendous snow mass, flanked on the east by great ice cliffs; number three is isolated and sheer, protected on all sides by a gigantic overhang – rock and ice both tower forbiddingly; number four seems a long rock ridge, while number five hides its northern drop behind a gentle southern snow slope."

Lyell was originally considered one mountain, named by the Palliser Expedition's James Hector for expedition patron Sir Charles Lyell, a lawyer with interests in geology and natural history. The individual peaks were later identified and numbered. In 1972, they were renamed to honour five long-serving Swiss guides who settled in Golden—Rudolph Aemmer (Peak 1), brothers Edward, Jr. (2), Ernest (3) and Walter (4) Feuz and Christian Hasler, Jr. (5). But most climbers still refer to the peaks by their numbers and to the collective whole as the Lyells.

From a high camp on the Lyell Icefield, it is possible to traverse all five peaks in one long day, as we did in 1989. The traverse can be done in either direction, though it's probably easier going from south to north and rappelling the steep rock step on Peak 4. Most parties, however, pick off a couple of peaks at a time on a four-to-six day trip, either from a base camp in Lyell Meadows or from higher on the glacier.

After ascending a steep snow slope, Peaks 1 and 2 are easy walk-ups from the intervening col. Peak 3 isn't much harder, the trick being to find a good route through some lower seracs.

Peak 4 is easily the hardest climb, particularly from the 3-4 Col. (5.4 rock step), while Peak 5 is primarily a snow ridge from either direction.

Several parties have approached the Lyells, and then climbed a few of the peaks, on skis. But the amount of trail breaking or, later in the spring, carrying of skis on the long lower approach demands an elevated degree of masochism. The col between Peaks 2 and 3 has also been used as a passageway for ski traverses from Jasper to the Wapta Icefield. It is reached by climbing 2000 metres from the Alexandra Valley floor along the 1902 first ascent route of Peak 2.

History

While the Lyell massif was viewed from afar by James Hector in the late 1850s, its exact location was unknown and had been confused with the nearby Mount Alexandra. Its highest point (Peak 2) was ascended by James Outram and guide Christian Kaufmann in 1902. The same summer, Norman Collie, Hugh Stutfield, Herman Woolley and guide Hans Kaufmann (brother of Christian) also made a half-hearted attempt at the summit after an approach that included building a raft to cross Glacier Lake and thus avoid burning forest. Their description provides perhaps the best example of the philosophical differences between a climber-explorer like Collie and more overt peak baggers like Outram.

"Starting as it does from an elevated plateau, Lyell, for its height, is a singularly uninteresting and unimposing mountain," wrote Collie and Stutfield in *Climbs and Explorations in the Canadian Rockies*. "However, some of the party, Hans and Woolley in particular, were anxious to make the ascent, which would have been merely a tiring trudge up a moderate slope of snow. But bad weather was coming up from the west, and all three peaks were already in mist, so the project was overruled. Hans was greatly shocked.

"'What, not climb Mount Lyell?' he exclaimed in horrified tones. 'You will regret it very much!' "Hans cared naught for geography: his business was to climb mountains, not to admire or map them; and he would much rather go up a high peak in a fog than get the finest view

Lyells 1-5 (r. to l.), showing traverse route.
Photo: Roman Pachovsky.

in the world from a lower one. We, however, who wished to study the surrounding country, thought that a small protuberance of snow near the centre of the glacier, and below the level of the now thickly gathering mists, would suit us much better; and the lazy ones of the party had their way."

They descended off the toe of the Southeast Lyell Glacier, long since impassable as an approach route because of glacial retreat. They were greatly impressed by the lower glacier's icefall, which they called "incomparably the finest we have seen in the Rockies" and "on a larger scale than anything of its kind in Switzerland."

Once the individual summits of Mount Lyell were identified as distinct high peaks, they attracted a couple of mountaineering parties in the mid-1920s. One such expedition was led by Ostheimer and Monroe Thorington and guided by Edward Feuz, Jr.; they claimed first ascents of Peaks 1, 3 and 5.

Glacier Lake Access and Approach From the Trans-Canada Highway just west of Lake Louise, drive 76 km north on Highway 93 to the Glacier Lake trailhead (1 km north of the Highway 11 junction at Saskatchewan River Crossing). The trailhead is 150 km south of Jasper on Highway 93. Follow the Glacier Lake trail—which soon crosses the impressively turbulent North Saskatchewan River—for 9 km to the lake's east end. A slightly rougher trail parallels the lake's north shore through up-and-down woods for another 3.5 km to its western end, which provides fine views up valley to the Southeast Lyell Glacier. Beyond, follow the indistinct, and in places washed-out, track along the Glacier River's meandering channels for about 5 km to more open river flats (old campsite).

Head up and right, above a glacial meltwater lake, to gain a bushy moraine, which is followed for a short ways above the right side of the glacier. Flagging should mark a trail to the right that climbs steeply through forest to Lyell Meadows, a lovely spot for a base camp (8-10 hours from trailhead). Beyond, go northeast up a basin of rock and scree towards the left end of Arctomys Peak, traversing left and descending slightly towards a col (GR 987541), where the Lyell Icefield is gained (any lower is impassably steep and fractured). Go west along the right side of the icefield to gain its centre below the five peaks (good high campsite on the glacier, 3-4 hours from Lyell Meadows).

Fly-in approach Some groups helicopter in from the Bush River Valley, setting up a 2150-metre camp (GR 962479) northwest of Mons Peak and just west of the Lyell Icefield, with spectacular views of waterfalls plunging into the chasm at the upper end of Icefall Brook (phone Alpine Helicopters in Golden at 250-344-7444). This camp was the site of the Alpine Club of Canada's 1996 and 2004 General Mountaineering Camps.

Such a camp places climbers midway between the Lyells and Forbes. From camp, take a rising line northeast, crossing a pocket glacier, to reach the top of a long ridge (roughly GR 977500) off the northwest end of Division Mountain. Follow this ridge northwest, along the divide, to gain the upper Lyell Icefield at GR 965514. Continue north-northwest to reach the Lyells. An advance camp on the icefield is needed to climb more than two or three of the peaks in one go.

Lyells Traverse

Route Described Traverse of all five peaks (III, 5.4)

Maps 82 N/14 Rostrum Peak and 82 N/15 Mistaya Lake (Glacier Lake approach)

Gear Glacier gear, rope, ice axe, crampons, small rack

Season mid-July to September

Time Trip – 4-6 days (see individual peaks for climbing times)
Climb – 12-14 hours to traverse all five peaks from a high camp

Traverse of the five Lyells (described from North to South, or 1 to 5)—A long but spectacular high traverse and a rare chance to bag five 11,000ers in one day. From the centre of the upper Lyell Icefield, head northwest up the glacier, aiming for the steep snow slopes that lead to the cols between Peaks 1 and 2. From the col, it's a short walk up and down the South Ridge of Peak 1 (Rudolph) and just as easily up the East Ridge of Peak 2 (Edward). Continue over the summit and down to the 2-3 Col and either head directly up the steep snow ridge of Peak 3 (Ernest) or contour right below small seracs and up through crevasses to the summit. Return the same way, contouring under the East Face to reach the 3-4 Col.

From the col, follow the narrow North Ridge of Peak 4 (Walter) on snow to a rock step (5.4) and then continue on exposed ice and snow to the summit. The descending South Ridge of Peak 4 involves climbing over and around pinnacles to reach the 4-5 Col. The North Ridge of Peak 5 (Christian) is enjoyable climbing on snow and rock and the descending South Ridge is all on snow, followed by a long detour around the south end to avoid fractured ice and cliffs to the east and safely return to the main icefield. (11-14 hours return).

Lyell Icefield from Mt. Forbes. A. Fly-in camp approach. B. Arctomys Peak. C. Lyell Meadows

Rudolph Peak (Lyell 1)

3507 metres (11,506 feet)

The most northerly of the Lyells, Rudolph has an impressive east rock face and an even more precipitous, and rarely seen, north aspect. Like many of the steeper lines on the Lyells, these potential hard routes remain unclimbed. After the long approach, most climbers are content to get up these peaks the fastest, easiest way possible.

No route on the Lyells is simpler than the standard South Ridge on Rudolph, the only challenge being the bergschrund and steep snow leading to the 1-2 Col from the upper Lyell Icefield. After that, it's a short snow ascent to the summit, with crevasse hazard almost all the way to the top. Because both Peaks 1 and 2 are a short walk from the intervening col, they are invariably climbed together, with Peak 3 thrown in as a bonus if time and energy permit.

Rudolph Aemmer worked as a guide in the Rockies for 40 years, retiring at age 65 and returning to his native Switzerland. A much-loved guide, he and Edward Feuz, Jr. promoted the building of the stone Abbot Pass Hut, now a national historic site in the Lake Louise/O'Hara area. He was also involved in the 1921 rescue on Mount Eon of Margaret Stone, who spent a week on a ledge after her husband, Winthrop,

fell to his death while descending alone from the summit. Aemmer, who carried Mrs. Stone for more than four hours on his back, was awarded an American Alpine Club citation, after which he said: "Real guides cannot be heroes. When somebody gets into trouble in the mountains, we go after him, take the necessary risks, and bring him down. Nothing else counts."

History

The first ascent of Lyell 1 was by the 1926 American team, guided by Edward Feuz, Jr., that also claimed Peaks 3 and 5. Its members included the energetic and ambitious 18-year-old Alfred Ostheimer III and Monroe Thorington, co-author of the first climbing guide to the Canadian Rockies and described by Ostheimer as an "expert mountaineer and walking encyclopedia."

The party left their camp in Lyell Meadows at 3:30 a.m. and worked their way through the soft snow of Lyell Icefield. "It was a long snow pull, but easily passed, and a bergschrund offered no hindrance," wrote Ostheimer of the 6.5-hour climb. They returned to the 1-2 Col and struggled through deep snow up Peak 2 and made their first, aborted attempt of Peak 3 before returning to camp.

Route

First Ascent July 5, 1926: Alfred Ostheimer III, Monroe Thorington, Max Strumia, *Edward Feuz, Jr.* – South Ridge

Route Described South Ridge (I)

Gear Rope, glacier gear, ice axe, crampons

Map 82 N/14 Rostrum Peak

Season mid-July to September

Time 4-5 hours return from high camp, 10-12 from lower camp

South Ridge From the middle of the upper Lyell Icefield, head north for the Lyell 1-2 col. Crevasses and the bergschrund may pose problems in low snow years. A steep final snow slope leads to the col (potential avalanche hazard), from which the South Ridge is easily ascended on snow and perhaps some scree to the summit. Some parties go up the west snow slopes slightly left of the ridge. **Descend** the same way to the 1-2 col.

Edward Peak (Lyell 2)

3514 metres (11,529 feet)

The snow peak of the Lyells, Edward is the highest of the five summits, though not by much. Indeed, the 1902 first-ascent party must have either been astute judges of elevation or lucky, since Peak 2, by current measurement, rises only three metres above Peak 3 and seven metres above the adjoining Peak 1.

If anything, Peak 2 is an easier ascent than Peak 1, being almost a hands-in-pocket snow climb along either the East or West Ridges. Typically, it is climbed along the former route from the 1-2 Col, after Peak 1 has been ascended. Often, it is then descended by the West Ridge en route to Peak 3. A more sporting route is to tackle the Southeast Face directly on snow and/or ice, with a superb finish on immaculate rock.

Edward Feuz, Jr. followed his father, Edward Sr., from Switzerland to Canada in 1903 to guide, first in Rogers Pass and later in the Rockies from his home in Golden. With nearly

50 years of guiding service with the Canadian Pacific Railway and on his own, he was the dean of Swiss guides in Canada. His record of more than 100 first ascents (78 of them virgin summits) in the Rockies and Selkirks is unmatched and includes mountains such as Sir Sandford and six Rockies 11,000ers. He guided more than two dozen ascents of his beloved Mount Victoria—once nearly dying in an avalanche—and last climbed it at the age of 85, 11 years before his death in 1981.

History

Unlike nearly every later climbing trip to the Lyells, the first ascent of Peak 2 came from the north and involved an elevation gain of close to 2000 metres. It was part of James Outram's and Christian Kaufmann's grand summer of 1902, which included first ascents of Columbia, Bryce, Alexandra and Forbes.

From a camp in the depths of the Alexandra River Valley, they departed at 2:30 a.m., crossed a stream on horses and ascended the valley to the East Alexandra Glacier. They followed the east edge of the glacier, scaling awkward cliffs and a steep lateral moraine to gain the glacier above an icefall. From there, it was a snow ascent to the col and then up the West Ridge to the summit, reached shortly before noon. Having hauled a large camera, tripod and measuring equipment to the top of this watershed peak, Outram spent three hours fiddling with the shaky theodolite in a keen wind, numbing his fingers.

During their 1926 expedition, Alfred Ostheimer, Monroe Thorington, Max Strumia and Feuz approached the Lyells from the south, via the Lyell Icefield. After climbing Peak 1, they made the first ascent of Peak 2's East Ridge and then descended the West Ridge en route to Peak 3, thus completing the first traverse of Edward.

Forbes Macdonald below summit of Lyell 1.
Photo: Roman Pachovsky.

Traversing below Lyells 3 (l.), 2 and 1. A. SE Face route. Photo: Helen Sovdat

Routes

First Ascent July 24, 1902: James Outram, *Christian Kaufmann* – West Ridge

Routes Described East Ridge (I), West Ridge (I), Southeast Face (II)

Gear   Rope, glacier gear, ice axe, crampons, perhaps a couple of ice screws

Map   82 N/14 Rostrum Peak

Season   mid-July to September

Time   4-5 hours return from high camp, 10-12 from lower camp

East Ridge From the middle of the upper Lyell Icefield, head north, crossing a bergschrund and steeper snow to reach the 1-2 Col (potential avalanche hazard). From here, it's a gentle rise up the East Ridge to the summit.

West Ridge From the upper Lyell Icefield, ascend easily north to the 2-3 Col and then up the low-angled West Ridge. The final section may be icy.

For the above two routes, **descend** the way you came or go down the opposite ridge for an easy traverse.

Southeast Face From left of the 1-2 Col, cross the bergschrund (could be challenging later in the season) and head straight up the middle of the face on 35- to 40-degree snow/ice for some 250 vertical metres, capped by a short stretch of steep scrambling up firm rock to the summit. **Descend** either the East or West Ridge.

Ernest Peak (Lyell 3)

3511 metres (11,519 feet)

The divide peak of the group, Lyell 3 was described by Ostheimer as suggesting "a giant tooth—isolated and sheer." He should know, as his 1926 first-ascent party nearly circumnavigated the peak looking for a reasonable path to the summit.

They finally found it along the north slopes, the route that most climbers now generally follow. It's usually a matter of finding a way around some lower seracs and then following a steep but short snow slope to the top. Because of Ernest's steeper rock arêtes, it's the only one of the Lyells without a standard ridge route to the summit.

Ernest was the middle of the three Feuz brothers who worked as guides in the Selkirks and Rockies. While overshadowed in accomplishments and personality by older brother Edward, he had a fine guiding record, with 40 first ascents of peaks and routes, including the hardest of the Lyells (Peak 4), Recondite and traverses of Hungabee and Victoria (south to north). Ernest led the rescue of those who survived the 1954 accident on Mount Victoria, in which four Mexican climbers fell to their deaths.

History

The first-ascent party had already zipped up Lyells 1 and 2 earlier on July 5, 1926 and were headed for a similar conquest of Peak 3 when they ran into a roadblock. "A great schrund blocked our farther upward moves on the ice, and the rock cliffs proved sufficient defence to keep us from the summit of one of the highest unclimbed peaks in Canada," wrote Ostheimer.

"After a short rest, we decided to have a look behind the peak, so we started around the great ice cascade to the north, but no way appeared up this great mass. The whole peak, in fact, impressed us as being one gigantic overhang; rock and ice both towered, leaned out forbiddingly, over these midgets, men who came to climb."

After finally crossing some rock to reach the 3-4 Col, they admitted defeat and headed back to their camp in Lyell Meadows. Four days later, a 1:25 a.m. start allowed them to cross, in four hours, the Lyell 3 bergschrund, above which they cut steps to gain rock ribs and then climb snow and ice on the North Slopes to reach the summit. Briefly soaking up panoramic views that extended as far as Mount Sir Donald in Rogers Pass, they scampered down the rotting snow, safely crossed the bergschrund by 7:30 a.m. and headed for the first ascent of Lyell 5.

Routes

First Ascent July 9, 1926: Alfred Ostheimer III, Monroe Thorington, Max Strumia, *Edward Feuz, Jr.* – North Slopes

Route Described North Slopes (II)

Gear Rope, glacier gear, ice axe, crampons

Map 82 N/14 Rostrum Peak

Season mid-July to September

Time 5 hours return from high camp, 10-12 from lower camp

North Slopes From the middle of the upper Lyell Icefield, ascend the glacier north to the 2-3 Col (or descend the West Ridge of Peak 2 to gain the col). From the col, contour right past the rocky East Ridge and below small seracs to gain steep north snow slopes. Cross the bergschrund (may pose problems) and stay clear of crevasses on the snow slopes, which soon lead to the top. The summit offers fine views of Lyell 4's North Ridge. **Descend** the same way.

Walter Peak (Lyell 4)
3400 metres (11,155 feet)

With its sheer East Face framed by sharply-etched ridges, Lyell 4 is the most imposing of the five peaks and the only one without a relatively simple route to the top. Indeed, on our north-south traverse of the five peaks in 1989, the ascent and descent of Walter took longer than the first three peaks combined.

In 1926, the intrepid Alfred Ostheimer was sufficiently intimidated by the sight of the unclimbed Lyell 4 to write: "From the 3-4 Col, a jagged arête looks at best most discouraging and hopeless. The best way would probably be to attempt a traverse of Peak 5 and cross the intervening arête to the summit of Peak 4, but even this presents great climbing problems and difficulties."

The good news is the climbing on either ridge is not that difficult, and the North Ridge is easily the best route on the Lyells. From the 3-4 Col, a narrow fin of snow rises to a short, steep rock step—partly protected by some fixed pitons and gingerly climbable in crampons—followed by more narrow snow ridge.

The South Ridge is somewhat easier but requires a long, south-north traverse of Lyell 5 to reach its base. Beyond, the chief difficulty is short roping over and around several pinnacles that guard the summit. Perhaps the most enjoyable day on this peak involves a north-south traverse of Lyells 4 and 5, starting from the 3-4 Col.

Walter was the youngest of the three Feuz brothers who guided in Canada and the only one without an official guide's licence. He was, nonetheless, a fine climber, recording 23 first ascents (20 of them peaks), many of them in the company of the ambitious Kate Gardiner in the southern Rockies.

History
Walter Peak was the last of the Lyells to be climbed, falling in 1927 to Dyson Duncan of New York, the delightfully named Twining Lynes, packer Jimmy Simpson and guide Ernest Feuz. After arriving by horseback from Lake Louise and sitting out four days of rain in a canvas tipi, they ascended the edge of the Southeast Lyell Glacier to a higher camp.

The ensuing climb, which consumed 30 hours round trip, involved a long march across the icefield to the south shoulder of Lyell 5, where soft, deep snow ruled out a planned traverse of that peak to reach Lyell 4. Instead, they reached the 4-5 Col by traversing around the west side of Lyell 5, a route no longer feasible because of glacial recession.

"In July," wrote Duncan, "the summit ridge (of Lyell 4) showed no signs of being the 'long rock ridge' which we had expected to find after reading earlier descriptions of the mountain. On the contrary, it was a narrow, heavily corniced snow ridge, similar to that of Mt. Victoria, but both the slopes which form it are somewhat steeper, and it is more irregular and broken. There were great mushrooms, waves and gullies; in fact the snow seemed to be blown into every shape which it could possibly assume. Fortunately the weather was extremely cold and the surface remained firm, for poor snow here would have made the climb impossible."

Before reaching the summit, Feuz accidentally knocked off a section of cornice that "left us standing on a ridgepole where a moment before there had been a regular sidewalk," said Duncan. "At last we crawled up onto an insecure knob of snow just big enough for two people to huddle on at the same time, and found it overtopped only by a huge cornice with a narrow base on which we did not dare trust our weight."

The North Ridge was not climbed until 1940, when Rex Gibson led an Alpine Club of Canada party up the sharp route.

Routes

First Ascent July 8, 1927: Dyson Duncan, Twining Lynes, Jimmy Simpson, *Ernest Feuz* – South Ridge

Routes Described North Ridge (II, 5.4), *Recommended, particularly when included in a traverse of Lyells 4 and 5,* South Ridge (II)

Gear Rope, glacier gear, ice axe, crampons, ice screws, plus a small rock rack and a few pitons for the North Ridge

Map 82 N/14 Rostrum Peak

Season mid-July to September

Time North Ridge: 6-8 hours return, via 3-4 Col, from upper Lyell Icefield
South Ridge: 10-12 hours return via Lyell 4-5 traverse

North Ridge From the upper Lyell Icefield, gain the 3-4 Col via steep snow. The first part of the ridge is a narrow but fairly level fin of snow, at the end of which two fixed pitons provide a good station for the short rock step above. Climb the step directly, trending slightly left to find an intermediate piton and then building a belay station, with pitons, at the top. Above, the snow ridge is followed (sometimes on its west side, where easier), with an intervening, 15-metre "Scottish" ice gully and possibly a few other icy sections requiring short ice screws. A last bit on rock leads to the summit.

South Ridge To reach the 4-5 Col, traverse Lyell 5 from the south (see page 138). While this col has been reached directly from the Lyell Icefield to the east, avalanche and crevasse hazard is high. From the col, follow a broad snow ramp on the west side of the ridge. Closer to the summit, climb over and around a number of rock pinnacles, a time-consuming process.

Descent The long way is to go down the South Ridge and then over Lyell 5, regaining the icefield via the lower South Ridge of the latter. This is a fine route if you're traversing Lyell 4 and 5 but tedious and repetitive if you've already traversed Lyell 5 to climb Peak 4. The much shorter but steeper descent is to down climb Lyell 4's North Ridge, rappelling where necessary, particularly the rock step.

Approaching 5.4 rock step on N Ridge of Lyell 4.
Photo: Helen Sovdat.

Christian Peak (Lyell 5)

3390 metres (11,122 feet)

Christian Peak is the lowest of the five Lyells but is aesthetically eclipsed only by Lyell 4. It is particularly impressive when viewed from Peak 4, with its north and south snow ridges rising elegantly above steep rock faces to a tapered summit.

As is often the case, the climbing on either ridge is easier than it looks. The simplest way up and down the mountain is via the South Ridge, a broad snow ramp that briefly steepens near the summit. The steeper North Ridge, an enjoyable combination of snow and fourth-class rock, is usually climbed on a north-south traverse of Lyells 4 and 5.

Lyell 5 can also be traversed from south to north and then continuing over Lyell 4. This is the slightly harder traverse of Peak 5, as the steeper North Ridge must be down climbed.

Like Edward Feuz, Jr., Christian Hasler, Jr. followed his father from Switzerland to guide in Canada. Arriving in 1912, he guided in the Selkirks and later the Rockies, making 23 first ascents, including 14 peaks. His life, however, was tragic. Following the death of a son and his wife, Hasler was badly mauled by a grizzly bear near Sherbrooke Lake in Yoho National Park in 1939 and died a year later after falling from the roof of his house. His last climb, during the Alpine Club of Canada's 1940 camp, was Lyell 5, the peak later named after him.

History

After making the first ascent of Lyell 3, the Thorington/Ostheimer party trudged across the icefield until they were below Lyell 5. "Some ticklish work followed on the lower schrund, which was really a miniature ice-fall. In fact, we literally swam across one poorly-bridged crevasse," wrote Alfred Ostheimer of their fairly direct approach to the South Ridge. The ridge was followed uneventfully to the summit, where "cameras clicked busily, pipes were smoked, and we snoozed in the sunlight." They then made the long march back down the icefield in the hot sun, their unprotected faces later "suffering the pains of severe blistering."

In 1973, J.K. Fox, J. Larson and D. MacFarlane made the first ascent of Lyell 5's North Ridge from the 4-5 Col, the narrow snow ridge and two rock pitches leading to the top.

Lyell 5 from Lyell 4.
A. S Ridge. B. N. Ridge

Opposite: N Ridge of Lyell 4 from Lyell 3, Lyell 5 in rear. Photo: Sandy Walker.

Magnificent traverse of Lyells 4 (r.) and 5. Photo: Dan Doll.

Routes

First Ascent July 9, 1926: Alfred Ostheimer III, Monroe Thorington, Max Strumia, *Edward Feuz, Jr.* – South Ridge

Routes Described South Ridge (II), North Ridge (II)

Gear Rope, glacier gear, ice axe, crampons

Map 82 N/14 Rostrum Peak

Season mid-July to September

Time South Ridge: About 6 hours return from a high camp, 10-12 from a lower camp
North Ridge: 10-12 hours return via Lyell 4-5 traverse

South Ridge From the Lyell Icefield, gain the lower ridge at the middle of its flat section by taking a rising line southeast up a snow ramp. Otherwise, swing farther south to access the ridge lower down. The ridge is followed on snow to the top, the angle increasing to about 40 degrees and the ridge narrowing just below the top.

North Ridge Gain the 4-5 Col, best done by first traversing Lyell 4 (north to south), but also accessible by masochistically following the example of the route's first-ascent party and first traversing Lyell 5 from south to north (this means, you'll descend the North Ridge before climbing it). Accessing the 4-5 Col directly from the Lyell Icefield is not recommended because of avalanche hazard and considerable crevasses. The ridge is followed on snow and fourth-class rock to the summit.

Descent After the first, steep 50 metres, the South Ridge is primarily a snow walk-off. Halfway down the flat section of the ridge, a contouring line can be safely followed to the icefield; any earlier shortcuts are likely to encounter considerably fractured ice and potentially steep slopes. Otherwise, continue down the South Ridge before dropping onto the icefield, a route that adds about a kilometre to the descent. The North Ridge can be down climbed to the 4-5 Col if a traverse of Lyell 4 is to follow.

Mount Forbes

3612 metres (11,850 feet)

Mount Forbes is the highest peak entirely in Banff National Park and one of the Rockies' climbing prizes. Its gleaming Northwest Face, a pyramid soaring above the surrounding mountains, is easily recognizable from almost any vantage point in the north-central Rockies. The rock precipices on the opposite side are perhaps even more impressive, rising more than 1500 metres from Forbes Creek, in the upper Howse River drainage.

The allure of Forbes is heightened by its relative isolation and inaccessibility, adding a sense of wilderness to any expedition to its glaciated slopes. The approach is a 21-kilometre march from near Saskatchewan River Crossing and involves a frigid plunge across the aptly-named Glacier River, followed by a steady climb to the toe of Forbes's North Glacier. The reward of this all-day push is one of the Rockies' finer bivy sites, with a glacial stream flowing past and expansive views across the Mons Icefield.

The climbing crux is sometimes finding safe passage around some immense crevasses in the middle of the North Glacier, particularly in a dry year. Once gained, the standard West Ridge is a straightforward though tedious scramble up loose shale. The recommended route is the Northwest Face, a classic, intermediate snow or ice line straight to the summit.

Rockies' explorer James Hector named the mountain in 1859 for Edward Forbes, his professor of natural history at the University of Edinburgh. It's one of numerous examples of prime Rockies' peaks named after folks who never set foot in this country.

History

Norman Collie first spied Forbes in 1897 from Mount Gordon on the Wapta Icefield, though he mistakenly thought the distant peak was Mount Murchison. A year later, bad weather thwarted his group's hopes of scaling Forbes, which he called one of the finest rock peaks in the Rockies, "a combination of the Weisshorn and the Dent Blanche (with) precipices on its eastern face that are exceptionally grand."

The 1902 first-ascent party was an all-star gathering that featured the two premier Rockies climbers at the turn of the century—Collie and James Outram. It was no doubt an uncomfortable alliance, as Outram had just scooped the prized Mount Columbia, which Collie had

discovered in 1898 and hoped to climb that summer on his third attempt. Joining this esteemed pair were Collie's companions—Hugh Stutfield, Herman Woolley and an American, George Weed—and the guiding brothers Hans and Christian Kaufmann. The latter was the real star on Forbes, doing all the leading on this most challenging climb.

Today, virtually all parties climb Forbes via its North Glacier. The approach is simpler, the elevation gain on the climb considerably less and the glacier ascent much easier than the rotten rock of the Southwest Ridge. Yet the 1902 party chose the latter, perhaps because in the era before crampons they were averse to ice climbs, though they did descend the north side.

The route turned out to be looser, steeper and more difficult than expected. Indeed, it was the hardest climb Collie did in four trips to the Rockies and was likely the most difficult of any completed in the range, until Outram's and Christian Kaufmann's daring ascent of the Northeast Ridge of Mount Bryce shortly thereafter.

Perhaps the only advantage of this approach from the southeast was the Forbes Creek canyon, which Collie described thus: "For a combination of peak, glacier, gorge and forest scenery, there is nothing to surpass it in the Canadian Rockies." The route up the Southwest Ridge was something else—a sharp rock arête interrupted by a pinnacle, followed by an ugly notch and topped by a heavily corniced snow ridge.

The lower ridge was steep and loose, with few holds and a "brown, scaly rock suggestive of rhinoceros hide… it must be admitted that Forbes is much more beautiful at a distance than when you are actually standing upon him," wrote Collie. Beyond the notch, the "*gymnase*, or sensational part of the climb," began up the knife-edged ridge.

"Very slowly, inch by inch, we edged our way upwards—now *à cheval*, astride of the uncomfortably sharp crest of the ridge, now clinging like limpets to the rocks at the side, for there was very little to catch hold of. On the left the cliffs fell perfectly sheer for some hundreds of feet, with mingled snow and rock declivities fifteen hundred feet or so below; on the right was the great precipice of the eastern face."

To exacerbate matters, the group was split into two parties, the latter with four on an 80-

Crossing the heavily-crevassed North Glacier below Mt. Forbes. Photo: Markus Kellerhals.

foot rope. At one point on this rope, a rock gave way under Hans Kaufmann's feet, and he fell a few feet before grabbing the arête with his hand. Feeling this many on a rope was too dangerous, Collie untied below one gnarly cliff band, content to stay behind. But after the cliff band was overcome, the guides went back down and brought him up.

Near the top, the rock became even more rotten, and "the narrow crest of the ridge seemed to be held together only by the snow frozen against its sides." Christian Kaufmann ably led this delicate climb all the way up. Then on the descent down the northwest side, he cut steps for nearly 500 metres to a col, below which they reached the South Glacier and traversed under the West Face to regain their bivy site, some 15 hours after setting out.

Two decades later, Joseph Hickson and Edward Feuz, Jr. made the second ascent of Forbes by the same execrable route. In 1926, Feuz returned with Monroe Thorington, Alfred Ostheimer and Max Strumia but this time from the north, after knocking off three of the five Lyell peaks. From a bivy near the toe of the Mons Icefield, they ascended the North Glacier to the West Ridge, which was followed over "extremely rotten shale and a long snow and ice ridge" to the top. On their way down, an avalanche roared past within seven metres of them.

In 1971, Jeff Lowe, Graham Thompson and Chris Jones made the first recorded ascent of the Northwest Face. Other than belaying through one short section of rock band, they front-pointed together up the 600-metre ice face, which was in excellent condition.

Opposite: Nancy Hansen (front) approaching the summit of Mt. Forbes, her last 11,000er. Photo: Markus Kellerhals.

Routes

First Ascent August 10, 1902: Norman Collie, James Outram, Hugh Stutfield, George Weed, Herman Woolley, *Christian Kaufmann, Hans Kaufmann* – Southwest Ridge

Routes Described West Ridge (II/III), Northwest Face (III), *Recommended*

Gear Rope, glacier gear, crampons, ice axe and ice screws (two ice tools and more screws for Northwest Face and for the West Ridge route later in the season)

Map 82 N/15 Mistaya Lake

Season mid-July to September

Time Trip – Three long days return
Climb – 7-10 hours return from camp below North Glacier; slightly longer via the Northwest Face

Glacier Lake Access and Approach From the Trans-Canada Highway just west of Lake Louise, drive 76 km north on Highway 93 (Icefields Parkway) to the Glacier Lake trailhead. The trailhead is 150 km south of Jasper on Highway 93.

Take the Glacier Lake trail to the east end of the lake (9 km), which is then followed along its north side. Beyond the lake's west end (12.5 km), follow an indistinct trail along the Glacier

River's north side. While most parties stay on this side all the way down to the valley draining the Mons Glacier, the river crossing here is usually more than waist deep, with chunks of ice floating past. By crossing the Glacier River lower down, where the channel is wider and more braided, the water may be below the knee.

Though some parties camp beside the river, it's worth pushing on to the North Glacier bivy if time and energy permit. On the right side of the Mons Glacier drainage, a trail works up and right to gain and follow a long lateral moraine. Scrambling up short rock steps takes you over a rocky shoulder to gain the lower Mons Glacier, which is easily crossed. Beyond, head southeast over a series of rubbly moraine ridges to reach a splendid bivy site (rock corrals, running water) near a small lake just below the toe of Forbes's North Glacier (10-12 hours from the car).

Fly-in approach Some groups helicopter in from the Bush River Valley, setting up a 2,150-metre camp (GR 962479) northwest of Mons Peak and just west of the Lyell Icefield, with spectacular views of waterfalls plunging into the chasm at the upper end of Icefall Brook. (Phone Alpine Helicopters in Golden at 250-344-7444). This camp was the site of the Alpine Club of Canada's 1996 and 2004 General Mountaineering Camps. From the camp, head east to gain the Mons Icefield and follow the glacier east-southeast to reach the above-mentioned North Glacier bivy site (about 4 hours), where a high camp makes for a much shorter summit day.

West Ridge From the bivy site, scramble east over rocks to gain the North Glacier. Swing toward its left side to avoid jumbled crevasses and then work back right past large crevasses to reach the bottom of the Northwest Face. Angle right on a snow/ice ramp of about 35 degrees to reach a col in the West Ridge. Follow loose shale on the ridgeline (or go left onto snow), which gives way to snow or ice shortly before the summit.

Northwest Face Follow the West Ridge route until almost directly below the summit, at the bottom of the Northwest Face. Head straight up the face on 40- to 50-degree ice or snow, joining the West Ridge just below the summit.

Descent For both routes, follow the West Ridge down to the col and then retrace your steps down the North Glacier.

Mount Cline
3361 metres (11,027 feet)

Mount Cline is one of a handful of 11,000ers well east of the Continental Divide in the front ranges. Located in the angle between the North Saskatchewan and Cline Rivers, it is just outside Banff National Park. Surprisingly, it is also farther north than Mount Bryce.

Despite its proximity to and visibility from the busy Saskatchewan River Crossing, Cline receives relatively few mountaineering visitors for a peak its size. For a modest effort, mountaineers will discover a stark but ruggedly beautiful landscape, highlighted by a lovely campsite beside two small lakes. Higher up are unique views of Cline's lower but more aesthetic neighbours, Mounts Wilson and Murchison, as well as the seldom visited White Goat Wilderness Area to the north.

For that reason, Cline is worth at least a two-day trip, though it can be climbed in a long day from the car (it has also been attempted on skis in the spring). Because it's on the edge of the dryer front ranges, Cline can often be tackled by early July, when many other big peaks are still entombed in snow.

The standard Southwest Ridge route is mostly a relaxed scramble, with a couple of notches thrown in for excitement. Rarely climbed, the North Ridge offers a recommended alpine mix of rock and ice, with superb positions. Cline's impressive East Face has yet to be climbed.

Norman Collie named the peak for area fur trader, trapper and one-time Jasper postmaster Michel Cline, who in the early 19th century commuted through the mountains from Jasper House to Kootenay Plains via "Old Cline's Trail."

History

Cline was first climbed in 1927, when most of the recognizable big peaks in the Canadian Rockies had already been claimed. The first ascent was led by the handsome and able guide Rudolph Aemmer and legendary outfitter Jimmy Simpson, who had escorted James Outram and Christian Kaufmann on their famous peak-bagging expedition of 1902. The clients on Cline included Honolulu attorney Alfred Castle and his son, Alfred, Jr.; their family owned what is now Dole Pineapple.

From the North Saskatchewan River, the party followed Owen Creek and then the west fork of Thompson Creek to today's customary lakeside bivy spot south of the mountain. The 50-year-old Simpson joined the ascent, which went well until the party encountered a notch in the ridge, which dropped down to a keystone with a thousand feet of air beneath it and overhanging rock above.

"I saw Rudolph go down and he got on the keystone. He stuck his axe in his belt, a sign it is going to be tough because he wants both his hands," Simpson recalled. "When he was nearly at the top of the other side, he found his left foot where his right foot should be. I saw him feel the rock with his hands and then this darn fool hung by his fingers and changed his feet. I saw every knuckle turn snow white. I thought, 'My God, if he falls will this rope hold?' He put his right foot on it and his left up a little higher and went up on top and said, 'Come on, it is all right.'"

The North Ridge was climbed in 1981 by Orvel Miskiw and Bruce Hart from a camp below Cline's big east wall. "The climb was mostly on good moderate ice (gullies) with two short sections of reasonable rock, alternating with rock rubble and snow. It provided more in length, challenge and enjoyment than we had expected from previous (foreshortened) views, and we recommend it," wrote Miskiw, who has done more exploratory climbing in the area than anyone. "We claim the first ascent of this route but I'm surprised if it has not been done before; an attractive route in scenic surroundings, to a prominent summit, the highest for many miles in all directions."

Opposite: Mt. Forbes. A. NW Face. B. W Ridge. Photo: Roman Pachovsky.

Mt. Cline N Ridge. Photo: Tony Daffern.

SW Ridge. A. notches. Photo: Markus Kellerhals.

Climbing up second notch on return.

Routes

First Ascent July 1927: J.H. Barnes, Alfred Castle, Alfred Castle, Jr., Jimmy Simpson, *Rudolph Aemmer* – Southwest Ridge,

Routes Described Southwest Ridge (II, 5.4), North Ridge (III, WI2, 5.3) *Recommended*

Gear   Rope, crampons, ice axe, a few pieces of rock gear and perhaps a couple of pitons for the notches. For the North Ridge, add a few more pieces of gear, a few ice screws and a second ice tool

Map   83 C/2 Cline River

Season   July to September

Time   Trip – 2 days

Climbs – Southwest Ridge: About 6 hours return from high camp

North Ridge: About 7 hours to the summit, another 2-3 down to the Southwest Ridge campsite

Access From just west of Lake Louise, drive 75 km north on Highway 93 (Icefields Parkway) to Saskatchewan River Crossing and then 9 km east on Highway 11 to the signed Thompson Creek campground. Park beside the creek or ask if you can use the campground's day-use parking area.

Southwest Ridge *Approach* From the parking area, take a good trail up the left (west) side of Thompson Creek, following the left fork as it bends west and then goes back north. A couple of kilometres beyond and shortly before a waterfall, go left, just before a cairn, on a good trail up a moraine into a rubbly bowl. Pick up an indistinct trail, leading into trees left of a cliff band, to reach a better trail heading right on a treed bench. When this trail peters out, continue contouring around into the upper valley. Go northwest along the upper stream to reach two small lakes, with good campsites at their north end (about 4-5 hours from the car).

Climb From the northwest end of the lakes, take a left-rising ramp that provides easy access into an upper basin and then traverse north on slabs to a col, from where the not-so-impressive-looking Cline is now visible to the northeast. Cross a small glacier to reach the Southwest Ridge at a low, U-shaped break in the rock.

A short distance along the ridge, two notches are reached. Crossing the first involves loose but straightforward down climbing onto a chockstone and then back up the other side; belay if necessary. The nearby second notch, while only a couple of metres across, is deeper and steeper, requiring about five metres of down climbing on solid holds and then stepping across a gap. Some foolhardy folks have jumped this notch. At last report, there were a couple of fixed pieces just above the near side of this second notch, allowing for a good belay, with the rope left attached for a top-roped return. Beyond the notches, it's easy going up the final slope on snow (preferred) or scree to the summit. **Descend** the same way.

North Ridge Note: Pack light, as you'll carry all your bivy gear up the route.

Approach From the parking area, go north along the eastern branch of Thompson Creek, mainly following the right side of the creek on an occasional, old outfitter's trail. After some early bushwhacking and a few creek crossings, the terrain starts to open up. Ascend to the broad col between Cline and Lion Peak, drop down to the glacier and continue north under the steep East Face of Cline until near the end of the North Ridge. Go left up a snow/ice gully between rock outcrops to reach a broad bivy ledge below the ridge proper.

Climb Follow the ridge up over a mix of moderate ice (one exposed, 60-degree pitch) and some low fifth-class rock interspersed with narrow sidewalks of rock.

Descend the Southwest Ridge route and follow its approach out to the highway.

Approaches for Recondite, Willingdon and Hector

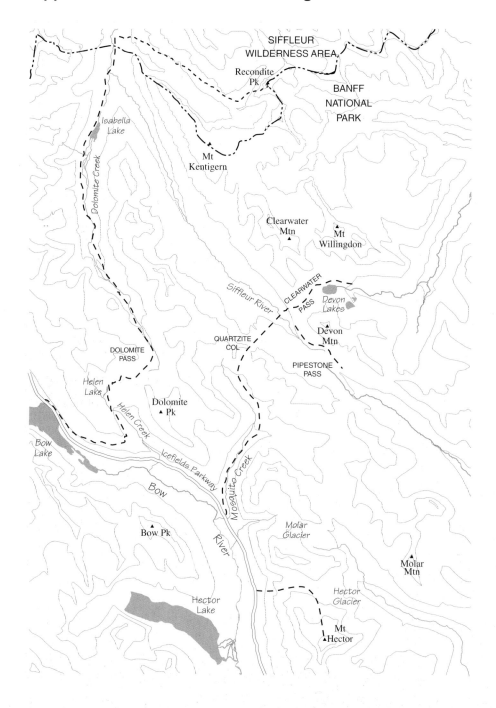

Opposite: A. Mt. Willingdon from Quartzite Col.
B. Crown. C. Willingdon 3. D. Clearwater Pass.
Photo: Markus Kellerhals.

Mount Willingdon
3373 metres (11,066 feet)

Bagging an easy 11,000er might be the mountaineering draw here, but the real lure is one of the Canadian Rockies' most beautiful areas. The peak itself is little more than a rubbly scramble under dry conditions, its difficulty sometimes eclipsed by a slippery down slope on the approach. But the broad alpine meadows of the upper Siffleur River Valley are superb, as are the turquoise Devon Lakes near Clearwater Pass, at the base of Mount Willingdon. The wilderness feel of this treeless expanse is enhanced by the occasional presence of wolves, grizzly bears and a remnant herd of woodland caribou, the most southerly in the Rockies.

The good news is this "remote" area, in the front ranges of the central Rockies, is accessible in a reasonable day's march, thanks to a short-cut known as Quartzite Col. This high perch provides a lovely overview of the Pipestone Valley and the first look at Willingdon and its two satellite peaks, though it's hard from this perspective to tell which is the 11,000er. Indeed, a few climbers have made a beeline for the 3337-metre (10,948-foot) Willingdon South (also known as Crown) to the right, not realizing their mistake till they're standing on the slightly lower summit.

Willingdon overlooks the headwaters of the Clearwater River, which swings northeast to feed the North Saskatchewan River; many of the violent hailstorms that sweep central Alberta originate at Clearwater Pass. To the north of Willingdon are a number of sizable peaks, most notably Recondite Peak, eight kilometres to the northwest. While this so-called Clearwater Group is considered a dry range, its highest peaks harbour a cluster of small glaciers. But from Willingdon's summit, the most impressive view is the exquisite trio of Devon Lakes, framed by Devon Mountain.

History
The route from Lake Louise up the Pipestone River and down the Siffleur Valley is one of the oldest in the Rockies and was followed by explorer James Hector in 1859 and by climbing

W Ridge route on Mt. Willingdon. A. Col. B. Cliff band. Photo: Gillean Daffern.

pioneer Norman Collie in the late 1890s. Although both parties passed close to Willingdon, they either didn't see or pay much attention to this high peak. Both Willingdon and Recondite were readily visible to early mountaineers on the Wapta Icefield, some 25 kilometres to the southwest. But these peaks' distance from the Continental Divide and unimpressive appearance led climbers to underestimate their elevation, though in reality they were the highest summits between Mounts Hector and Forbes.

"These peaks have comparatively little snow and for that reason are apt to be shunned by mountaineers as merely uninteresting shale piles," wrote Osgood Field as an added reason why the Clearwater peaks were overlooked as a climbing objective. "This conception is to a certain extent true, but there are still climbers who exult in the mere attainment of a virgin summit of high altitude."

Field was certainly interested, having heard of a rumoured near-11,000er known as Mount Clearwater. So in 1925, he and four others traveled by horseback into the upper Clearwater area and discovered their quarry among a surprising number of peaks exceeding 10,000 feet. From a high camp, they ascended snow and ice slopes (now gone) to reach the West Ridge, which was followed to the summit.

Field's exultation at a first ascent was short lived. Upon returning to civilization, he learned Willingdon had been climbed six years earlier by a topographical survey party. In a Rockies' history replete with ambitious climbers knocking off big peaks, it's fitting that one 11,000er fell first to anonymous surveyors, who as a whole did so much to identify and map the peaks of the Canadian Rockies. Field's suggestion to name the peak Clearwater was also ignored. It was instead called Willingdon, after Canada's thirteenth governor general, and Clearwater Mountain was assigned to a peak two kilometres west.

In 1977, Judy Cook and Scipio Merler ascended the Northeast Glacier to a col and then went up the South Ridge. The *Rocky Mountains of Canada–South* calls this an elegant snow route, the best in the surrounding Dry Ranges.

Routes

First Ascent 1919: Topographical survey party – West Ridge

Routes Described West Ridge (I); traverse (I)

Gear Ice axe, crampons (optional) and perhaps a short piece of rope for the final cliff band

Maps 82 N/9 Hector Lake and 82 N/16 Siffleur River

Season Late June to early October. The approach has been done on skis in spring.

Time Trip – 2-3 days return

Climb – About 6 hours return from Devon Lakes, add 2-3 hours for traverse

Access From the Trans-Canada Highway just west of Lake Louise, drive 24 km north on the Icefields Parkway to the Mosquito Creek Youth Hostel parking lot.

Approach Follow the Mosquito Creek hiking trail for about 4 km and then angle left on game trails along the creek's north fork, traversing through open forest and grassy slopes on either side of the creek. About where the creek bends west (GR 477255), head north up steep grassy slopes dotted with low evergreens to a large, rocky amphitheatre. Pick your way though these tedious boulders (left side longer but easier) to a notch in the ridge known as Quartzite Col (476283). A plaque and wreath have been placed nearby in honour of fallen mountaineer Gary Pilkington. It's worth walking along the ridge to the right to scout out the best way down the steep snow and rock slope into the valley below (crampons and an ice axe may be necessary if it's icy).

The hummocky meadows beyond are surprisingly undulating, but three small headwater branches of the Siffleur River are easily hopped across. Continue northeast to intersect a deeply-furrowed horse trail leading up to Clearwater Pass. Follow this often muddy trail around the north shore of the largest Devon Lake, and camp near a small inlet stream south of the objective (6-8 hours from the road).

West Ridge Angle northeast onto a grassy moraine that leads, by easy scrambling, up a ridge of sharp, rotten rock with interesting pitting to a col marked by a large crown-shaped rock. From here, follow the West Ridge up back-sliding scree (snow if you're lucky). Just before the summit, there is a sting in the tail—a loose and down-sloping, five-metre cliff band, which can be slippery if wet or icy. If so, good holds on solid, though steeper, rock can be found by traversing a short distance to the left, or north.

Descent Return via the ascent route. The presence of a couple of pitons above the northern route through the cliff band indicates some groups have rappelled from here, rather than down climb.

Option From the summit of Willingdon, it's worth taking an extra couple of hours to traverse southeast over two near-11,000ers—Willingdon South (3337 metres) and Willingdon 3 (3325). Despite first appearances, the connecting snow ridge can be directly followed to the middle peak (from where the snowy top of Willingdon is much more impressive), followed by an easy walk up the third peak. The most straightforward return to camp is to go back over the middle summit and down a scree ridge between it and Willingdon, traversing right as you descend to reach a gully to the left of the Willingdon ascent moraine (it's worth studying the best line into the gully while ascending the moraine in the morning).

Recondite Peak

3356 metres (11,010 feet)

Recondite is the runt of the 11,000ers, stretching a mere three metres of shattered limestone above the benchmark. This dubious status was reinforced by the omission of its name from the 1:50,000 imperial topo map, which was belatedly rectified on the newer, metric version. Not surprisingly, "Recondite" means obscure. Under dry conditions, the climb is mostly a scree slog—with a bit of loose, exposed scrambling—that usually demands a rope only for a short rappel from the false summit.

Recondite's chief attribute is its splendid isolation. Straddling the boundary between Banff National Park and the Siffleur Wilderness Area, the peak is a 40-kilometre trudge from the Icefields Parkway. Thus the approach, and the return, through this stark but beautiful wilderness is considerably more memorable than the climb. It includes knee-deep stream crossings, swamp wallowing, boulder hopping and bushwhacking through mossy forest. Worse, the 600-metre elevation gain to reach Dolomite Pass is all lost descending into the Siffleur Valley. Indeed, after some 30 kilometres, you are actually 100 metres lower than when you started, with a 1,600-metre gain to the summit still ahead.

By the time you're ascending the shifting rock, another definition of Recondite, "incomprehensible," starts making sense. But when you hear wolves howling at night in the untouched Siffleur Valley or gaze at a semicircle of steep walls from one of the finest high bivy sites in the Rockies, the journey begins to feel worthwhile.

Of all the storied 11,000ers, Recondite Peak was my bugaboo. It took me five attempts and about 400 kilometres on foot to finally reach the top. The failures included an April attempt on skis that ended when the snow ran out; climbing the wrong peak in a further, parallel valley when we forgot the map; forgetting the tent poles and later turning around in a summer snowstorm; and being stopped by verglas within spitting distance of the summit. When I finally made it to the top on a Labour Day weekend, it was snowing, with a biting wind and almost no visibility.

Crossing Dolomite Creek above Isabella Lake on Recondite approach.

After his 1927 first ascent, on his last major climbing trip to the Rockies, Howard Palmer called the peak Recondite because it was hidden from sight.

History
In 1925, Osgood Field led the first mountaineering party into the upper Clearwater area and identified Recondite as Peak No. 5. Looking north from Mount Willingdon, he described a rudely pyramidal mass that is "one of the outstanding rock towers of the Canadian Rockies. (It) will never be considered as a mere pile of shale by anyone who attempts its ascent. It is a beautiful rock peak and, from what we could see, may present very considerable problems to mountaineers."

He was wrong on both counts. Recondite is today regarded, by its relatively few summiteers, as a shale pile rather easily ascended by its Southwest Ridge (the Southeast Face that so impressed Field has not been climbed). While his party ran out of time before mounting a serious attempt, they did identify the best way to attack the peak, from the southeast branch of the Siffleur River.

From a camp in this valley in 1927, Howard Palmer and guide Ernest Feuz made the first ascent of Recondite, via the Southwest Ridge, without incident; they thought they had climbed a 10,990-foot peak. "The peak is composed of friable, shattered rock, against which one must particularly guard at the final pitch," wrote Palmer, who was impressed with the sharp summit, guarded on three sides by forbidding cliffs.

Route

First Ascent August 26, 1927: Howard Palmer, *Ernest Feuz* – Southwest Ridge
Route Described Southwest Ridge (II)
Gear 50-metre light rope, long piece of webbing, ice axe and crampons
Map 82 N/16 Siffleur River, 82 N/9 Hector Lake
Season August to September best (lower creeks)
Time Trip – 3 long days
Climb – About 8 hours return from high camp

Access From the Trans-Canada Highway just west of Lake Louise, drive 33 km north on the Icefields Parkway to the Crowfoot Glacier Viewpoint parking lot on the right, the start of the Helen Lake and Dolomite Pass trail. A more direct route to Dolomite Pass starts 4 km south on the highway and follows the ski route via the Helen Creek trail, but is less scenic, involves some route finding and is often closed because of grizzly bear activity.

Approach Note: While there is a shorter approach, with less elevation gain, north up the Siffleur River from Highway 11, the trail is not maintained and involves much log hopping. The more common approach, described below, is about 37 km to a high bivy (12-plus hours).

From the Crowfoot Glacier parking lot, follow the justly famous Helen Lake trail, with its sweeping Bow Valley views and lovely alpine meadows. Beyond the lake (6 km), the trail switchbacks steeply to a high ridge, then quickly descends past Katherine Lake to Dolomite Pass (9 km). Descending north from the pass,

Returning to false summit on Recondite Pk.

151

SW Ridge route on Recondite Pk. A. False summit. B. Col. Photo: Roman Pachovsky.

a rougher trail initially follows the left side of Dolomite Creek, which is crossed twice. Shortly after the second crossing, the valley opens up leading to Isabella Lake. Rather than follow the trail as it swings muddily left into trees, it's generally more direct to don running shoes and slosh straight across a number of small channels, angling left to regain the trail in trees just before the lake (24 km).

From a lakeside warden's cabin, follow the trail north for 4 km to a crossing of Dolomite Creek (generally below the knee in late summer). Disregarding the upper Siffleur Valley trail going southeast, follow the right bank of the creek briefly to a short but slightly deeper crossing of the Siffleur River. Continue north along game trails to the entrance of a sizable valley to the right, the Siffleur's southeast branch, just inside the Siffleur Wilderness Area (campsites).

If time and energy permit, press on up this drainage, following the mossy right bank until it's feasible to cross the stream. After about 2 km, the valley opens up and levels off, revealing an austere, dry landscape. It's nearly another 4 km of plodding before Recondite finally reveals itself to the northeast. Just before a creek drops down from the left, head left up through trees to a streamside grassy bench ringed by high peaks, a lovely reward after many hours of toil.

Southwest Ridge From the bivy site, contour around the stream's left side and go east up a tedious scree slope to a col at the foot of the Southwest Ridge, which provides impressive views of the glaciated Mounts Kentigern (southwest) and Augusta (east). The ridge is followed up pavement-like gray limestone towards a tower, circumvented by traversing right and then down climbing a small notch onto the more exposed South Face. The ridge is regained (very loose rock) just before a false summit. Secure a long webbing anchor around this friable block and rappel some 10 metres into a notch, leaving the rope for the return ascent. It's a short, exposed scramble around the left of the summit block to reach the top. **Descend** the same way.

Mount Hector

3394 metres (11,135 feet)

Mount Hector is the dominant peak north of Lake Louise, from where it looks remarkably like the cartoon Peanuts character Snoopy lying atop his doghouse. Its lofty isolation offers summiteers grand views of the Wapta and Waputik Icefields to the west and the infrequently visited peaks of the Drummond Glacier to the east.

While the first-ascent party tackled the direct west slopes from the Bow Valley, most climbers today approach via the 5.5-kilometre North Glacier route. The latter is one of the most popular spring ski ascents in the Rockies, with a long, scenic climb punctuated by an exciting bit of exposed, sometimes slippery, scrambling at the end. The reward is a fast 1600-metre run back to the car.

Hector is one of the few 11,000ers named after the Canadian Rockies early explorers and climbers. James Hector was the surgeon and geologist of the Palliser Expedition, which explored the western prairies and mountains in the late 1850s. In a 38-day push, the tireless Hector and two guides traveled through the major river valleys of the central Canadian Rockies, passing close to the peak and lake that bear his name as they headed north towards the North Saskatchewan drainage.

History

Mount Hector was the second Rockies 11,000er to be scaled. The 1895 first-ascent party was an estimable trio of Appalachian Mountain Club members—Charles Fay, Charles Thompson and the fine young climber and Boston lawyer Philip Abbot, who died famously a year later while attempting Mount Lefroy.

"Our party that climbed Mt. Hector cannot, I am afraid, lay claim to much glory there from. We had no hair-breadth escapes; we did not even encounter great hardships, except such as are familiar to every bricklayer's apprentice. We did not need to exercise great generalship; the mountain was in plain sight, we walked to its base—some distance, I admit, and not exactly over a paved road—and then walked on till we reached the summit," Abbot wrote in an entertaining account in *Appalachia.*

"Furthermore, it cannot fairly be said that the expedition was one of unusual beauty. Grandeur of one sort there certainly was. In the single element of savage desolation—unrelieved, monotonous, boundless, and complete—I have never seen anything which equaled the view from the summit of Mt. Hector, and I do not expect to see anything which will excel it... There was nothing visible but the one unbroken wilderness of ice and snow and crag, an ocean without shores whose waves were mountain ranges."

Led by outfitter Tom Wilson and laden with heavy packs, the Appalachian Club party was the first climbing group to venture up the fire-swept and swampy Bow Valley north of Laggan (today's Lake Louise). While their later hopes of mountaineering on the unexplored Wapta Icefield were dashed by the bushwhacking elements, they managed to bag Hector in a 13-hour day.

From a valley camp north and west of the peak, they ascended through open trees and steepening slopes of grass and shale to reach a rounded shoulder that split shattered cliffs of limestone. Upon surmounting this dry western flank, they were surprised at the sudden dazzling white of the upper North Glacier, which they climbed to reach the summit rocks. They left a jam jar record, found in almost perfect condition by a 1923 party.

In 1902, Edward Holway and guide J. Muller climbed Hector's South Face, descending by the Southwest Ridge. In 1933, R.G. Cairns, A.A. McCoubrey, Jr. and R. Neave approached from the northeast and then ascended the North Glacier route that is commonly followed today.

1600-metre ski descent from Mt. Hector.

Ascending N Glacier of Mt. Hector.

Mt. Hector and N. Glacier in summer. Photo: Markus Kellerhals.

Route

First Ascent July 30, 1895: Philip Abbot, Charles Fay, Charles Thompson – West Face

Route Described North Glacier (I) *Recommended as a ski ascent*

Gear Rope, glacier gear, ice axe, crampons recommended

Map 82 N/9 Hector Lake

Season mid-March to early May on skis, July to September on foot

Time 8-11 hours return on skis, longer on foot

Access From the Trans-Canada Highway turnoff just west of Lake Louise townsite, drive 19 km north on the Icefields Parkway (Highway 93) and park in a small pullover on the left.

North Glacier This describes the ski route, though the summer approach is essentially the same. The lower valley is exposed to unavoidable avalanche slopes, which tend to slide on warm spring days. Pick a clear day when the hazard is low and the snow conditions are still good, and get an early start.

Cross the highway and follow the Hector Creek bed through woods (the summer trail is on the right) for less than 1 km to steep, open slopes (avalanche hazard). Angle up a short gully that splits the cliff band, kicking steps as the slope steepens for about 100 vertical metres. When the valley widens, aim right of a large, rocky shoulder, traversing left onto its higher crest if snow conditions ahead are unstable. Similarly, the avalanche slopes of Little Hector on the right can be avoided by going left of a small moraine below the North Glacier's toe. As you ascend, the fine double summit of Molar Mountain comes into view to the northeast.

Rope up for the glacier (at least one skier has fallen into a crevasse here) and continue the long, steady climb towards Hector. The usual route swings slightly right and then back left before the final, steep snow slopes, though a more direct line is often feasible in good snow years. Switchback up these steep slopes to gain a bench to the right of the summit block and then traverse up and left to reach a small saddle between the summit and an impressive sheer rock face to the left.

Leave your skis here and scramble up the final 50 vertical metres to the small rock summit (a bergschrund is crossed in summer and low-snow springs). When windswept, the rocks can be slippery, in which case crampons and good short-roping/belaying technique are valuable guards against a short bit of considerable exposure. **Descend** the same way.

Lake Louise/Lake O'Hara Peaks

Next to the Columbia Icefield, the Lake Louise/ Lake O'Hara area contains the greatest concentration of 11,000ers—seven tightly-bunched peaks. Other than the highest of the group, Mount Temple, they are perched on a north-south axis along the Continental Divide, overlooking Banff, Yoho and Kootenay National Parks and a slew of jewel-like lakes. Because of the immense popularity and scenic grandeur of the Louise and O'Hara areas, these giants are among the most visible in the Rockies—especially Temple, the two peaks of Victoria, Mount Lefroy and, to a lesser extent, Hungabee Mountain.

Despite their proximity to roads and one another, these peaks are mostly climbed individually. One exception is South Victoria and Lefroy, which can both be scaled from the hut at Abbot Pass, though they're often not in shape at the same time. South Victoria and Huber are sometimes combined in a long loop trip, and the two peaks of Victoria can be attained in a traverse of the massif, if you don't mind a precariously loose ridgeline.

The peaks of this region offer something for every type of alpine climber. There is the classic walk along the snowy Southeast Ridge of South Victoria, the snow/ice face of Lefroy, and the delightful glacial ascents of North Victoria and Mount Huber. From a rock perspective, there's the scramble up the southwest side of Temple, the big, wandering south flanks of Hungabee and the long, challenging rock route up Temple's East Ridge.

The rock in these parts tends to be loose, and occasionally nasty, especially along the long Northwest Ridge of Deltaform Mountain. A low band of solid Gog quartzite, however, is found on such peaks as Deltaform, Hungabee and Temple's East Ridge; it's the portable holds above that seize climbers' attention. The crumbling turrets that mountaineers traverse below on Huber are at least aesthetically and geologically interesting, consisting mainly of Cathedral limestone and dolomite layers that have been vertically fractured.

Facilities

Lake Louise has two gas stations, an outdoor shop and a limited supply of groceries. It's better to stock up in Banff, Canmore or Calgary. There are several restaurants and a bakery, Laggans, which opens daily at 6 a.m. and is a popular congregating spot for climbers.

Go to the Lake Louise Visitor Centre (403-522-3833) to register for climbs and to check for climbing conditions, trail restrictions and weather forecasts. If you're heading into Lake O'Hara from the west, stop at the Yoho National Park office in Field.

For much of the summer and early fall, hikers are legally required to travel in tight groups of six in areas around Moraine Lake frequented by grizzly bears. This can particularly affect those approaching and returning from Deltaform and those climbing the Southwest Face of Mount Temple or descending that route after climbing Temple's East Ridge. It can be a problem finding other hikers or climbers to hook up with in these areas if you're making a very early start or late exit. Contact the Lake Louise Visitor Centre for up-to-date information on these restrictions.

Accommodation In Lake Louise, these range from a nearby national park campground and an upscale hostel, the Alpine Centre (403-522-2202) to the famed but expensive Chateau Lake Louise (a post-expedition beer on the patio, though, is a worthy celebration). Closer to Lake O'Hara is West Louise Lodge and, not much farther west, several small motels and bed and breakfasts in Field.

A base camp can be established at Lake O'Hara, either in the campground (phone 250-343-6433 for reservations) or the cozy Elizabeth Parker Hut, which sleeps 24 (phone the Alpine Club of Canada at 403-678-3200 for reserva-

Mts. Lefroy (l.) and Victoria from Mt. Whyte.
A. Fuhrmann Ledges. B. Death Trap.
C. Abbot Pass.

tions). Huber can comfortably be climbed from here, but it's a long day to get up and down Hungabee; most parties bivy below Opabin Pass (check at the park visitor centres in Lake Louise or Field for permits).

Access There are two main access roads running south into this area off the Trans-Canada Highway. The easternmost road leaves the hamlet of Lake Louise, in Banff National Park, and shortly splits. A southwest branch soon leads to Lake Louise, providing access via the Plain of Six Glaciers Trail to North Victoria and to Abbot Pass, the launching point for South Victoria and Lefroy. The other branch continues south to Moraine Lake, providing access to the two described routes on Temple and to Deltaform, the latter via the Eiffel Lake Trail.

To reach the Lake O'Hara access road, drive 11 km west of Lake Louise into Yoho National Park and turn left (south), crossing railway tracks to reach the O'Hara parking lot. A 12-km gravel road leads south to Lake O'Hara. The O'Hara road is only open to bus traffic in summer (it's a ski trail in winter), with four departures each day from mid-June through September. While a few seats are set aside for day-before-departure bookings, earlier reservations are recommended (phone 250-343-6433). Thrifty hikers can plod up the road, adding 3-4 hours to their approach. The good news is the bus ride back to the parking lot is free.

Abbot Hut Approaches Note: The route up to Abbot Pass from Lake O'Hara may be more tedious and slightly less aesthetic than from Lake Louise but is safer, shorter and requires 300 less metres of elevation gain, if you take the bus to Lake O'Hara. If you're planning a one-day ascent and need an alpine start, however, the Lake Louise approach is your best bet.

From Lake Louise Take the tourist trail around the northwest side of Lake Louise, continuing past the Plain of Six Glaciers Teahouse to the toe of the Victoria Glacier (7 km). The traditional route goes up the glacier's Death Trap, which is exposed to avalanches from Mount Victoria and is becoming increasingly difficult, and in some years impossible, to ascend because of yawning crevasses.

Access and Approaches for
Lake Louise/Lake O'Hara 11,OOOers

A safer alternative that avoids the Death Trap is a traverse of the Fuhrmann Ledges, a few hundred metres above the valley floor on Lefroy's lower slopes. Cross the Victoria Glacier and ascend a large scree slope left of Lefroy's north buttress. At the top of the scree slope, traverse right to access the start of the ledges, marked by red paint spots and bolted for running protection at exposed sections. At the ledges' end, take a rising line across a broad scree slope to reach the upper slopes of the Victoria Glacier, angling upwards across snow/ice to reach Abbot Pass (about 10.5 km and 4-5 hours from the lake).

From Lake O'Hara From the warden's cabin, cross the bridge and follow the trail around the north side of the lake and then east to Lake Oesa (3 km). Above Oesa's north shore, take a rising line on a good trail northeast across scree and low-angled rock to access a steep, narrow scree bowl (beware of rockfall). In 2001, a single trail was built up this loose chute, eliminating much of the backsliding agony of years past, though you may still have to bash your way up some sections of this non-maintained trail (about 5.5 km and 3-4 hours from Lake O'Hara).

Abbot Pass Hut The pass is home to the historic, stone Abbot Pass Hut. When it was built in 1922 at an elevation of 2925 metres, it was the highest permanent building in Canada, later supplanted by the nearby Neil Colgan Hut. The hut sleeps 24 and has sleeping pads, complete cooking equipment, propane stoves and lights and a wood stove. For reservations, phone the Alpine Club of Canada in Canmore at 403-678-3200.

Mount Victoria

For slack-jawed tourists staring southwest across Lake Louise, the gleaming mass of Mount Victoria fills nearly the entire backdrop. Its huge East Face is guarded by a hanging, active glacier and capped by an undulating ridge some three kilometres long.

Victoria contains two 11,000ers, the higher South Summit and the North Summit, at the far end of the long ridge. Some agitators suggest there is a third 11,000er, a so-called Centre Victoria, which although higher than the north peak appears to be no more than a high bump on the ridge.

Traverses of the entire Mount Victoria ridge-line were intermittently popular in the early decades of the 20th century, most often led by guide Rudolph Aemmer. The traverse sees considerably less traffic these days, with some experienced mountaineers saying it is frighteningly loose and best avoided. Such sentiments were echoed by the 1909 first traverse party of Aemmer, Edward Feuz, Jr. and client G.W. Culver, who traveled from north to south, encountering a large depression midway between the two summits, which necessitated lowering themselves by a sling.

"It seemed almost incredible that any such saw-toothed formation could exist as the remaining part of the Victoria arête proved to be," Culver wrote. "Jagged pinnacles, or gendarmes, jutted sharply upward from the ridge in countless numbers. Some of these we surmounted; others we were forced to circle around, but always upon the left side of the face for the wall upon the right was absolutely sheer. Almost everywhere the rock was terribly treacherous. So rotten was it indeed that time and again a projecting portion which appeared to offer a firm hold would break off at the slightest touch."

In the mid-1930s, though, it held no such horrors for Georgia Engelhard, who traversed the peak from south to north with Eaton Cromwell. "The Victoria traverse, with its airy ridges, jagged pinnacles and sensational pitches is by far the best climb of the district, comparable to some of the good routes in the Alps and although, to quote Val Fynn 'nur fur schwindel freie' (only for those free of giddiness), offers no real technical difficulties, " she wrote.

Early mountaineers called this peak Mount Green for William Spotswood Green, an Episcopal clergyman whose 1888 visit to the Selkirks and Rockies and subsequent book *Among the Selkirk Glaciers* heralded the birth of mountaineering in Canada. After Norman Collie's group climbed the main, South Summit, the name was changed to honour Queen Victoria.

Mt. Victoria. A. South Summit. B. North Summit and NE Ridge route.

159

Mount Victoria – North Summit
3388 metres (11,115 feet)

Most mountaineers have eyes only for the higher, more storied South Summit of Victoria. That's unfortunate, because the North Summit can offer a wonderfully pleasant climb on firm snow or ice, or on rock, via the standard Northeast Ridge route. The views are also stunning, particularly of the fractured and noisily calving glacier on the massif's East Face, as well as of surrounding big peaks like Lefroy, Temple and Huber.

The same route can be considerably more challenging under adverse conditions, which can range from soft, avalanche-prone snow to open crevasses and a yawning bergschrund on the lower glacier. In dry years, an additional difficulty is getting over a bare and often dripping black band of rock just below the North Victoria-Mount Collier Col. From the col, there's a choice of following the Northeast Ridge over a rock step or bypassing the step on the right, on snow or ice, and regaining the ridge below the summit.

The North Face (III) offers a harder, steeper route from the Lake O'Hara Fire Road up the North Glacier. Unfortunately, glacial recession has made route finding through the crevasses and seracs of the lower glacier much more problematic in recent years.

History

Samuel Allen of Philadelphia was one of the first mountaineers to explore the Lake Louise area. After his first visit in 1891, he was back two years later, making two attempts to climb North Victoria, repulsed each time by avalanche conditions below the Victoria-Collier Col.

The short-lived but meteoric Rockies career of James Outram got kick-started with the first ascent of North Victoria in 1900. Ironically Outram, an Anglican vicar in England, had just come to Canada to recover from a breakdown from overwork. Apparently, the cure was to bag as many big unclimbed peaks as possible, often in exhaustingly rapid succession.

The first of these was North Victoria, where Outram got a lesson in the value of a good guide. Although Outram had climbed in the Alps, he and his brother, William, and Joseph

Scattergood were unknown to their Swiss guide, who felt a second guide was needed to get them up the peak. "But the addition proved to be a great hindrance and a source of weakness, almost amounting to danger, to the party," Outram wrote.

After rowing across Lake Louise and traversing under Mount Whyte and Popes Peak, they reached a steep, narrow snow ridge not far below the summit. "Cautioning Zurfluh to be particularly mindful of the cornice and give it a wide berth, for I have a special antipathy to these dread traps for the unwary climber, I followed in his and my brother's footsteps with a confidence which received a rude and sudden shock when, in an instant, I felt my previously solid resting place quiver, totter, disappear, and I shot downward into space surrounded by a whirling mass of snow and ice," Outram wrote.

The tight rope limited the fall through the cornice to a few feet, and the annoyed Outram was quickly able to regain the ridge. "There would have been no accident at all had the guide taken ordinary precautions," wrote Outram, who thereafter climbed with elite guides, principally Christian Kaufmann. Soon after this slip, the group reached the summit, where Outram was suitably impressed with the sharp ridge connecting Victoria's north peak to the higher, south summit. But his later plan of making a first traverse of Victoria along this ridge was dashed by poor weather.

The steep, glaciated North Face of the north peak resisted several attempts by elite Rockies' climbers of the 1960s including Brian Greenwood, Glen Boles, Dick Lofthouse and Eckhard Grassman. Finally in 1969, a party of Murray Toft, Charlie Locke, Urs Kallen and Fred Roth succeeded on the May long weekend. After climbing through a crevasse and surmounting an overhanging bergschrund on the lower glacier, they reached the crux, a prominent ice band running across the face. This they tackled at its most challenging point, an eight-metre, steep wall topped by a vertical inside corner. Hand and foot holds were laboriously chopped up the lower wall and then Roth, trying a strenuous move, went flying backwards when an ice block broke off in his arms. But his fall was held by a nearby screw, and the difficulties were soon over.

Opposite: Forbes Macdonald on NE Ridge of North Victoria. A. 5.3 rock ridge option.
Photo: Roman Pachovsky.

Route

First Ascent August, 1900: James Outram, William Outram, Joseph Scattergood, *C. Clarke, H. Zurfluh* – Northeast Ridge

Route Described Northeast Ridge (II, 5.3 if rock ridge followed) *Recommended*

Gear Rope, glacier gear, a few ice screws, plus slings and a few pieces of gear if tackling the rock step

Map 82 N/8 Lake Louise

Season July to September

Time About 12 hours return from Lake Louise

Access and Approach From the hamlet of Lake Louise, drive 4 km east up the hill to Lake Louise. Take the tourist trail around the northwest side of the lake, continuing on to the Plain of Six Glaciers Teahouse (5 km).

Northeast Ridge Just past the teahouse and a large slide path, head right on a scantier trail up a scree slope and then, below cliffs, traverse left on moraines, bearing for the right side of the glacier toe below Mount Collier. Rope up and follow the glacier's right side past some large crevasses till below the North Victoria-Collier Col. Cross the bergschrund (challenging if melted back) and go up a steepening snow slope to a black and often wet rock band, sometimes in excess of 50 metres, and scramble up it to reach the broad col.

From the col, follow the snow ridge towards a prominent rock step. This step can be circumvented by traversing right and then going up a 40-degree snow/ice slope until the ridge can be regained. The other option is to climb the 10-metre rock step, bypassing its prow via ledges on the left (5.3) and then moving back right. The final stretch of the Northeast Ridge is low-angled snow leading to a small rock summit.

To **descend**, either down climb the snow/ice slope or rappel down the rock step. From the col, down climb the black rock band or rappel it. A single rope won't clear the rock band in one rap.

N Face of North Victoria from Narao Pk. A. N Victoria-Collier Col

The Classic SE Ridge of South Victoria. The "Sickle" in centre of picture. Photo: Roman Pachovsky.

Mount Victoria – South Summit
3464 metres (11,365 feet)

The Southeast Ridge of South Victoria is one of the great alpine climbs in the Canadian Rockies. A long, elevated sidewalk in the sky, the ridge follows the narrow spine of the Continental Divide and offers spectacular views of surrounding high peaks, particularly Lefroy, Hungabee and Deltaform on the return journey. In places, the exposure is exhilarating, especially in the Sickle, a slender snow notch with long drops towards Lake O'Hara on the B.C. left and Lake Louise on the Alberta right. As a guide once said, it's just walking, but it's fancy walking. Or as another guide said to his fearful companions crawling along the Sickle, "Stand up gentlemen, you won't hit your heads."

Though it is essentially a scramble on loose rock to reach the ridge and then a long, exposed walk, the route can be more demanding and even dangerous with too much snow on the ridge or ice among the lower rocks. Combined with unpredictable weather, it's perhaps not surprising a considerable number of climbers turn back well shy of the summit. Try to tackle the route when it's reasonably dry.

Even under good conditions, round-trip times from the hut can range from under four hours for fast, experienced parties to a long day for fledgling mountaineers. Those attempting the route should be comfortable with short roping or solo-ing most of the route, since the only protection against a slip along narrow sections of ridge is for a roped mate to jump off the other side.

Though it can be done more comfortably in one day, the Southwest Face route is considerably less aesthetic. It follows the standard Mount Huber approach to the Huber-Victoria Col and then ascends a long gully to intercept the Southeast Ridge just below the summit. Some climbers, traveling light, do a loop journey, going up to the hut, climbing the Southeast Ridge and then descending the Southwest Face back to Lake O'Hara, thus saving several hours on the way out.

History
Compared with the tribulations and tragedy on Mount Lefroy next door, the first ascent of Victoria's main, South Summit was decidedly routine, though the unguided Walter Wilcox and Samuel Allen failed on an attempt in 1893. Two days after Lefroy was finally toppled in 1897, four members of the same party headed up Victoria, including perhaps the leading British and American alpinists of their day—Norman Collie and Charles Fay, respectively.

Having just been up the Death Trap between Lefroy and Victoria, the climbers quickly found their way up the lower Victoria Glacier to Abbot Pass. They then went up "a series of small ter-

Descending SE Ridge of South Victoria. A. Mt. Lefroy. B. Deltaform Mtn. C. Hungabee Mtn.

races of excessively rotten rock," wrote Collie, who didn't appear overly awed by the subsequent walk along the narrow Southeast Ridge and didn't even mention the Sickle. "The climbing along the arête was not difficult but required care, and it was only the last five hundred feet that were at all narrow. About midday, after breaking many steps in soft snow, the summit was finally reached—a small pinnacle of snow, 11,500 feet above sea level." In his account, Fay admired all the leading Collie did, especially through the knee-deep snow; no mention was made of Sarbach, the Swiss guide.

In 1909, the Southwest Face was climbed by an Alpine Club of Canada group led by John Forde, who had been on the first ascent of Goodsir's North Tower the same year. The party included Elizabeth MacCarthy, whose husband, Albert, was on the first ascent of the highest peaks in the Rockies and in Canada—Robson and Logan. Forde reported the route provided a much shorter and easier access to the summit, "with the long and tedious walk along the ridge from Abbot's Pass to the summit avoided."

After four defeats because of bad weather, the illustrious team of Val Fynn and guide Rudolph Aemmer finally succeeded on the Northeast Face (III) in 1922, though nasty conditions on the upper glacier and brittle outcrops of rock made things interesting. "The bergschrund was easily crossed just below the main summit but the following ice slope was covered with deep powdery snow which all but defeated us," wrote Fynn, undoubtedly the best amateur climber of his generation in the Rockies and perhaps the first to deliberately seek out harder face routes, such as the one on Victoria.. "A hard, two-inch crust was all that enabled us to negotiate this nasty bit. All protruding rocks were glazed and very treacherous."

Several decades later, new routes were fashioned on the South and West Faces and the South Ridge, the latter with rock climbing up to 5.3 in difficulty. In February of 1968, a winter ascent of the Northeast Face was completed by an all-star collection of local climbers—Brian Greenwood, Eckhard Grassman, Charlie Locke and Don Gardner.

Like Lefroy, Victoria had a famous tragedy, albeit more than half a century later. In 1954, four Mexican climbers descended from the South Summit but made the mistake of traversing onto the Northeast Face in soft snow. They perished when an avalanche sent them tumbling some 600 metres to the Death Trap, the worst accident in Canadian mountaineering at the time.

Routes

First Ascent August 5, 1897: Norman Collie, Charles Fay, Arthur Michael, *Peter Sarbach* – Southeast Ridge
Routes Described Southeast Ridge (II) *Recommended*, Southwest Face (II)

Gear	Rope, ice axe, crampons, glacier gear for South Face
Map	82 N/8 Lake Louise
Season	mid-July to September
Time	Trip – 2 days
	Climbs – Southeast Ridge: 6-9 hours return from Abbot Pass
	Southwest Face: 8-10 hours return from Lake O'Hara

Approach For the Southeast Ridge route, hike into Abbot Pass either from Lake Louise or Lake O'Hara (see pages 157-58). The Southwest Face is accessed from Lake O'Hara.

Southeast Ridge From Abbot Pass, go behind the hut outhouse and under a cliff to where it peters out. Begin scrambling up loose ledges on a somewhat zigzagging line; it's quite easy to wander off course here. Gradually work your way left (cairns) to gain the ridge proper about 200 vertical metres above the hut. A short section of snow ridge leads to the first buttress, which is climbed to the right of the ridge on fourth-class rock to reach a subsidiary summit. The more level ridge now begins an undulating course over snow and along the U-shaped Sickle, which can be quite exciting if narrow and icy. Beyond, bypass a prominent rock step, the second buttress, by scrambling up easy rock on the right (east) side of the ridge. Regain the ridge and follow it over alternating patches of snow and easy rock to the distant summit, again going onto the right, or Lake Louise, side of the ridge where necessary but not straying too far onto more exposed slopes.

Descend the same way, taking care on the loose ledges above the hut. An alternative is to go down the Southeast Ridge for a few hundred metres and then, at a prominent notch, descend the Southwest Face to the Huber-Victoria Col (see below for details, in reverse). If time permits, it's a relatively short ascent to the summit of Mount Huber via the Northeast Ridge, before descending to Lake O'Hara by the lower Huber route.

Southwest Face Follow the standard Mount Huber route from Lake O'Hara to the Huber-Victoria Col (see page 168). Go slightly north across the glacier to a prominent gully, aiming for the highest point of snow meeting the rock. Cross the bergschrund (may be difficult in dry years) and ascend the gully on snow/ice towards a prominent bulb of rock. From here, one option is to continue up the gully a short ways and then take a rising traverse left through a break in a rock rib, scrambling up the left side of the rib to reach a prominent notch in the Southeast Ridge. The other option is to take a rising line left earlier, from the rock bulb, going through a slot to reach the left side of the rib, which is ascended on good rock to the Southeast Ridge. The summit is reached in about half an hour over a relatively level ridge. **Return** the same way or go down the Southeast Ridge to Abbot Pass.

SE Ridge route on South Victoria from Mt. Lefroy.

Mount Huber
3368 metres (11,050 feet)

Mount Huber is the 11,000er orphan of the Lake O'Hara/Lake Louise group. The lowest of the seven such area peaks, it is particularly over-shadowed by the long mass of nearby Mount Victoria, which hides all views from the east. While visible from Lake O'Hara, its castellated structure on the west gives an impression of active decay and offers no clue of its handsome glaciated north aspect.

Ascending Huber by this standard northern route is a fine day's outing. It starts with a scrambling traverse up Huber's west side, turns onto its North Glacier and finishes with a steep bit of snow and/or ice. Speedy folks with time and ambition can continue up, and then come back down, the snowy Southwest Face of South Victoria, thus bagging two 11,000ers in a long day.

Walter Wilcox named the peak for Swiss climber Emil Huber, part of the 1890 first-ascent team of Mount Sir Donald, in Glacier National Park to the west.

History
The first ascent of Huber might still, a century later, be the longest return route on the peak. It featured guides Christian Bohren, who was on the first ascent of Mount Assiniboine, and the great Christian Kaufmann, who made more first ascents of Rockies 11,000ers (nine) than anyone. One of the clients was British climber George Collier, who the same summer climbed the nearby Mount Collier with his brother, Thomas, and Kaufmann; that peak is named for Thomas.

Unfortunately, there is no first-person account of Huber's first ascent in 1903. The entry, in the *American Alpine Journal*, is as follows: "Their route, little likely to be repeated, is nonetheless remarkable. Leaving the Lake Louise chalet at 4:30 a.m., they reached Abbot Pass at 9, ascended Victoria ridge to within 30 minutes of the summit, where a couloir was descended to the saddle and Mount Huber attained by its North Face. On returning, the party went to the summit of Mount Victoria and were back at Abbot Pass at 5:30 p.m. and the chalet by 8 p.m."

In 1907, several parties from an Alpine Club of Canada camp at Lake O'Hara ascended Huber via today's standard route, traversing the West Face, going up the North Glacier and then the Northeast Ridge. This route was equally popular at an ACC camp in 1909, prompting club president Arthur Wheeler to write: "At one point in the cliffs, it was considered advisable, though not absolutely necessary, to place a rope, which much helped those making their first ascent."

This Northeast Ridge route was reached in 1933 by Sterling Hendricks and guide Ernest Feuz, who descended south from Abbot Pass, traversed west above Lake Oesa and then went north up a snow basin between Huber and Victoria. The first winter ascent was done in February 1973 by Chris Perry, later the author of several area rock climbing guidebooks, and photographer Pat Morrow, the second Canadian to climb Mount Everest and arguably the first to ascend the highest peak on all seven continents. They bivied in a snow cave, on the north side, on the way up and down.

NE Ridge to summit of Mt. Huber from South Victoria. A. Easier finish. Photo: Clive Cordery.

Opposite: Mount Huber from South Victoria.

Route

First Ascent 1903: George Collier, Ernst Tewes, *Christian Bohren, Christian Kaufmann* – North Face

Route Described North Glacier/Northeast Ridge (II)

Gear Rope, glacier gear, ice axe, crampons, a few ice screws

Map 82 N/8 Lake Louise

Season July to September

Time Trip – 1-2 days
Climb – 8-10 hours return from Lake O'Hara

Access and Approach Take the bus or hike into Lake O'Hara (see pages 156-57). While Huber can be climbed in a day from the road, most parties spend the previous night at the O'Hara campground or the Elizabeth Parker Hut. From the warden cabin, cross the Cataract Brook bridge, go around the north end of Lake O'Hara for a few hundred metres and then head left up the steep 1.5-km trail to Wiwaxy Gap. From this saddle, take a subsidiary trail northeast to the southwest base of Mount Huber.

North Glacier/Northeast Ridge From the base of Huber, angle up and left on an indistinct trail that traverses left on rubbly ledges (cairns). At one spot, there is a delicate move around a slight rock bulge, with considerable exposure. It's easier scrambling beyond, moving up and left, though it can be easy to get off route following some misplaced cairns. Eventually, the route heads straight up and then slightly back right to gain the North Glacier partway up its right side. Angle left up this lower glacier and scramble up a small rock band to reach an upper glacier, which is followed on its right side towards the Huber-Victoria Col. One can either head straight up the Northeast Ridge to the summit on steep snow or ice or swing farther left to the edge of some rocks, where the angle is a more modest 30-35 degrees.

Descend the same way.

N Glacier/NE Ridge route on Mt. Huber.

Mount Lefroy

3423 metres (11,230 feet)

Mount Lefroy is the only 11,000er whose greatest fame is tied to tragedy. American Philip Abbot's fatal fall in 1896 shocked the international climbing community and, with the resulting introduction of Swiss guides, changed the nature of Canadian climbing for the next four decades.

Lefroy's natural features are equally formidable. Straddling the Continental Divide in the heart of the Lake Louise/Lake O'Hara group, it has a long and precipitous east flank, rising 1000 metres from Paradise Valley, and an equally impressive north snout that overhangs the Victoria Glacier. For climbers, the most arresting view, from the nearby slopes of South Victoria, is of the less steeply tilted West Face, with parallel gullies of snow or ice offering several reasonable lines to an undulating ridge and thence the summit.

These long gullies can range from good step-kicking snow early in the season to mostly ice later in the summer. While the ascent can be made in under two hours with good snow conditions, climbers should be aware that at least several climbers, besides Abbot, have suffered long, tumbling falls after slipping on the 40-degree slopes or on flanking bits of loose rock.

Like South Victoria, Lefroy can be climbed in a long day from either Lake Louise or Lake O'Hara, but most parties prefer to overnight at Abbot Hut and tackle Lefroy early in the morning, when there is less danger of rock fall. Although it makes logistical sense to climb both Lefroy and South Victoria from a base camp at the pass, they are often not in shape at the same time.

There is some confusion as to whether this peak was named by James Hector during his Palliser Expedition explorations of the late 1850s or by surveyor and geologist George Dawson in the mid-1880s. In both cases, the name is for General Sir John Henry Lefroy, an astronomer whose interest in terrestrial magnetism led him to map and visit the north magnetic pole.

History

While South Victoria today draws the lion's share of attention from mountaineers and Lake Louise tourists, it was the neighbouring Lefroy that most intrigued early climbers. In 1894, Walter Wilcox, Yandell Henderson and Lewis Frissell tackled the north side and were going up an icy couloir "which no Swiss guide would venture to enter" when Frissell was struck by a boulder and had to be lowered down the mountain. He recovered sufficiently to get up Mount Temple later that summer.

Just after their 1895 success on Mount Hector, the Boston-area group of Abbot, Charles Fay and Charles Thompson turned to Lefroy, none with more ardour than Abbot. "The failure of that endeavor, a failure fraught with possibilities of ultimate success, increased our desire," Thompson wrote of this unsuccessful first attempt. "All winter we had planned and plotted to overcome the difficulties of that mountain."

A year to the day later, the threesome, accompanied by George Little, rowed a boat across Lake Louise and made their way up the Death Trap to what is now known as Abbot Pass. Looking up at the remaining western slopes, Abbot exuberantly declared: "The peak is ours," Fay wrote. Leaving the pass around noon, they ascended to the base of the couloir where, without the benefit of today's crampons, they faced a sobering reality.

"The first blow of the axe upon the ice, heavy, dull, resistant, altered our plans, dashed our hopes of easy success, and, little suspected, turned the fortune of the day," Thompson wrote. "No longer an easy, rapid ascent along footholds carelessly taken, kicked in the snow; instead, a long, arduous scramble over intermittent ledges, changing to ice, and toilsome step-cutting only as a last resort."

One of the best American alpinists of his time, Abbot led throughout, dragging the ropes, untethered to his companions, up a chimney in a final cliff band in the waning afternoon. "In the impressive silence came the dull thud of a falling body, faint and rattling at first, heavy and crashing as it came bounding nearer," Thompson wrote. "Crying to Fay that a great stone was coming, I made two steps toward him, turned, saw Abbot pitch through the left-hand crevice, strike upon the top of the (rock) knee, turn completely over, and, clearing the scree, plunge headlong down the ice-slope. Some seconds thereafter we saw him lying at the edge of the escarpment, the ropes wound about his body." Three painstaking hours later, the three reached Abbot, who died soon thereafter.

Following this first death in North American mountaineering, Abbot's family requested the peak be climbed in his honour. To mollify the criticism surrounding the tragedy, the returning climbers enlisted the services of Swiss guide Peter Sarbach and invited experienced British climber Norman Collie. After some warm-up climbs in the Selkirks, to the west, an unwieldy party of nine headed up Lefroy on the first anniversary of Abbot's death. In three rope teams, they kicked firm steps up the lower West Face, scaled a band of steep and rotten rock and continued up the right-hand couloir, bypassing Abbot's treacherous cliff on a slender patch of snow between rock and ice. Reaching the summit at 11 a.m., they soon headed down, fearful their precarious ladder of snow steps would melt away.

"From the top rocks downwards we were mighty polite to the snow of Mount Lefroy," Harold Dickson wrote. "I cannot speak for all the party, but I know that three men, including Sarbach, came down 1,500 feet with their faces to the mountain."

In March 1966, American legend Fred Beckey along with Ron Burgener and Jim Madsen made the first winter ascent. After sitting out a storm in the hut—"temperatures being so low that spilled tea froze instantaneously on the table's oilcloth"—they cramponed up the standard route in two-and-a-half hours, placing one ice piton for protection. "The howling, cold wind added zest," Beckey wrote. "Crampons usually bit in well, although some powdery sections required careful belaying."

In 1971, Pierre Lemire and A. Doherty scaled the huge Southeast Ridge/East Face (IV, 5.7) on a steep rock rib and then snow, reaching the summit on their second day. Eight years later, wardens Clair and Gerry Israelson and Cliff White overcame the Northeast Face (5.7, A1), also in two days.

Icy conditions on W Face of Mt. Lefroy. Photo: Roman Pachovsky.

Foreshortened view of W Face of Mt. Lefroy from South Victoria.

Route

First Ascent August 3, 1897: Harold Dixon, Charles Fay, Arthur Michael, J.R. Vanderlip, Charles Noyes, Charles Thompson, Herschel Parker, Norman Collie, *Peter Sarbach* – West Face

Route Described West Face (II)

Gear Rope, glacier gear, crampons, ice axe (two tools and ice screws if icy)

Map 82 N/8 Lake Louise

Season July to September

Time Trip – Usually 2 days
Climb – 5-6 hours return from Abbot Pass

Approach Hike to Abbot Pass from Lake Louise or Lake O'Hara (see pages 157-58).

West Face The face contains three parallel snow/ice gullies, any of which, depending on conditions, can be ascended directly to or near the summit. The middle and left-hand (most northerly) gullies are perhaps slightly steeper and exposed to bigger drop-offs to the Victoria Glacier. The right-hand, or southern, gully is most commonly followed and is thus described here in more detail.

From Abbot Pass, go straight up scree/snow to the foot of the broad right-hand gully. Kick snow steps or crampon your way up under a triangular rock step, which is skirted on the right. Continue straight up on slopes of about 40 degrees, again bypassing cliff bands on the right. Closer to the ridgeline, where the snow steepens straight above, it's usually easier to angle your way up and left through a narrow snow/ice gap between loose rock steps to gain the South Ridge. Follow the ridge north over several rises to a small summit, with sharp drop offs on both sides.

Descend the same way.

Hungabee Mountain

3493 metres (11,457 feet)

Hungabee is the highest peak in the Lake O'Hara area. Straddling the Continental Divide, this handsome, pyramid-shaped peak overlooks four lovely, lake-dotted valleys and offers summit views that include three surrounding 11,000ers—Delataform, Temple and Victoria.

From a climbing perspective, though, Hungabee is another crumbling Rockies' classic. Val Fynn, who climbed Hungabee by two routes, aptly said, "This mountain, like all the others in the district, is more dangerous than difficult, requiring very careful selection of a route on account of the very rotten rock."

Although the standard West Ridge route is rated at 5.4, much of it is a traversing scramble up rubbly ledges and loose gullies—the ridge proper is followed only at the bottom and nearer the top—with little belayed climbing for competent parties. This is a route for boots, not rock shoes.

The overall difficulty, and danger from rock fall and avalanche, is often determined by how wet or icy the route is; it is best avoided until relatively free of snow, which in some years isn't until August. The biggest technical challenges come high on the mountain, chiefly a cap of rotten black rock and, just below the top, a short but exposed traverse, unnerving in soft snow.

In 1894, pioneer Rockies climber and explorer Samuel Allen named the peak Hungabee, the Stoney Indian word for chieftain or savage chief, on account of its prominence among its neighbours.

History

In 1901, Charles Thompson, George Weed and guide Hans Kaufmann nearly reached the summit of Hungabee before being rebuffed by difficulties. Two years later, Herschel Parker had the luxury of two guides, Hans and Christian Kaufmann, the latter who had carefully looked for the best line of attack. After hiking from Lake Louise over Wenkchemna Pass, they camped in a silk tent in Prospectors Valley. They started up the mountain just south of Opabin Pass and appeared to follow the West Ridge to vertical cliffs, which Christian penetrated via a perilous, ice-filled chimney.

"It was only by watching the rope that Hans and I could judge the progress Christian was making above us," Parker wrote. "For minutes at a time, it seemed, the rope would be motionless, then inch by inch it would slowly disappear

Hungabee Mtn. Photo: Glen Boles.

NE Face Hungabee Mtn. from Mt. Temple.

up the chimney, and the crash of falling rocks and ice would warn us that we must cling even more closely and find what protection we could beneath the rocky wall."

Above, a steep slope of snow over treacherous rock led to the broad shoulder on the North Ridge below the final summit block. Barred by a vertical step from following the ridge to the summit, they traversed right on an airy snow slope and, regaining the ridge, had to step across an exposed notch just before the summit. Shortly after retracing their snowy traverse on the descent, some of the now slushy slope slid over the cliffs below. After a final soaking descending the now pouring chimney, they stumbled back to camp, ending a 14-hour day.

Val Fynn and Oliver Wheeler followed much of this route on the mountain's second ascent, in 1909. The same year, guide Rudolph Aemmer discovered the now standard route that wanders left of and then back to the West Ridge. Sixteen years later, Aemmer and Fynn pioneered the North Ridge, scrambling from Opabin Plateau to a gap between Ringrose and Hungabee and following the somewhat loose and moderately steep ridge to the top. "I believe that this is by far the best route up Hungabee, and it is very little more difficult than the two others," wrote Fynn, adding there was no exposure to rock fall.

In 1936, Georgia Engelhard and guide Ernest Feuz made the first traverse of Hungabee, climbing the North Ridge and descending the South-east Ridge, which featured a long, overhanging rappel. "The traverse is not nearly as enjoyable as that of Victoria and the (Southeast) ridge has little to recommend it beyond the sensational rope-off," Engelhard wrote.

In 1963, Dick Lofthouse and Walter Schrauth spent two days going up the Southeast Ridge, a series of infirm vertical steps, ending in the "dreaded Black Band—loose and nasty," wrote Lofthouse. Here he led up an overhang, protected only by a knotted sling in a narrow crack, with "loose holds (coming) off one after another" and a hard traverse to the rappel sling left by the 1936 party. "The top part of the ridge was a series of crumbling black towers. Over the top of one, around the next and so on, it was slow going, but at 11:30 we were on top, well satisfied to have the whole ridge behind us."

In December 1966, Brian Greenwood, Charlie Locke and Chic Scott skied up to Opabin Pass and climbed the West Ridge, with one bivouac. The crux was a 40-foot, ice-filled chimney just below the upper ridge. Four years later, Greenwood returned with John Moss, Chris Jones and O. Woolcock to climb Hungabee's big Northeast Face in July. They made good time up moderate-angled slopes interrupted by the odd short pitch over steep rock bands. After bivouacking in a serendipitous cave, they reached a vertical band of the infamous black rock, which was overcome by traversing until a chimney could be climbed to the North Ridge below the summit.

173

W Ridge route, Hungabee Mtn.

Route

First Ascent July 21, 1903: Herschel Parker, *Christian Kaufmann, Hans Kaufmann* – Southwest Face

Route Described West Ridge (III, 5.4)

Gear Rope, glacier gear (for approach), ice axe, crampons, small rock rack

Map 82 N/8 Lake Louise

Season mid-July to mid-September

Time Trip – 2 days

Climb – 10-12 hours return from a high bivy

Access Take the bus or hike up to Lake O'Hara (see pages 157-58). While one can stay at the nearby campground or Elizabeth Parker Hut, it saves about two hours each way to hike up, the afternoon before the climb, to bivy sites near Opabin Pass (overnight wilderness permit required).

Approach From Lake O'Hara Lodge, walk around the south side of the lake and take the East Opabin trail up steeply through trees to lovely meadows, following the beautiful stone pathway laid out by Lawrence Grassi to Opabin Lake. Continue southeast up the valley on a rougher trail and ascend the small Opabin Glacier to Opabin Pass (about 2 hours from Lake O'Hara).

West Ridge From Opabin Pass, scramble east over a hump. Continue up the ridge on green-black quartzite, traversing left below an orange-coloured cliff band and then taking a long, steeper line left up ledges, crossing two shallow couloirs. Just before reaching the steep and usually snowy Northwest Face, climb directly up an indistinct rib that breaks through cliffs. Bypass a steeper, higher rock band by traversing right and then go up the left side of the first gully on chimneys and ledges. Above are more loose but lower-angled gullies, which lead to the crumbling black rock of the North Ridge. Partway along this summit ridge, an exposed traverse is made to the right to bypass a steep step, with the ridge regained via some low-angled rocks just before the top. **Descend** the same way, usually with several rappels.

Opposite: Upper W Ridge on Hungabee Mtn.
Photo: Roman Pachovsky.

Mount Temple
3543 metres (11,624 feet)

Location and elevation make Mount Temple the most visible of all the 11,000ers in the Canadian Rockies. The second-highest peak entirely in Banff National Park, this massive mountain is the only one of the Lake Louise-Lake O'Hara giants east of the Continental Divide and the only one close to the Trans-Canada Highway and its millions of motorists.

Its steep, stepped East Ridge is a prominent landmark for those driving west of Castle Junction, and its towering North Face, capped by an immense hanging glacier, overlooks the tourist masses in the hamlet of Lake Louise. Scores of hikers see its gentler southwest aspect up close from Larch Valley.

Temple was the first Rockies 11,000er climbed, in 1894. Today, it is often the first 11,000er scaled by budding mountaineers. Indeed, its Southwest Face and Ridge is essentially a scramble from Sentinel Pass. On a nice summer's day, dozens of folk—some trailing young children, others hauling dogs—can be seen toiling up its rubbly slopes. To avoid the scrambling hordes, set out early or late in the day (some even do it as a moonlight ascent) or in the last stages of fall, when the golden alpine larches make this a rewarding ascent.

That said, Temple is still a big peak—with unpredictable weather, slippery scree, some exposure, rockfall (especially from fellow climbers), some route finding and altitude for novices to contend with. In 1955, seven American teenagers were killed in a summer snow avalanche when they strayed too far onto the face, the worst mountaineering accident in Rockies history. A couple of other scramblers have died, falling over cliffs after getting off route.

Temple also offers tremendous hard routes for seasoned climbers, though nearly all have seen fatalities. The three-kilometre East Ridge, with its mix of steep rock and long summit snow ridge, attracts many international climbers, in part because of its inclusion in *Fifty Classic Climbs of North America*. The 1500-metre North Face, exposed to rock and ice fall, boasts five big routes that still draw experts looking to test their skills on a big, committing face.

N Face, Mt. Temple.

Ascending SW Face of Mt. Temple. A. Hungabee Mtn. B. Mt. Lefroy.

Surveyor George Dawson named the peak for Sir Richard Temple, an economist with the British Association for the Advancement of Science. Temple was fortunate to have his name bestowed on such a spectacular peak considering he made just one trip to the Rockies, as leader of an association field trip in 1884.

History

For 70 years, Temple was the scene of milestones in North American mountaineering. Its initial ascent in 1894 marked the first 11,000er to be scaled in the Canadian Rockies. The climb of the East Ridge in 1931 was one of the hardest alpine routes of its time in North America; even today, it is a stiff test for hardened mountaineers, most of whom bypass the heinous Black Towers of the original ascent. And the 1966 ascent of the North Face, considered the Eiger of the Rockies at the time, opened the door for many of the Rockies' big wall climbs of the 1970s.

Today, Temple's Southwest Face and Ridge is considered a moderate scramble at most. But in the early 1890s, it took considerable effort just to get to the peak and find the one side of the mountain without high, intimidating walls. This exploration fell to the enthusiastic but unguided members of Yale University's Lake Louise Club. Principal among them were Samuel Allen and Walter Wilcox, the latter who went on to explore as far north as the Columbia Icefield and write the classic *The*

Rockies of Canada. A noted photographer, Wilcox later returned to the summit of Temple with an enormous eleven-by-fourteen camera.

In 1893, Wilcox and Allen went south from Lake Louise (then called Laggan) and briefly up Paradise Creek before striking south and camping beneath the northeast flank of Temple. Following an old glacial bench around the mountain's southeast corner, they then went up loose southern slopes and gullies to a vertical wall that ended their hopes. Their one consolation was a glimpse into the Valley of Ten Peaks.

A year later, they looked down from Mitre Pass on Paradise Valley, which became their new approach for tackling Temple. From a camp in the upper valley, Wilcox, Allen and Lewis Frissell set out, "our minds filled with mingled feelings of hope and wonder and uncertainty," Wilcox wrote. "We were approaching the crisis of two years of hard effort and of failure and of an unknown future." Reaching the top of Sentinel Pass, they saw the Southwest Face for the first time and roped up for its ascent.

"The mountain was already ours though we did not realize it at the time," Wilcox wrote. "It was now a slow and careful ascent of scree slopes and a few rather steepish rock cliffs where ordinary care was necessary and was used." At noon, they were on top after an eight-hour ascent. "Many a hearty cheer rent the thin air as our little party of three reached

177

the summit, for we were standing where no man had ever stood before, and... at the highest altitude yet reached in North America north of the United States boundary."

In 1931, after pioneering an impressive rock route in Wyoming's Teton Range, guide Hans Wittich and client Otto Stegmaier traveled north to Lake Louise, with Wittich's family along for a holiday. At 5:30 a.m., the pair left the then Moraine Lake campground and hiked along the trail above the road to the base of the East Ridge. They quickly gained elevation till they reached a 100-metre wall, where they changed from hobnailed boots to light climbing shoes.

"Then started a very strenuous climb with the aid of a rope," Wittich wrote of their two-and-a-half hour ascent of what later became known as the Big Step. "Once in a very exposed position, standing on a hand-wide ledge, an overhanging rock forced me almost down to the abyss. Abundant energy only can overcome such moments."

A higher step offered "a terrible climb... on massive, stratified rock, knife-sharp on the edges," succeeded by a stretch of lower-angled but very loose shale. "A disgusting and most dangerous climb followed... as almost every grip and step broke off and down at the slightest touch." Then came the seemingly endless succession of "Black Towers," involving thin holds, small cracks and exposed traverses.

Finally, in the evening sun, they reached the hanging summit glacier. They inched their way below the corniced ridge, which got progressively steeper and icier, requiring step cutting, as they had no crampons. "The ice ridge was now cruelly steep and sharp as a knife," Wittich wrote. "With determination, I worked hard below the knife edge, hewed a saddle on the very crest and swung myself on the saddle in cowboy fashion. Now we rode and jumped from saddle to saddle, up the ice-edge."

They reached the summit at 8:30, thirteen-and-a-half hours after setting out, and bivouacked in the pitch dark partway down the Southwest Face. Today, most climbers are hard pressed to match this ascent time, even though they carry crampons, are spared the morning walk from Moraine Lake and avoid the ugly Black Towers.

In the early 1960s, two teams—first Brian Greenwood and Jim Steen and later Americans Yvon Chouinard and Doug Tompkins—went part way up the North Face's prominent dolphin-shaped snow patch before being turned around by bad conditions and weather, respectively. In Chouinard's case, they escaped the

face just before a large rock fall swept across their tracks. In 1966, Greenwood and Charlie Locke forged a route up a steep rib right of the Dolphin (V, 5.8, A2). More than halfway up this huge wall, a vertical buttress forced a delicate traverse left on a down-sloping shelf covered in soft snow over ice. They continued up the face on an indistinct buttress to a bivy ledge.

"Just as we reached the small ledge where we spent the night, an ominous roar deafened us and a large amount of snow and ice parted company with the glacier, swept the depression, shattered on a small ledge we had just traversed, and crashed into the depths below," Locke wrote. "We were thankful that we had veered from our intended route and succumbed to the safety the buttress offered."

Greenwood was the best local climber of his generation, pushing the known limits on both hard rock climbs and big alpine faces, most notably Temple's North Face and Mount Babel's East Face (5.10, A1). On Temple, he led most of the second day, in a wet snowstorm, on steep but firmer limestone until reaching the summit ridge. "Even though we veered from our proposed route, we felt a great sense of achievement," Locke wrote. "The centre of the face, continually swept by rock and icefall and capped by a glacier through which the possibility of exit appears uncertain, remains unclimbed. Perhaps some day its lure will attract some climbers who will push the perfect route up the north face."

Though the perfect line above the Dolphin remains unrealized for obvious safety reasons, four other routes, with assorted variations, have since been fashioned up the North Face. The most daring was the 1970 North Ridge, which American stars and cousins George Lowe and Jeff Lowe ascended beneath the teetering seracs of the north glacier. Greenwood was back with James Jones in 1969 to put up a much safer route on the Northeast Buttress.

As often happens on faces once considered at the upper limits of ability, some of Temple's North Face routes have been climbed in winter—starting with a five-day epic by Carlos Buhler and Phil Hein in January 1976—and some soloed in half a day. In February 2004, local hardmen Ben Firth and Raphael Slawinski made a winter ascent of the Greenwood-Locke route, spending one night on the face and another on the way out. Though the face was in reasonably good condition (i.e. not plastered in snow), "still it was far too cold and snowy for rock climbing, so we dry tooled the whole thing," says Slawinski.

Routes

First Ascent August 17, 1894: Samuel Allen, Lewis Frissell, Walter Wilcox – Southwest Face and Ridge

Routes Described Southwest Face/Ridge (I), East Ridge (IV, 5.7) *Recommended*

Gear Southwest Face: Helmet and ice axe
East Ridge: Double ropes, ice axe, crampons, alpine rock rack, perhaps bivy gear

Map 82 N/8 Lake Louise

Season Southwest Face: late June to early October
East Ridge: late July to early September

Time Southwest Face: 7-10 hours return
East Ridge: 14-16 hours return, perhaps a bivouac

Southwest Face/Ridge Despite the considerable traffic on this route, various lines of ascent and descent are taken, especially through the lower cliff bands; some route-finding skills are needed. Also, take care not to knock loose rock down on lower parties.

Access and Approach From Lake Louise townsite, drive south on the Lake Louise road for 2 km, turn left and go 13 km to the Moraine Lake parking lot. Briefly walk along the lake's north shore and then start up the Larch Valley trail, which switchbacks steeply through trees and then goes right at a level junction. Hike north through Larch Valley, following the trail up through scree to Sentinel Pass (6 km from parking lot).

Route From Sentinel Pass, bash up a loose scree trail on the left side of a gully to prominent cliffs, bypassed by traversing right and then going up the third, broader gully. Above, scramble up rubbly ledges, working right to find the easiest line through a gray rock band. Continue up a firmer, lighter-coloured rock band to reach the broad Southwest Ridge, where the divergent trails merge into a more defined track up a last scree slope. On the final stroll to the summit, overlooking the vibrant Moraine Lake, stay well clear of any cornices on the right.

Descend the same way. Once safely below the last cliff bands, a more direct line down to Larch Valley can be taken over good scree and remnant snow patches, though lower down one must traverse left to bypass a final cliff band.

SW Face and Ridge, Mt. Temple.

179

E. Ridge, Mt. Temple. A. Black Towers. B. Big Step.

Route bypassing Black Towers on E Ridge, Mt. Temple.

East Ridge *Access* From Lake Louise townsite, drive 2 km south on the Lake Louise road, turn left on the Moraine Lake Road and follow it for 9.7 km, parking at a small viewpoint pullover on the left at the base of a slide path.

Route This is a long, committing route, the hardest in this book. To avoid a bivouac, parties should be prepared to climb mainly unroped up to the base of the Big Step, with the occasional fifth-class move on good quartzite. There are also route-finding challenges, particularly on the lower sections and on the traverse around the Black Towers.

From the parking area, walk west for 50 metres and scramble up an obvious avalanche slope to its top, left of a distinct pinnacle on the ridge. Continue up the gully, veering right below a headwall and following the gully to a broad bench and then walking left to reach the start of the ridge proper. Beginning in a gully just right of the ridge, follow the ridge on generally good, fourth-class quartzite, again moving right in a couple of places (cairns).

This leads to the Big Step, a 200-metre buttress that is half technical climbing (up to 5.7), with good protection and some fixed pitons. Start up the ridge crest to the top of a pillar (25 meters) and, moving up and left around the crest, climb the steep wall to its left until it's possible to move back right to a good ledge (50 metres). Move up a steep wall past a pin onto a rubbly ledge (20 metres), where the angle eases. Move left into a gully and chimney system, which is followed to its top, with some awkward moves getting over two chockstones. Alternatively, climb straight up the ridge. Above, scramble up the ridge to a flat spot, where an alternative access to the upper ridge known as the Aemmer Couloir tops out.

Follow the ridge easily to where it begins to steepen beneath the Black Towers, the buttresses guarding the summit snow slopes. Traverse left on a prominent ledge system into the moat beneath the towers, the difficulty varying greatly depending on the amount of residual snow and ice. Aim for a gully that breaks through the black bands of the towers, to the right of gullies topped by large cornices. If you go up a gully too soon or too far, the climbing becomes considerably more difficult. The start of the correct exit gully is marked by a small pinnacle,

Doug Fulford climbing quartzite on lower E Ridge, Mt. Temple. Photo: Nancy Hansen.

which you have to squeeze past while moving along the moat. Climb to the gully's top in about five pitches (up to 5.4), on down-sloping rock covered with gravel and offering little protection, with some old fixed piton stations. Beyond, the glacial summit ridge is followed over snow and possibly ice to the top (beware of cornices and crevasses).

Descend the Southwest Ridge and Face route, following well-beaten paths and cairns to Sentinel Pass and then hiking down through Larch Valley to Moraine Lake.

Deltaform Mountain
3424 metres (11,233 feet)

Deltaform is an imposing, triangular peak, its North Face rising 1000 metres above the Wenkchemna Glacier and the Valley of the Ten Peaks. Brooding black from a distance, it reveals, closer up, alternating bands of light and dark limestone, much of it shattered.

Deltaform nearly rivals the Goodsirs for the rankest rock in the southern Canadian Rock-ies, though the holds are generally solid on the occasional pitches of fifth-class climbing. Indeed, the standard Northwest Ridge route starts up a cliff of blocky quartzite on the nose of Neptuak Mountain, which must be traversed before Deltaform is tackled. A couple of alternative starts avoid this steep nose, and some folks avoid Neptuak altogether by going up a gully to the Neptuak-Deltaform Col from Prospectors Valley.

Because of the route's length and crumbling nature, most parties need a long day to get up and down Deltaform from a high camp near Wenkchemna Pass. The ability to route find and climb long sections of loose, fourth-class rock unroped greatly diminishes the chances of a bivouac on this big, serious mountain.

The Northwest Ridge has a sting in the tail—a short, deep notch separating the false and main summits, with a few thin, strenuous moves to surmount this final obstacle. Two friends once reached this notch, a literal stone's throw from the top, after a long day, only to have a lightning storm force a hasty, scary retreat. A few years later, they came all the way back to go up those last 10 metres and say they had truly reached the summit.

On his 1896 map, pioneering American alpinist and explorer Samuel Allen named the mountain Saknowa, the Stoney word for "eight." Allen's mountaineering colleague Walter Wilcox renamed it Deltaform because the north face resembled the shape of the Greek letter "Delta." Unfortunately, all of Allen's Stoney names for the Ten Peaks were dropped, save Neptuak (nine) and Wenkchemna (ten). Allen, a Yale graduate, had a similarly unhappy fate, confined the last four decades of his life to an asylum for the insane. It's questionable if this scholar, one of the few early mountaineers to appreciate Canada's native heritage, would have been pleased that Peak Six (his Shappee) was renamed Mount Allen.

Upper NW Ridge, Deltaform Mtn.
Photo: Roman Pachovsky.

History

The 1903 first ascent of Deltaform—on steep, exposed and rotten rock—was undoubtedly one of the hardest rock climbs in the Canadian Rockies at the time. Yet this challenging route received relatively little fanfare, then or since.

The first ascent capped a banner year for American professor Herschel Parker, who had earlier made first ascents of two similarly loose and demanding peaks, Goodsir's South Tower and Hungabee Mountain. Mind you, he had the best Rockies guide of the era, Christian Kaufmann, leading the way on all three, with brother Hans Kaufmann along for all but Goodsir. In 1906, Parker accompanied Frederick Cook on the latter's alleged and discredited first ascent of Mount McKinley. Six years later, Parker got to within some 100 vertical metres of McKinley's summit before turning around in a gale.

From a camp below Neptuak in Prospectors Valley, Parker, August Eggers and the two Kaufmanns delicately made their way up crumbly couloirs, loose ledges and a chimney to reach Deltaform's South Ridge. Though the summit was now less than 100 vertical metres above, it took them another four hours to reach it following an airy traverse beneath a buttress and alternate stretches of rotten rock and step cutting of hard ice.

"Although we had been successful in conquering what is doubtless one of the most difficult mountains on the American continent, no word of mutual congratulation was spoken," Parker wrote of the 10-hour ascent. "Our position was far too serious to permit any feeling of exultation. We had no sooner reached the summit than Christian said, 'We must not stay here; we must get down.' If the climb had been difficult, the descent was decidedly worse," consuming 11 hours. After carefully reaching the foot of the buttress in a snowstorm, they "plunged downward over treacherous rock slopes, difficult cliffs and a dubious couloir," returning to camp at 3 a.m.

Six years later, Joseph Hickson climbed the same route considerably faster under better conditions. Still, it was far from easy, with guide Edward Feuz, Jr.'s head bloodied by a dislodged rock and the other guide, Rudolph Aemmer, having to stand on Feuz's shoulders to reach holds in a gnarly chimney. This South Ridge route has since fallen out of favour.

It wasn't until 1961 that today's standard route, which traverses Neptuak and then ascends Deltaform's Northwest Ridge, was tackled by Brian Greenwood and Glen Boles, whose photographic portfolio of the Rockies is unrivalled from a mountaineering perspective. Their time of 7-1/2 hours from Moraine Lake to the summit may also be unmatched, as they didn't rope up until 150 vertical metres below the top. This dynamic duo was back in 1968 with Charlie Locke and Joe Farrand to pioneer the 800-metre North Glacier route, which involved numerous pitches of steep, hard snow and ice, with traverses around several icefalls and other difficulties. Glacial recession has since made this route virtually unclimbable.

Three years earlier, Locke and Don Gardner made the first ascent of Deltaform's fairly solid East Ridge as part of their amazing seven-day, 32-kilometre traverse of the so-called Lake Louise Horseshoe. This odyssey began at Mount Babel, traversed the Ten Peaks and then continued over Hungabee, Ringrose, Glacier, Lefroy, Victoria, Collier and Popes, ending at Lake Louise. Deltaform's 650-metre East Ridge featured four gendarmes, the second of which required two rope lengths of steep climbing to circumvent.

In early July of 1973, American alpine stars George Lowe and Chris Jones went up a 1300-metre North Face route known as the Super Couloir (IV, 5.8/9), which was plastered in snow. To avoid avalanches, they started at 5 p.m., climbing the lower couloir before bivouacking. The next day, 12 ice pitches brought them under the top rock band, when an enormous cornice and then a large rock fall crashed down the route they had just climbed. The final two pitches took eight hours, with Lowe leading the last, first on good but overhanging rock and then a groove with bits of rock sticking out of thin ice.

"No crampons, no hauling line, no protection," wrote Lowe. "Metres of chopped holds, balancing carefully—so carefully—between them. Hours passed in tense concentration until the rope ran out, just as I heaved over the cornice on the ridge. It was the most horrible pitch of my life." Three years later, Carlos Buhler and Mark Whalen made a February ascent of the Super Couloir in abysmal conditions.

NW Ridge route, following right skyline. A. Deltaform Mtn. B. Neptuak Mtn. Photo: Roman Pachovsky.

Route

First Ascent September 1, 1903: August Eggers, Herschel Parker, *Hans Kaufmann, Christian Kaufmann* – South Ridge

Route Described Northwest Ridge (II, 5.5)

Gear	Rope, alpine rock rack, a few pitons and extra sling material, plus crampons and ice axe if the route is not dry
Map	82 N/8 Lake Louise
Season	late July to early September
Time	Trip – 2-3 days
	Climb – 12-14 hours return from high camp

Access From Lake Louise townsite, drive south on the Lake Louise road for 2 km, turn left and go 13 km to the Moraine Lake parking lot.

Approach Take the Larch Valley trail up switchbacks, going left at the Larch Valley junction and following the trail to Eiffel Lake. Traverse above the lake's north side and head southwest on a less distinct trail towards Wenkchemna Pass. While it is conceivable to climb Deltaform's Northwest Ridge in a very long day from Moraine Lake, most parties wisely choose to bivouac in the last level spots before the pass (about 2 hours to bivy sites, permits needed).

Northwest Ridge From Wenkchemna Pass, the normal start tackles the nose of Neptuak Mountain directly in one pitch on quartzite—following a crack then a steep chimney—to reach Neptuak's Northwest Ridge. This direct start can be avoided and the ridge gained by either going a short distance left before the pass and then up a snow slope (sometimes thin and icy) or by going over the pass into Prospectors Valley and traversing right on ledges and then up a prominent couloir of steep, firm rock. Above the nose, scramble up mostly scree along the ridgeline, deviating to the right to avoid most difficulties, though one or two short fifth-class pitches can be climbed directly. From the summit of Neptuak, descend along or near the ridgeline (perhaps one short rappel needed) to reach the broad Neptuak-Deltaform Col (bivy corral).

Pick your way up the Northwest Ridge of Deltaform above, traversing right to pierce fourth-class cliff bands of shattered rock and then returning to the ridge for the odd pitch of belayed climbing. The angle steepens on the 150-metre summit tower, featuring more loose rock and scant protection. A false summit reveals a surprise—a 15-metre-deep notch, which requires either a rappel or delicate down climbing. A short, vertical wall with thin but good holds (5.5) on the other side is then scaled to reach the true summit.

Descend the same way, rappelling into the notch and climbing steeply up through a chimney on the other side. Below, about half a dozen rappels are needed to overcome steeper sections.

Mount Goodsir

Located at the south end of Yoho National Park, the North and South Towers of Mount Goodsir are among the highest peaks in the southern Canadian Rockies. Because of their size, distinctive shape and relative isolation, these twin peaks are among the most recognizable landmarks in the Rockies, visible from high vantage points throughout the range, in the Columbia Mountains to the west and on Highway 93 northbound from Radium. The flat "col" separating the two towers is actually a third 11,000er, the Centre Goodsir, though many would dispute its authenticity as a distinct peak.

Despite their lofty prominence, the Goodsirs are infrequently climbed, for two reasons. First, the rock is among the most rotten of all the 11,000ers, rivaled only by Alberta and perhaps Deltaform. Although the climbing by the standard routes is technically not difficult and considerably easier when firm snow covers the lower sections, mountaineers must continually watch for holds breaking off, feet slipping on loose rock and airborne rocks whistling past. Almost no one comes back to climb these peaks twice, and many thwarted parties swear never to return to complete the job.

The second deterrent is the approach. While not terribly long, it involves some bushy route finding and one short stretch of avalanche debris unrivalled in the Rockies for nastiness. As I crawled with heavy pack over fallen trees—mindful a slip could either impale me on a sharp branch stub or break a leg in the deep holes between logs—I thought only a deranged climber would brave this gauntlet. Happily, this section can often be bypassed by a safer, if wetter, detour onto the river flats below.

If one can look past these difficulties, the Goodsirs are situated in a lovely Ice River Valley in the heart of the Ottertail Range. Climbers are likely to have the place to themselves, even though the Goodsirs are only 12 kilometres, as the crow flies, from the nearest point on the Trans-Canada Highway. The summits also provide fine views northeast over the Rockwall Trail to the Lake O'Hara peaks and northwest to the nearby Mount Vaux. The most impressive sight from either tower, however, is the looming presence of its twin.

Aptly, the Goodsir towers are named for two Scottish brothers, both medical doctors. One, John Goodsir, was the Edinburgh University anatomy professor of James Hector, who was impressed by these soaring peaks during his Rockies explorations in the late 1850s.

Access From Lake Louise, drive 54 km west on the Trans-Canada Highway (24 km east of Golden) and turn south on the signed Beaverfoot Road, a very good gravel logging road. Cross the railway tracks and the Kicking Horse River bridge and follow the fairly new kilometre signs, which begin, at 0, just beyond. Stay on the main road, passing Beaverfoot Lodge around 13 km. Midway between the 19- and 20-km signs, go left on the old Ice River Main Road, which although decommissioned is still fine for two-wheel drive vehicles.

At 3.4 km on this side road, go left into a logged clearing; the tops of the Goodsirs are visible to the north. One can drive another couple of hundred metres on a good grassy track through young lodgepole pine to its end in a smaller clearing (1 hour from Lake Louise).

Approach From the parking area, walk north on a good trail that swings east into mature forest above Ice River. The trail is briefly interrupted by a logging road and then picked up again in a clear cut, just before a side road enters from the right. When the Ice River trail is intersected at the bottom of the jumbled clear cut, turn right and follow the trail along the right side of the Ice River for about 7 km to a warden's cabin (2-3 hours).

From the warden's cabin, head down to the edge of the Ice River and follow an intermittent

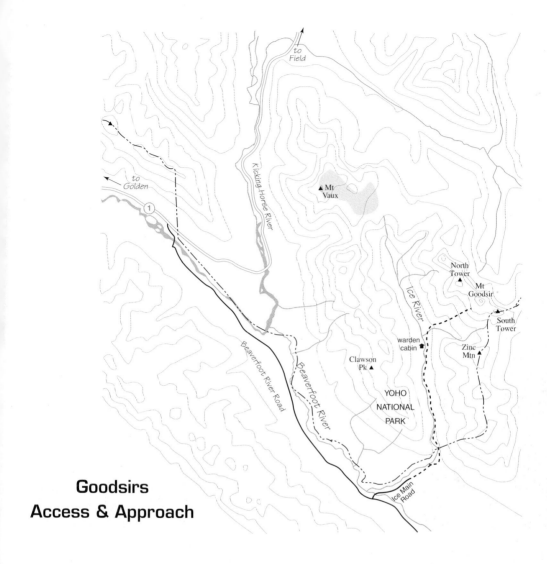

Goodsirs
Access & Approach

trail north along its right side. Preferably with running shoes and shorts, slosh around the left side of two ensuing ponds and, where the river forces you onto its right bank, go up an open slide path for about 20 metres to intersect a faint trail. Follow this trail left through forest to another, alder-strewn slide path and go up its left edge for about 150 metres and then into the trees to reach a broad trail, which is followed left around the shoulder of Zinc Mountain.

To climb the South Tower, continue up the Zinc Creek Valley to tree line and set up a camp wherever you can find a near-level spot in the shrubby gravel southwest of the peak. If you're planning to approach the mountain's standard route from the south, you can continue up the creek's right-hand branch nearly to its source before camping.

To climb the North Tower and/or Centre Goodsir, leave the Zinc Creek trail (below the end of the Northwest Ridge on Zinc Mountain) by crossing the main creek and following its left, or north, branch, setting up camp in any flat spot above tree line, below Centre Goodsir. An alternative is to keep ascending through shrubs and then snow slopes to a flat spot below the North Tower-Centre Goodsir col, a convenient bivy site if one plans to climb both those peaks.

Bill Corbett on upper crux of Mt. Goodsir, North Tower. Photo: Roman Pachovsky.

Mount Goodsir – North Tower

3525 metres (11,565 feet)

Slightly lower than its twin, Goodsir's North Tower is nonetheless the fourth-highest peak in the southern Canadian Rockies. The climbing quality is slightly better than on the South Tower, if only because in good snow conditions, one can stay off the rotten rock until shortly below the summit. But if bad snow or ice conditions or rock fall force one onto the execrable limestone, all bets are off. The key is hitting the route in prime shape, usually around the August long weekend.

Unlike the South Tower, the North Tower's normal route is pretty obvious. Just follow the peculiar horizontal V—broad scree ledges etched in snow and easily visible from a distance—up the lower South Face. From here, it's a mere half hour of groveling up loose but mostly fourth-class rock to the summit. No one has yet braved the North Tower's Northeast Face, which doesn't offer the long, elegant line of the route up the South Tower's North Face.

History

Just after his success on Goodsir's South Tower in 1903, guide Christian Kaufmann and his brother Hans almost led August Eggers—a Norwegian-born doctor from Grand Forks, North Dakota—up the North Tower. A severe snowstorm some 350 vertical metres shy of the summit forced a turnaround and a difficult return to camp in the dark.

Six years later, Eggers was back, this time with John Forde, P.D. McTavish and guide Edward Feuz. Despite starting from a camp way down in the Ice River below the Northwest Face and making a very long traverse south on "some of the rottenest rock" they had ever seen to reach the Southwest Ridge, they made it to the top. All, that is, except their unwell leader, Eggers, who stayed behind some 350 metres below the summit and insisted the rest carry on. From high on the Southwest Ridge, the remaining climbers traversed right to intercept the upper arm of the V, climbing the rock right of the upper gully to avoid cutting steps. After painstakingly reaching the summit at 4 p.m., they carefully made their way down, picking up Eggers en route and down climbing for two hours in the dark before finally stopping to bivouac. They reached their camp early the next morning, after spending 25 hours on the mountain.

"The climb was not a particularly exciting one," Forde wrote, "the long time taken to reach the summit being more on account of the extreme caution with which it was necessary to move than because of any difficulties encountered." About two hours after their return, guide Rudolph Aemmer and two American clients arrived in camp, two days late in their bid for a first ascent. They made the second ascent the following day.

At an Alpine Club of Canada camp in 1961, Calgary climber Glen Boles and a Boston group that included *Rocky Mountains of Canada* guidebook co-author Robert Kruszyna and Charles Fay (grandson of the famed Rockies climber of the same name) made the first ascent of today's standard South Face route, intercepting the original route on the upper leg of the V. Neglecting to bring their crampons, they had to cut steps up hard snow and venture onto rotten rock, dodging considerable rockfall all the way up the V.

John Derick climbing chossy rock on North Tower, Mt. Goodsir. Photo: Nancy Hansen.

Route

First Ascent August 16, 1909: John Forde, P.D. McTavish, *Edward Feuz* – Southwest Ridge
Route Described South Face (III, 5.4)
Gear Rope, ice axe, crampons, very small rack perhaps including a few pitons
Map 82 N/1 Mount Goodsir
Season mid-July to early September
Time 8-12 hours return

South Face From a camp below the Centre Goodsir, work your way up and left across grass and hard scree to a long snow slope that climbs to a small snow bench beneath the North Tower-Centre Goodsir Col. Make a rising traverse left to gain the bottom of the horizontal V, which is followed left and then back right, either on low-angled snow or scree. The upper leg of the V leads to a gully, which with good snow provides step kicking up a 35-degree slope (watch for rockfall) to a notch at the base of the summit block, with a sharp drop down the Northeast Face. From the notch, take a rising traverse left on thin holds (crux) to get past a short, steep section, then work your way right to the ridge, where better rock leads to the summit.

Descend the same way, a rappel from a three-piton station helping to get past the short, steep section of rock, and regain the couloir at the top of the upper V.

S Face route, Mt. Goodsir, North Tower

Mount Goodsir – Centre Peak

3384 metres (11,102 feet)

Is the Centre Goodsir a peak? Perhaps. On the affirmative side, it looks like a peak on the map, with sufficient distance from the bookend Goodsir Towers and enough elevation gain from the intervening cols to merit consideration. On the dissenting side, it's not mentioned in *The Rocky Mountains of Canada–South* guidebook.

The Centre Goodsir is usually climbed only by those a) already in the Goodsirs area and b) intent on bagging all or many of the 11,000ers. They climb it just to be safe, so they don't wake up in the nursing home 40 years later, wondering about that one piece of unfinished business.

Though the Southwest Face is essentially a fourth-class route, it is exposed and loose and would be difficult to protect; one should take care going up and climbing down.

The Centre Goodsir can be climbed in a couple of hours from the connecting col with the North Tower. Though both peaks can be bagged in a long day from a valley-bottom camp, a high bivy site on a small snow bench below this col makes things easier.

History

The first recorded ascent of Centre Goodsir was by Don Forest, Ian Rowe and Gary Pilkington in 1979. It was Forest's fifth trip into the Goodsirs—one February attempt to climb the North Tower was thwarted by bottomless snow. On this last trip, they got too far east on their intended target, the North Tower, and ended up climbing the centre peak instead. A day later, they got up the North Tower.

Pilkington died soon thereafter when he and Eckhard Grassman fell while attempting the North Face of Mount Edith Cavell. A memorial plaque and wreath for Pilkington is located at Quartzite Col, on the shortcut approach from North Mosquito Creek to Mount Willingdon.

The Goodsirs. A. North Tower. B. Centre Peak. C. South Tower.

Routes

Centre Peak, Mt. Goodsir.
A. SW Face. B. South Tower.

First Ascent August 17, 1979: Don Forest, Gary Pilkington, Ian Rowe – Southwest Face
Routes Described Southwest Face (II)
Gear Helmet
Map 82 N/1 Mount Goodsir
Season mid-July to early September
Time 4-6 hours return

Approach As for Goodsir's North Tower, follow the upper left-hand branch of Zinc Creek over hard scree and grass, usually kicking steps up steep snow beyond. A flat spot just below the North Tower-Centre Goodsir Col provides a good bivy site with fine views to the south and west. Otherwise, camp in the valley bottom.

Southwest Face From just below and right of the North Tower-Centre Goodsir Col, pick the easiest line up the broken ledges of the face, taking care on the rotten rock. At the top of the face, follow the Northwest Ridge, which narrows higher up, over a false summit to the higher, south summit.

Descend same route.

Mount Goodsir – South Tower
3562 metres (11,686 feet)

Goodsir's South Tower is the second highest peak in the southern Canadian Rockies, topped only by Mount Assiniboine. But it may be unrivalled among these southern peaks for the atrocious quality of its shattered limestone rock.

Just below the summit block on the standard route, a short stretch of level but narrow, rickety ridge can be all but impassable if covered with snow, especially if corniced. For that reason, the route is usually not tackled until at least mid-July. On the summit rocks beyond, one has a choice of an easier but very loose face or a narrow and steeper ridge on firmer holds. Other than this latter ridge, it's hard to protect any of the climb. Throw in some route-finding challenges, and it's easy to see why this peak, though technically not that demanding, is among the most nerve-wracking of all the 11,000ers in the Canadian Rockies.

But this is child's play compared to the two routes put up on the tower's north flank, which rises 1850 sheer and somewhat rotten metres above Goodsir Creek. Quite possibly, neither route has been repeated.

History

In 1901, Charles Fay, James Outram, Joseph Scattergood and guide Christian Hasler gingerly made their way up the snowy, rotten rock of the Southwest Ridge, only to be repulsed by cornices and avalanche-prone slopes just below the summit. It was the only 11,000er to defeat Outram in his three whirlwind years of climbing in the Canadian Rockies. "Never did I feel less certain of the safe outcome of a climb, or breathe more freely on leaving snow, surely the worst condition in which it was ever my fortune to meet it," wrote Fay.

Two years later, Herschel Parker and guiding brothers Hans and Christian Kaufmann were also turned back by heavy snow high on the mountain. But shortly thereafter, Parker, Fay, Christian Kaufmann and Hasler took another crack at it. This time, the snow was in perfect condition and they made steady progress up the arête and subsequent cliff, though "the hand and foot holds on one occasion lost their grip on the man passing between the first two anchorages, and left him for a moment in a state of what might be called 'suspended animation,'" wrote Fay, who considered the South Tower his finest climb.

The final arête "was so narrow and thin that one astride it could have his left leg vertical over a sheer drop, at first indeed overhanging, of hundreds if not thousands of feet, while its mate pointed down that 70-degree slope of snow. At eleven o'clock we were on the summit—Goodsir was ours. The repulse of two years before was forgotten, and our affections went out to the graceful peak, no longer a sullen monster, and for the joys of that one glorious hour spent on its pure snowy summit, we granted it our love for a lifetime."

In 1915, Joseph Hickson and guide Edward Feuz, Jr. climbed the Southwest Ridge route and then descended most of the Northwest Ridge. In 1933, this traverse was done in reverse by Kate Gardiner, Lillian Gest and guides Christian Hasler, Jr. and Feuz, Jr., who was perhaps the only person to climb this peak twice.

The South Tower's Northeast Face (V, 5.6) was climbed in 1970 by the redoubtable team of Tim Auger, Don Vockeroth, Charlie Locke and Lloyd MacKay, among the elite Rockies climbers of their era. After crossing the lower glacier and climbing 150 metres of solid limestone, they went up the glacier's "ugly face" to a bivouac. The next day, Vockeroth wrote, "the rock is unbelievably bad. There were moments where I was scared and wished I was elsewhere. Does this damn mountain ever give up? Lead after lead, up chimneys, gullies, sloping ramps and open face climbing, but always loose. At times I swore the rock was vertical scree glued together with frozen soil."

In 1983, two stalwarts of the next Rockies generation, David Cheesmond and Kevin Doyle, tackled the North Face (VI, 5.7) in April, hoping to avoid rockfall. Leaving their bivy gear at the base of the climb, they went up overhanging ice to the level glacier, beyond which they climbed six pitches of steep snow- and ice-covered rock to reach a left-trending ramp and their first unplanned bivy. In a storm the next morning, they continued up the ramp to the summit ridge, where Doyle fell 10 metres through a cornice before the rope pulled him tight.

In the now-raging storm, they attempted to descend the south side of the mountain but instead went down the steep northeast side, where Doyle was almost avalanched off the face. Six vertical rappels later, they "crawled into a crevasse for another night of stomping, brewing and the beginning of a fascinating hallucinatory experience," Cheesmond wrote. "Behind us as the storm cleared (the next morning) we could see both the way up the north face and our misguided descent down the north-east; the former greatly recommended and the latter unimaginably scary."

Climbing upper SW Ridge of Mt. Goodsir's South Tower. Photo: Roman Pachovsky.

Mt. Goodsir's South Tower, North Goodsir in background. See route line page 190. Photo: Glen Boles.

Route

First Ascent July 16, 1903: Charles Fay, Herschel Parker, *Christian Hasler, Christian Kaufmann* – Southwest Ridge

Route Described Southwest Ridge (III, 5.4)

Gear	Rope, ice axe, crampons, small rack, including a few pitons
Map	82 N/1 Mount Goodsir
Season	mid-July to early September
Time	10-13 hours return from a camp below the peak

Southwest Ridge From a camp above tree line southwest of the peak, there are several starting options. The standard choice is to work your way up scree and boulders to reach the Southwest Ridge, where it starts to get steeper. At least one party, though, has found the rock more solid (especially on the descent) if one swings around well to the right onto a more south-southeast aspect towards Sentry Peak, near a waterfall in Zinc Creek; the Southwest Ridge is gained higher up. The most direct line, if there's sufficient and solid snow, is left of the Southwest Ridge in an obvious, broad gully, which halfway up angles right and steepens to about 40 degrees, intercepting the Southwest Ridge near a flattish shoulder. An early, cold start is recommended for this shortcut to avoid rockfall.

From the shoulder, climb through a small basin and then ascend a few easy towers of rotten rock to reach a short stretch of knife-edged ridge on loose, orange rock. Beyond, one option is to traverse rightward around a steep cliff and onto the very loose and exposed Southeast Face for a bit of unnerving scrambling to a short, solid crack, which rejoins the ridge just before the summit. The safer but technically harder and more exhilarating option is to climb up the left side of the steep cliff and stay on the narrow, broken ridgeline, which offers belayed climbing on generally good rock.

Descend either all the way down the Southwest Ridge or, from the lower shoulder, go down either the lower South-Southeast Ridge or the snow gully. The latter is exposed to rockfall from high cliffs on the left (looking up) and should be avoided late on a hot afternoon.

Mount Assiniboine

3618 metres (11,870 feet)

Though far from any road, Assiniboine is one of the most recognizable and striking peaks in the Rockies. As the loftiest mountain in the southern Canadian Rockies and more than 500 metres above its nearest neighbours, Assiniboine is also a distinctive landmark for distant mountaineers. Up close, its massive pyramid rises high above the helicoptered tourists and backpackers that throng to Lake Magog in Assiniboine Provincial Park. Surprising to some, it also straddles the boundary with Banff National Park, making it the highest peak in that park.

Assiniboine is aptly named the "Matterhorn of the Rockies." It is the quintessential horn-shaped mountain, with steep rock walls and huge spurs carved by four or more glacial cirques. The remnant glaciers are receding rapidly, most notably on the north side above Lake Magog.

Assiniboine's North Ridge is a classic route that attracts many international climbers. They come as much for the mountain's aesthetics and stellar surrounding scenery as for the actual climbing (a hut below the ridge is an added incentive). Under dry conditions, the 900-metre North Ridge is mostly an advanced scramble on somewhat loose rock, with the prominent red and gray cliff bands offering short stretches of fifth-class climbing. After ascending this route in 1919, Joseph Hickson offered this blunt assessment: "The country of Assiniboine is splendid; as a mountaineering problem the peak is overrated."

But the North Ridge can certainly bare its teeth, becoming treacherous when wet, snow covered or glazed with ice. Even under relatively benign conditions, it can be a demanding climb for those unaccustomed to the route finding and loose rock typical of most Rockies alpine ascents. Higher on the ridge, the view down the precipitous East Face is sensational.

Hickson was equally dismissive of the Southwest Face route, calling it "nothing more than a long, steep walk... because every one of the precipitous bluffs can be circumvented in a more or less easy way." Indeed, this route is primarily a scramble, albeit a wandering one, the crux being a short, loose section through cliff bands below the summit. The true reward of this route is the lovely, untrammeled environs

Mt. Assiniboine from Lake Magog.
A. Gmoser Highway ledges. B. R.C. Hind Hut.
Photo: Don Beers.

Mt. Assiniboine from Lake Magog. Photo: Gillean Daffern.

on the mountain's south side, far removed from the north side's hordes.

In 1885, surveyor George Dawson spied the peak from afar and named it after the nearby Assiniboine Indians, who sometimes hunted in these mountains. Assiniboine means "stone boiler" (hence the common local name of Stoneys), from the practice of putting hot rocks into water-filled, hide-lined holes to cook food.

History

Mount Assiniboine, with its steep-walled perfection, both haunted and intimidated early mountaineers, who were more explorers than seasoned climbers. Chicago businessman Robert Barrett and guide Tom Wilson were the first white men to get a close look at Assiniboine after venturing from Banff over Simpson Pass and down the Simpson River in 1893. Subsequent visitors included Samuel Allen and Barrett, the latter in 1895 with Walter Wilcox, J.F. Porter and guide Bill Peyto. They traversed below the steep northern flanks and discovered the easier Southwest Face.

In 1899, Wilcox returned with H.G. Bryant and L.J. Steele. The latter two went up the Northwest Arête to 3,050 metres, where an approaching storm forced a descent. On the retreat, Steele slipped on an ice slope, dragging Bryant with him and avoiding disaster only by a "skillful lunge with his ice axe" into a crevice below a large rock.

In 1900, the two Walling brothers of Chicago arrived with three guides. As Outram later noted, "with larger enthusiasm than experience in matters mountaineering," the Wallings were rebuffed by the lower cliff band on the North Face. On the return to Banff via the Spray Valley, the guides went ahead and the Wallings became lost, apparently killing a horse for food before being rescued. A year later, Wilcox, Bryant and guides Edward Feuz, Sr. and F. Michel went up the Southwest Face, turning around in avalanche-prone snow late in the day some 300 vertical metres below the summit.

Climbing with Edward Whymper's entourage that summer in the Yoho Valley, an ambitious and more skilled Outram heard of these attempts but felt "the distance and expense placed the enterprise beyond my reach." Fortunately, Peyto offered to zip Outram in and out of Assiniboine in five days, and in late August they set out from Banff with guides Christian Hasler and Christian Bohren. Taking a direct line from Lake Magog, they skirted Assiniboine's North Face to the Assiniboine-Sturdee Col.

"From this point, the lower portion of the unknown side of the mountain lay in full view, and, to our joy, we saw that the anticipated difficulties were non-existent," Outram wrote. But they didn't account for route finding and visibility. After traversing on ledges to the Southwest Face, they worked their way up the face in enveloping cloud, only to discover the summit they reached was the attached and lower Lunette Peak.

Undaunted, they returned the next day. As often happens when a seemingly insurmountable goal is finally attained, the breakthrough is fairly mundane. So it was with Outram's party, which despite some "brittle and extremely insecure" rocks, bits of verglas and frequent detours, reached the summit around noon. Perhaps the real coup was Outram convincing his guides to go down the North Ridge, thus making the first ascent also the first traverse of the mountain.

W. Douglas and guides Christian Hasler and Christian Kaufmann made the first ascent of the North Ridge in 1903. Sixteen years later, Hickson noted: "The climbing affords most pleasant and not too strenuous exercise on a fine ridge presenting several sharp rock noses. But throughout, its quality altogether falls below that afforded by the northwestern ridge of Mt. Sir Douglas." Not many contemporary climbers, however, would agree, as this route easily gets 20 times the traffic of the standard line up Sir Douglas. Don Gardner, Eckhard Grassman and Chic Scott climbed the North Ridge in the winter of 1967.

In 1910, the Northwest Face was climbed by guide Rudolph Aemmer and British legend Dr. Tom Longstaff, the first man to climb a 7000-metre peak (India's Mount Trisul), a famed Himalayan explorer and member of the 1922 British Everest expedition. Although similar in difficulty to the North Ridge, the adjacent North Face (5.5) wasn't climbed until 1967, when Yvon Chouinard, Chris Jones and Joe Faint ascended it over hard ice. Amazingly, French climber Raymond Jotterand soloed this route in three hours on a bitterly cold New Year's Day in 1978, forced by high winds to crawl the final metres to the summit.

By far the toughest line on Assiniboine is the East Face. We were "appalled by its appearance," the hardened Chris Jones wrote in 1967. "It seemed to be a problem of another order of magnitude." Indeed, it wasn't until 1982 that local big wall legend David Cheesmond and Tony Dick scaled this 1700-metre face (5.9, A2) over three days.

Ascending SW Face, Mt. Assiniboine. A. Mt. Eon. B. Mt. Aye.

Climbing upper N Ridge, Mt. Assiniboine. Photo: Nancy Hansen.

Routes

First Ascent September 3, 1901: James Outram, *Christian Bohren, Christian Hasler* – Southwest Face

Routes Described North Ridge (II, 5.5) *Recommended*, Southwest Face (II)

Gear	Rope, ice axe, crampons, plus alpine rock rack and a few pitons for North Ridge, and glacier gear if approaching the North Ridge from the south
Maps	82 J/13 Mount Assiniboine and 82 J/12 Tangle Peak (Assiniboine Creek approach) or 82 J/14 Spray Lakes Reservoir (Bryant Creek approach)
Season	mid-July to mid-September
Time	Trip – 2-3 days
	Climb – North Ridge: 8-11 hours return
	Southwest Face: 10-12 hours return

Access and Approach The quick and dirty way is to fly from Canmore to Assiniboine Lodge and then scramble up to the R.C. Hind Hut. On foot, the traditional route departs from the Spray Valley, follows Bryant Creek and goes over Assiniboine Pass. But the banning of mountain bikes along Bryant Creek makes this approach a very long day at the least. A much faster approach, even for the North Ridge, is from the south, leaving Settlers Road, off Highway 93, and later following Assiniboine Creek north (see map on page 205).

Bryant Creek Approach From Calgary, drive 60 km west on the Trans-Canada Highway and go 50 km south on Highway 40. Turn right on the Kananaskis Lakes road and 2 km later, head north on the Smith-Dorrien/Spray Trail for 30 km to the Engadine Lodge/Mount Shark Road turnoff. This turnoff can also be reached by driving 38 km south of Canmore along the Smith-Dorrien/Spray Trail. From the turnoff, drive 7 km west to the Mount Shark parking lot.

Hike or bike west, past Watridge Lake, crossing the Spray River bridge (6 km) and turning right at a junction to follow Bryant Creek (no bikes allowed beyond the warden cabin). Follow the Bryant Creek trail for 11 km, turning west to climb steeply over Assiniboine Pass and dropping southwest to Lake Magog (27 km total, about 8 hours on foot). Staying at the campground or Naiset Cabins here allows the approach to be broken into two days if one so chooses.

Follow a trail around the west side of the lake, taking a right fork beyond the lake's end that leads to a rising traverse left across scree to a headwall well right of the central gully. Scramble up to good ledges (the Gmoser Highway), follow them left (cairns) and, shortly before reaching the upper part of the central gully, go straight up to snow slopes and beyond to the R.C. Hind Hut (2-3 hours from Lake Magog).

N Ridge Mt. Assiniboine. Photo: Don Beers.

SW Face of Mt. Assiniboine from Mt. Eon. Photo: Markus Kellerhals.

Assiniboine Creek Approach This approach can be used for both the North Ridge and Southwest Face routes, the latter departing from Assiniboine Creek at Lunette Lake. From the Castle Junction on the Trans-Canada Highway midway between Banff and Lake Louise, drive 84 km south on Highway 93, turning east onto the gravel Settlers Road (highway sign). The ensuing roads are excellent, other than the final 5 km on a spur road, which is still drivable in a low-clearance vehicle. Follow the numbered kilometre signs. The Baymag mine signs will also keep you on track (see map on page 205).

Just before the 12-km sign, take the left fork onto the Kootenay/Palliser Road. Stay on the main road by taking the next left fork and, just after crossing the Kootenay River, go left again beyond the 14-km sign. Turn left onto the Cross/Mitchell Road at 32.7 km. At 37.5 km and just before the bridge crossing to the mine, go right (Aurora sign) on a rougher side road for 5 km. Park just after crossing the Aurora Creek bridge and wrap your vehicle in chicken wire (about one hour from Highway 93).

From the parking area, go up left past berry patches on an old skid road, heading for the upper left side of a cut block. In the trees beyond, a good trail climbs steeply above the right side of Assiniboine Creek before leveling off. A couple of kilometres from the trailhead, a second and major side stream can be safely crossed on a leveled log bridge with a cable hand rail about 25 metres above the main trail.

If you are climbing the Southwest Face from the south, continue north along Assiniboine Creek through open forest for about another 4 km and then branch right onto a side trail (cairn) along a creek draining from Lunette Lake. Cross the outlet stream and follow a faint trail up the steep bushy shoulder extending off the South Ridge of Mount Sturdee. After some 400 metres of sweaty elevation gain, where the trees thin out, traverse right under cliff bands into a scree basin. Resist the temptation to go straight up and instead continue traversing right to some wet scree ledges, which are ascended to a mossy plateau, offering a superb, streamside bivy site (roughly GR 94345, elevation 2400 metres; about 6 hours from the car).

If you are heading to the North Ridge, continue north along Assiniboine Creek, bypassing Lunette Lake and following the trail to Assiniboine Lake (6 km from the car). Go around the right side of the lake and then grovel up a light gray scree gully right of a moraine under Mount Sturdee. Continue up to the right of a black wall and, at the top of the scree gully, angle left up loose rock to gain the toe of the glacier. Rope up to ascend the left side of the crevassed glacier and then bash your way up a final slope of nasty, back-sliding scree to the Strom-Assiniboine Col. Drop down the other side to the R.C. Hind Hut, below the east side of Mount Strom (6-7 hours from car).

Accommodation Assiniboine Lodge is a one-stop source for booking helicopter flights and accommodation, both at Lake Magog and at the R.C. Hind Hut. Reservations are recommended for both. Helicopter flights, from the Mount Shark heliport, are on Sundays, Wednesdays and Fridays (Fridays and Mondays on August and September long weekends) For staying at Lake Magog, on the way in and out via the north approach, the choices range from the campground to the Naiset Cabins to the luxurious Assiniboine Lodge. Phone 403-678-2883 or check www.assiniboinelodge.com. The Hind Hut is located below the east end of Mount Strom at GR 945375. It sleeps up to 15 and is equipped with a propane stove, mattresses and dishes. Potable water from snowmelt is nearby. Camping is not allowed outside the hut.

North Ridge Under dry conditions, generally try to avoid the gullies (danger of rockfall, especially from climbers above) and instead stick to steeper but firmer rock. From the hut, cross to the bottom of the North Ridge and scramble up its broad shoulder on loose scree (cairns) through a small black rock band and up to the red band, which is pierced by following a ramp to a break well right of the ridge. Regain the ridge and continue up to the gray band, also penetrated to the right of the ridge on good holds, with some fixed pitons (5.5). Follow the ridge up a couple of short, fifth-class rock bands and over a snow crest, staying well below the corniced final ridge to the summit.

Descend the same way, with two or three rappels under dry conditions and many more rappels and cautious down climbing if wet or icy.

Southwest Face Note: It is also possible to climb this face from the Hind Hut, heading north over a glacier to the Sturdee-Assiniboine Col and then traversing left on ledges to intersect the route described below.

From the bivy site southwest of the peak, contour around to the right to bypass small cliffs and then ascend grassy ledges northeast into a scree bowl. Aim for a long gully, usually snow filled, that leaves the middle of the bowl and trends left up a broken face. Kick steps up the steep snow as far as you can before scrambling onto rocks on the right (under low or no snow conditions, an earlier exit can be a bit nasty on down-sloping rock). Once out of the gully, scramble straight up on easier, blockier rock to a plateau and go clockwise until halfway around the bowl.

Ascend small steps in a basin and surmount a cliff band via a short, narrow gully, which if wet may require a belay. Continue up over rock and snow, working right to a prominent orange block of rock, a good landmark from below. Traverse under the block to its right end and then take a rising line left on snow, passing below the Lunette-Assiniboine Col. Work your way up through a cliff band via a loose, shallow gully (sometimes snow covered) to reach the South Ridge, which is followed on snow to the summit.

Descend the same way. One or two rappels may be needed to get down the upper gully, plus perhaps one more farther down.

Upper W Face route, Lunette Pk.
A. Mt. Assiniboine. B. Lunette.

Lunette Peak

3400 metres (11,155 feet)

Lunette is also known as Lost Peak, because the first-ascent climbers in 1901 briefly and mistakenly thought they were on top of Mount Assiniboine. More than a century of neglect later, Lunette has become almost literally lost in the shadow of its higher and much more famous neighbour. If it weren't for 11,000er peak baggers, Lunette would scarcely be climbed at all.

The reason, many would claim, is Lunette is not really a peak but just an extension of Assiniboine's South Ridge. In fact, when the former is viewed from the south, it's hard to make it out as an independent peak. Nonetheless, Lunette is officially a mountain, named on the map and in the standard guidebook.

Along with the adjoining South Face of Mount Assiniboine, Lunette is worth climbing if only for the lovely lower approach along Assiniboine Creek, the superb bivouac site with expansive vistas to the south, and the utter isolation on this side of the mountain. From this lofty bivy, it is quite feasible to climb Assiniboine and Lunette in a day. Indeed, both have been climbed in a very long day from the car.

Under good conditions, the ascent of Lunette is primarily a difficult scramble, and the rope may not be needed by a competent party. But the climb should not be taken lightly, because of loose rock, hazard from rockfall and route-finding challenges.

In 1913, the Alberta/B.C. Boundary Commission named this peak for obscure reasons. Lunette means "glasses" in French.

History

Of all the first ascents of 11,000-foot peaks in the Canadian Rockies, Lunette was perhaps the only one where the mountaineers, upon reaching the top, were disappointed. In 1901, James Outram made his initial mark on Canadian mountaineering by being the first up the much-coveted Assiniboine. But it took him two tries, the first netting Lunette by surprise.

Leaving Magog Lake at 6 a.m., Outram, guides Christian Hasler and Christian Bohren and outfitter Bill Peyto ascended to the Assiniboine-Mount Sturdee col. Here, Peyto stayed behind to do some mineral prospecting, while the others swung around to the southwest side of Assiniboine.

Unfortunately, the upper portion of the mountain became increasingly obscured in mist and light rain. After ascending to Assiniboine's South Ridge, they scrambled through cliff bands to reach what they thought was the top.

But their joy was short-lived, as their barometers indicated they were far too low and their shouts echoed off the obscured East Face of Assiniboine above them. So they descended from the summit of Lunette in the gloom, and a day later got it right on Assiniboine.

Lunette was the last of the 11,000ers climbed by Calgarian Don Forest, in 1979. He thus became the first to ascend all these peaks in the Canadian Rockies.

Route

First Ascent September 2, 1901: James Outram, *Christian Bohren, Christian Hasler* – West Face
Route Described West Face (II)
Gear Rope, ice axe, crampons, perhaps a few pieces of rock gear
Maps 82 J/13 Mount Assiniboine, 82 J/12 Tangle Peak (approach)
Season July to September
Time Trip – 2-3 days
Climb – About 8 hours return from high camp

Access From the Castle Junction on the Trans-Canada Highway, drive 84 km south on Highway 93, turning east onto the gravel Settlers Road (highway sign), which provides access to the south side of Mount Assiniboine. The road—a sparkling white from the magnesite ore trucked from the Baymag mine—is excellent, other than the final 5 km on a spur road, which is still drivable in a low-clearance vehicle. **Note:** Follow the numbered kilometre signs. The Baymag mine signs will also keep you on track (see map on page 205).

Just before the 12-km sign, take the left fork onto the Kootenay/Palliser Road. Stay on the main road by taking the next left fork and, just after crossing the Kootenay River, go left again beyond the 14-km sign. Turn left onto the Cross/Mitchell Road at 32.7 km. At 37.5 km and just before the bridge crossing to the mine, go right (Aurora sign) on a rougher side road for 5 km. Park just after crossing the Aurora Creek bridge and wrap your vehicle in chicken wire (about one hour from Highway 93).

Approach From the parking area, go up left past berry patches on an old skid road, heading for the upper left side of a cut block. In the trees beyond, a good trail climbs steeply above the right side of Assiniboine Creek before leveling off. A couple of kilometres from the trailhead, a second, major stream can be safely crossed on a leveled log bridge with a cable hand rail about 25 metres above the main trail. Continue north along Assiniboine Creek through open forest for about another 4 km and then branch right onto a side trail (cairn) along a creek draining from Lunette Lake. A lakeside lunch spot provides superb views of the southern flanks of Mount Assiniboine and the bump on its right skyline (yes, that's Lunette).

Cross the outlet stream and, as best you can, follow a faint trail up the steep bushy shoulder extending off the South Ridge of Mount Sturdee. After some 400 metres of sweaty elevation gain, where the trees thin out, traverse right under cliff bands into a scree basin. Resist the temptation to go straight up and instead continue traversing right to some wet scree ledges, which are ascended to a mossy plateau (roughly GR 943345, elevation 2,400 metres; about 6 hours from the car). It's a spectacular bivy site, with a stream flowing by, expansive views to the south and perhaps visits from ptarmigan and mountain goats.

West Face From the bivy site, contour around to the right to bypass small cliffs and then ascend grassy ledges northeast into a scree bowl, aiming for a long gully, usually snow filled, that leaves the middle of the bowl and trends left up a broken face. Kick steps up the steep snow as far as you can before scrambling onto rocks on the right (under low or no snow conditions, an earlier exit can be a bit nasty on down-sloping rock). Once out of the gully, scramble straight up on easier, blockier rock to a plateau and go clockwise until halfway around the bowl.

Ascend small steps in a basin and surmount a cliff band via a short, narrow gully, which if wet may require a belay. Continue up over rock and snow, working right to a prominent orange block of rock, a good landmark from below. Traverse under to its right end and then take a rising line left on snow, with superb views south to Eon and Aye Mountains. From here, the route up Assiniboine's South Face continues left and then goes up through cliff bands.

For Lunette, go more directly up on steeper snow, swinging around the left end of cliffs guarding the summit block. Just before the Assiniboine-Lunette Col, traverse right onto wide ledges beneath a couple of rock towers. Either carefully head up a shallow gully on loose black rock below the summit (it's hard to tell from below which tower is the highest) or continue traversing right to find a slightly easier line to the summit ridge, which is followed back left to the top.

Descend the same way. One or two rappels may be needed.

Mount King George
3422 metres (11,227 feet)

King George is the dominant mountain of the Royal Group, a gorgeous cluster of isolated peaks above the Palliser River on the B.C. side of the Continental Divide. Though the Royal Group is less than 10 kilometres due west of the busy Peter Lougheed Provincial Park, the circuitous logging road access, the lack of an established approach trail and the sometimes exciting crossing of the Palliser River add up to relatively few mountaineering visitors.

That's a shame, because the area is well worth visiting, for two reasons: climbing a lovely peak, and enjoying perhaps the finest base camp of all the 11,000ers. Here, one's tent is pitched in a meadow fringed by alpine larches, with a stream meandering past and views of sharp-sided peaks emerging from small glaciers. Though there is an area horse camp and some heli hiking, their activities tend to be farther north, leaving mountaineers to relish a true wilderness experience. From the summit, one can see the other southern 11,000ers, from Harrison in the south to Assiniboine in the north, with Sir Douglas and Joffre to the near east.

There are two well-established, moderate routes up King George. The standard line curves up the west side, while the more aesthetic and slightly harder and steeper route follows the Southeast Ridge to the summit plateau. In low snow years, the latter can be more challenging than expected, even for experienced mountaineers, while open crevasses can similarly imperil the former. Taking the Southeast Ridge up and the Southwest Face down makes a fine loop trip.

The Alberta/B.C. Boundary Commission named the Royal Group for eight immediate members of the British royal family circa World War I. The family head was King George V, also emperor of India.

History

Like nearby Sir Douglas and Joffre, King George was revealed as an 11,000er to ambitious mountaineers in a 1917 map of the area by the Alberta/B.C. Boundary Commission survey. Two years later, talented British-American climber Val Fynn and guide Rudolph Aemmer led a horseback expedition south from Banff up the Spray Valley, bound for King George. Upon

SE Ridge route on Mt. King George.

Access and Approaches for Assiniboine, Lunette and King George

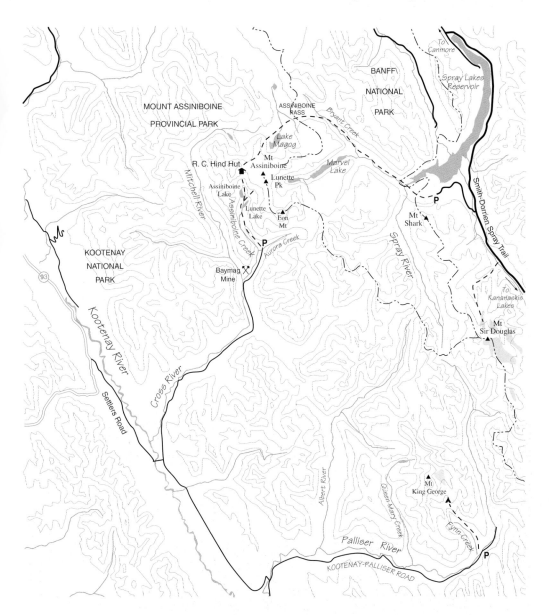

crossing Palliser Pass, they became bogged down in heavy, fire-strewn timber, taking all day to cover six kilometres near LeRoy Creek, with two packhorses needing rescue after rolling down steep hillsides.

After another day of bushwhacking down the Palliser Valley, Fynn and Aemmer left their companions and headed up a side valley northeast of Mount Prince Albert on an approach that was "clearly beyond the reach of the ladies," Fynn wrote. "For hundreds of yards we walked on tree trunks without ever touching the ground." The next day, the pair took a circuitous route (undoubtedly not since repeated) over the South Ridge of Mount Prince George, went back north up a glacier between Prince Albert and King George and then up a rib to the North Ridge of the latter.

Ascending upper SE Ridge, Mt. King George.

The rocks "proved excessively steep in the lower part of the rib, but were very firm and afforded one of the best climbs we had had anywhere in the Rockies," wrote Fynn. "Unfortunately this welcome condition did not last, the upper third of the ridge being composed of a very brittle kind of rock requiring very careful handling." After taking turns cutting steps up an intervening ice rib, they reached the North Ridge, which "gave us a most enjoyable climb, partly on ice and partly on rocks, with an occasional fairly difficult passage." Reaching the summit at 5 p.m., they made the long, tortuous journey down, reaching their bivouac site at 1 a.m.

The second ascent of King George was not made until 1970, when Gerry Brown, John Carter and William Hurst of the Kootenay Mountaineering Club went up the Southeast Ridge. The chockstone couloir above the King George Glacier proved the "most difficult and messy part of the climb, with small mud-cov-ered ledges to our left and a vertical rock wall to our right forcing us directly under a large chockstone, from which a small stream of water issued," Hurst wrote. Upon reaching the summit, they found the first-ascent record, complete with Aemmer's professional guide's calling card, in remarkably good condition after 51 years. They went back down the Southeast Ridge, rappelling two of the trickier spots as well as the lower chockstone.

In 1984, Calgarians Frank Campbell, Karl Nagy and Russ Varnam went up the East Face, left of the first-ascent route and right of a couloir pioneered by Everest conqueror Dwayne Congdon along with Dave McNab. "The route is highly recommended, quite similar to the Victoria North Face but with two pitches of steeper ice," wrote Nagy of the mostly ice and some mixed route. "The rock is excellent compared to that of the loose grunt standard south-east ridge."

Routes

First Ascent August 10, 1919: Val Fynn, *Rudolph Aemmer* – East Face/North Ridge

Routes Described Southeast Ridge (II, 5.3), Southwest Face (II)

Gear Rope, glacier gear, crampons, ice axe, small rock rack for Southeast Ridge, perhaps a few ice screws later in the season

Map 82 J/11 Kananaskis Lakes, 82 J/12 Tangle Peak (approach)

Season mid-July to September, late summer better for crossing the Palliser River

Time Trip – 3 days

Climb – About 12 hours return, slightly longer on Southeast Ridge

Access From the Castle Junction on the Trans-Canada Highway, 30 km west of Banff, drive 84 km south on Highway 93 (or 20 km north from Radium), turning east onto Settlers Road (highway sign). The route beyond follows the Kootenay and then Palliser Rivers on good gravel roads that get slightly rougher near the end but are still fine for low-clearance vehicles. Watch for logging trucks, and follow the kilometre signs (about 1 hour from the start of Settlers Road).

Note: The description below describes two parking spots. The first provides access to a good log crossing of the Palliser River. The second, a couple of kilometres farther, allows the river to be waded where it is considerably wider but should be tackled only when the water is low (late summer or early fall).

Drive south on Settlers Road and at a major junction, go left onto the Kootenay/Palliser Road (12-km sign). After a bridged crossing of the broad Kootenay River (13 km), go right at the 14-km sign to stay on the Kootenay/Palliser Road. Just after crossing the Palliser River on a bridge (35.7 km), stay left on Kootenay/Palliser Road. At a junction at 39.9 km, turn right on to the higher, unmarked Joffre Creek Road, continuing straight ahead at a couple of minor junctions. At the 54- km sign, stay to the right on a rougher road, ignoring fresher, spur logging roads beyond. At 59.7 km (100 metres past a faded "39" plywood sign), park just over the crest of a small hill (cairn), if you want to tackle

Mt. King George.

207

the log crossing of the Palliser River. The south end of the Royal Group, including King George, is visible to the north through a gap. If you plan to wade across the river, drive another couple of kilometres to more open flats.

Approach If you're parked at 59.7 km, head straight down through bush (slight trail) for a couple of hundred metres to where a large tree has been felled over a narrowing of the Palliser River. It has since been leveled and a cord hand railing installed, making the crossing much easier.

If you're parked beyond in the flats, wade across the river at its widest point. If the water is much above the knee, the current will probably be too strong to make this a safe option (in early July, one year, we needed a canoe to get across). Once across, head downstream on a trail to intersect the log-crossing route.

From the north side of the Palliser log crossing, go downstream on a broad trail that soon diagonals right through woods. Just before Fynn Creek, head north on a wide trail that goes to the end of the valley and then angles to the right up a headwall.

Above this headwall, angle up left toward the bottom of the valley between Mounts Princess Mary and Prince George. Camp in a lovely meadow at tree line beside the upper right fork of Fynn Creek. If you're planning to climb the Southwest Face route via the west side of Mount Princess Mary and want a shorter ascent day, a higher and equally lovely campsite can be reached by heading west up the left-hand fork of Fynn Creek and going steeply through trees right of a waterfall to tree line (GR 140036).

Southeast Ridge From the lower camp, cross a moraine and work north-northwest to gain the King George Glacier, which is followed briefly on its left side. Go up the first, or most southerly, of two steep snow couloirs. Getting past a large, dripping chockstone at mid-height can be the crux of the entire climb, and may be virtually impassable, if the surrounding snow has exposed too much wet rock. At the top of the couloir, ascend a snow/ice slope of up to 35 degrees and, just before the King George-Princess Mary Col, angle right up a small snow/scree gully to reach the broad Southeast Ridge.

Follow the narrowing ridgeline up loose rock (up to about 5.3 in difficulty), which improves higher up, with great views down the ridge crest. Depending on snow conditions, you may have to traverse left to bypass a cornice and gain the level upper ridge, which is followed

right for about 15 minutes. Beyond, angle left and cross a bergschrund to reach the 35-degree Southwest Face, which is ascended to a false summit. A short, corniced ridge then leads to the true summit.

Southwest Face There are two routes for approaching the Southwest Face. One follows the Southeast Ridge route (see above) up the chockstone couloir and the snow slope above. Cross the King George-Princess Mary Col and then take a rising right line up scree to broken cliffs, penetrated by your choice of gully. The route now traverses on scree and rock slopes far beneath the upper Southeast Ridge, gaining the hanging upper Southwest Glacier (not shown on the map) along its unbroken right side. In low snow years, crevasses here may prove impassable. Continue up the glacier's right side, intercepting the top of the Southeast Ridge just below the Southwest Face. Go up the 35-degree slopes of the face, first on glacier and then up a final snow slope through a broad gully to reach the corniced summit ridge.

A slightly easier start to the Southwest Face follows the upper left-hand branch of Fynn Creek to the valley on the west side of Princess Mary. Ascend the valley over snow, remnants of a glacier (much smaller than appears on the topo map) and scree to the King George-Princess Mary Col. From here, follow the rest of the Southwest Face route as described above.

For both routes, **descend** the Southwest Face to the top of the level Southeast Ridge. Work your way southwest, angling left at one point to avoid an ice cliff and down climbing through cliffs on easy rock to gain the glacier near the King George-Princess Mary Col. From here, either follow the lower Southwest Ridge route or head down the chockstone gully (harder to find if you didn't go up this way) to the glacier east of King George, as described in the Southeast Face route. A rappel off boulders (long slings needed) may be required to get past the chockstone.

Mount Sir Douglas

3406 metres (11,174 feet)

The unobstructed views from the second-highest peak in Kananaskis Country are outstanding, particularly south across the Haig Glacier to the white fang of Mount Joffre. On a clear day, they are a fine reward for fairly tedious climbing up the loose West Ridge (standard route). The nearby Northwest Face offers a somewhat harder but more aesthetic snow/ice route, with some risk of rockfall. Glacial recession has made the start of both routes and the upper Northwest Face more challenging, particularly in dry years.

Straddling the Kananaskis-Banff National Park and Alberta-B.C. boundaries, Sir Douglas is commonly seen by skiers ascending the Robertson Glacier and by skiers and hikers venturing up to Burstall Pass—the latter offering fine views of the Northwest Face. Given the relatively easy access, it's not surprising Sir Douglas's steeper face routes have attracted top local climbers in both summer and winter.

Sir Douglas is the loftiest peak in the British Military Group, which honours leading commanders from World War I. Prominent among these soldiers was Sir Douglas Haig, who led British forces in France.

History

Mount Sir Douglas offers perhaps the most blatant example of the often fierce but usually understated competition to bag the big, virgin summits in the Canadian Rockies. In 1917, an Alberta/B.C. Boundary Commission map of this part of the southern Rockies identified three 11,000ers—Sir Douglas, Joffre and King George. This inspired two parties in 1919 to leave Banff on horseback and head south up the Spray Valley to establish separate climbing camps near Palliser Pass.

Hearing that Val Fynn and guide Rudolph Aemmer had just claimed nearby King George, Joseph Hickson and guide Edward Feuz, Jr. immediately headed for Sir Douglas at the unusually late hour of 9 a.m. on August 11. Despite burnt timber on the approach, step cutting on the lower glacier and rotten rock on the West Ridge, the pair reached the summit at 5 p.m. and were relieved to see it "bare of everything in the shape of human workmanship," wrote Hickson.

"On the descent, which was tedious, we followed very closely the route by which we had come up. The footholds were for the most part poor; and loose and sharp rocks worked havoc with our foot-gear (they had changed from nailed boots to rope-soled shoes on the ascent), through which bare toes later protruded." They stumbled back into camp as daylight was fading.

Meanwhile, Fynn and Aemmer were returning to Palliser Pass from their King George triumph and hoping to beat their two competitors up Sir Douglas as well. Thus on August 12, unaware of the first ascent a day earlier, they tackled the southwest flank but were eventually turned back by steep, difficult rock on the south face.

NW aspect of Mt. Sir Douglas from near Burstall Pass

Roman Pachovsky near top of W Ridge,
Mt. Sir Douglas.

"Neither of us had ever seen such vile scree or so much of it in one valley," wrote Fynn, perhaps the only amateur of his era good enough to climb as an equal with a guide. In perhaps a sly dig at his less accomplished rival, he said: "Ed Feuz had taken Dr. Hickson to the summit of Sir Douglas."

A philosophy professor at McGill University, the wealthy Hickson was the only prominent Canadian in the early decades of Rockies mountaineering. Although slowed by an old leg injury, he made first ascents of four 11,000ers (Sir Douglas, Joffre, Fryatt and King Edward) and 26 other first ascents in the Rockies and Selkirks, invariably with Feuz, Jr. as his guide.

This dynamic duo certainly appeared skilled and speedy alpinists on Sir Douglas compared with the large Alpine Club group that needed 25 hours, round trip, to make the second ascent of the peak in 1922. T.O.A. West described that West Ridge climb as steep, loose and nerve wracking and the slabby descent as "infinitely worse and without an enjoyable moment."

West's lengthy, colourful account contrasts sharply with Charlie Locke's brief and breezy tale of the first ascent of the East Ridge, and its 5.6 rock, in 1971: "No one had brought any gear. No matter. After assuring myself that the Gods would look after us, I started up. The first few belays were mind shattering as we had no protection and my stances were horrible. After a few pitches, better belay stances were found and we were no longer in danger."

The same summer, Glen Boles, Don Forest and Gordon Scruggs pioneered a fine snow and ice route up the Northwest Face (III). They followed a tilted snow ramp left to the middle of the face and then kicked steps straight up steep snow for about 150 metres. Fearing the fresh snow above them might avalanche in the warming sun, they traversed left to the Northeast Ridge, which was followed to the summit. Two years later, Murray Toft and Mel Reasoner added a harder, direct finish (IV) to this route on firm blue ice, with sustained climbing between 45 and 55 degrees.

To show how far climbing standards had advanced since the early 1920s, Don Gardner made a solo winter ascent of the original Northwest Face route in 11 hours return in 1987. And after many attempts by some of Calgary's finest climbers, Jeff Marshall and Eric Trouillot made the first winter ascent of the challenging Southeast Face (IV, 5.6/5.7) in 1992.

Routes

First Ascent August 11, 1919: Joseph Hickson, *Edward Feuz, Jr.* – West Ridge

Routes Described West Ridge (II), Northwest Face (III)

Gear	Rope, glacier gear, ice axe, crampons, ice screws, plus two tools for Northwest Face
Maps	82 J/11 Kananaskis Lakes, 82 J/14 Spray Lakes Reservoir (approach)
Season	mid-July to mid-September
Time	Trip – The climb has been done as a very long day trip, but most parties take two days, with a bivouac near South Burstall Pass
	Climb – 10-12 hours return from high camp

Access From the Trans-Canada Highway 60 km west of Calgary, drive 50 km south on Highway 40. Turn right and, 2 km later, head 22.5 km north on the Smith-Dorrien/Spray Trail to the Mud Lake parking lot. The parking lot can also be reached in 45 km from Canmore, via the Smith-Dorrien road.

Approach Follow the signed Burstall Pass trail along the old Burstall Creek logging road and then across braided stream flats and up the treed headwall into the upper Burstall Valley. Where the trail turns right to climb to the pass, continue south up an open depression for about 2 km to South Burstall Pass (GR 155229), which offers wonderful views of the Northwest Face, the lush Spray Valley below and the Royal Group of peaks to the southwest. Climbers often camp just beyond and below the pass, where water can be found (10 km, 3-4 hours).

West Ridge From South Burstall Pass, descend south to a valley of rock debris, ascend a shoulder and traverse a bushy, west-facing slope. Briefly descend again and cross a small moraine to reach the lower of two small parallel glaciers below the west side of Sir Douglas. Ascend the snow and/or ice of this glacier, which steepens as it nears a notch on the West Ridge.

The ridge is a long rise of rotten rock and scree, but the exposure is minimal and the climbing mostly a steep scramble when dry. About halfway up the ridge, traverse right onto the Southwest Face and ascend a gully (usually snow or ice) until the ridge can be regained above some pinnacles. Beyond a false summit, a short, exposed ridge leads to the true summit.

Northwest Face From South Burstall Pass, follow the same initial route as for the West Ridge and, after crossing moraines, gain the toe of the higher, or left-hand, of the two glaciers. Work your way up the right side of this crevassed glacier to reach a prominent snow/ice ramp, which angles up left all the way across the Northwest Face. Follow this ramp, the crux sometimes being the crossing of an exposed, rotten avalanche chute part way along. Beyond, go straight up for 150 vertical metres, then angle left over steep snow along a continuation of the ramp system, under a protecting overhang of rock, to gain the Northeast Ridge just below the summit.

For both routes, **descend** the West Ridge.

Mt. Sir Douglas. A. NW Face. B. W Ridge.

Mt. Joffre. A. NE Ridge. B. N Face. Photo: Clive Cordery.

Mount Joffre

3450 metres (11,319 feet)

Mount Joffre is one of two 11,000ers in Kananaskis Country and the highest peak between the U.S. border and Mount Assiniboine. Tucked into the southwest corner of Peter Lougheed Provincial Park and perched on the Continental Divide, Joffre and its shining, glaciated North Face is infrequently seen, except from nearby high vantage points. Even fewer folks wander up Joffre Creek to Sylvan Pass to gaze in awe at its nearly 1000-metre west rock wall, as yet unclimbed. Summiteers enjoy unique views of the Italian Group of peaks to the south and the Royal Group to the northwest.

Joffre's North Face is a fine, moderate route of up to 40 degrees on snow and/or ice. If the face is not in shape, the Northeast Ridge offers an alternative route, on snow and rock, of comparable difficulty. For a nice loop, you can go up one route and down the other. While Joffre has been climbed in a very long day, car to car, the approach and Aster Lake environs are sufficiently lovely to warrant a more leisurely three-day trip.

When avalanche conditions are stable, Joffre is also a recommended ski ascent, with the last bit up the North Face usually done on foot. Certainly, it is much more enjoyable swooping down the lower Mangin Glacier and ensuing moraines on skis than descending on foot.

The Alberta/B.C. Boundary Commission named the peak for Joseph Jacques Joffre, commander in chief of the French army at the outset of World War I. The area peaks are collectively known as the French Military Group and include the nearby Mount Pétain, for the French World War I hero Henri Petain, later vilified for apparently collaborating with the Germans in World War II.

History

After narrowly beating Val Fynn and Rudolph Aemmer up Mount Sir Douglas in 1919, Joseph Hickson and Edward Feuz, Jr. continued south to Joffre, which they had to themselves. The worst part of the journey was descending from Palliser Pass through deadfall that slowed the horseback pace to a mile an hour, and then ascending the trail-less Le Roy Creek to North Kananaskis Pass. They continued on to Kananaskis Lakes and then to a bushy camp at Hidden Lake, from which they mounted a very long day's ascent of Joffre. After some nasty bushwhacking, they got above tree line, crossed Aster Creek and gained the bare Mangin Glacier, which they followed to Joffre's summit block. Eschewing a route up the right side of the North Face, they instead went left through sharp rocks to a saddle in the Northeast Ridge.

"Under a rock band from which stones were being dislodged by the melting snow, some hard ice had to be traversed by step-cutting, after which several sharp and none too solid excrescences of rock had to be ascended," wrote Hickson. "These being gingerly overcome, we reached the easier rocks above, which were cov-ered with fresh snow on which large hail stones were still intact." Beyond, the Northeast Ridge was followed, above a tremendous drop to the Petain Glacier on the left, to the summit. They returned to camp in mid-evening, exhausted from a 15-hour day.

In 1952, a group from an Alpine Club of Canada camp at Elk Lakes ascended the Petain Glacier to the Northeast Ridge and then went over the subsidiary north summit to the true summit. In early March 1970, hardened alpinist Eckhard Grassman and companions Archie Simpson and James Jones made both the first ascent of the North Face and the first winter ascent of Joffre, skiing to the base of the summit block and then kicking steps up the headwall.

Routes

First Ascent August 18, 1919: Joseph Hickson, *Edward Feuz, Jr.* – North Glacier
Routes Described: North Face (II) *Recommended*, Northeast Ridge (II)
Gear   Rope, glacier gear, crampons, ice axe
Map   82 J/11 Kananaskis Lakes
Season   March-April on skis, July-September on foot
Time   Trip – 2-3 days
             Climb – 8-10 hours return from Aster Lake

Access From the Trans-Canada Highway 60 km west of Calgary, drive 50 km south on Highway 40, turn right and follow the Kananaskis Trail for another 13.5 km to the Upper Lake day-use parking lot. The trailhead is at the far end of the parking lot.

Approach From the parking lot, follow the trail along the south side of Upper Kananaskis Lake for 5 km. Shortly after the trail turns north at the end of the lake, take a subsidiary path left, which leads through heavy forest to Hidden Lake in less than 1 km. If you're in luck, the water will be sufficiently low to enable walking along the left-hand shoreline and thus avoiding some nasty bush. Beyond the lake, a trail climbs steeply through thick forest to reach an open basin at tree line. Angle left up scree slopes below Mount Sarrail to reach a thin trail traversing to the right above cliffs and then through easy ledges to leveler ground above the aptly named Fossil Falls. In winter or early spring, it is considerably safer to avoid this high traverse and instead ski up the valley bottom, picking a line up a treed headwall to the right of the falls.

Above the falls, the trail tends to peter out past a small, occasional pond. If it does, make your way across the rolling country to the right, using Aster Creek as a right-hand rail guiding you to Aster Lake, which has a backcountry campsite, with bear-proof food containers. Bivy sites can also be found along gravel flats south of the lake (11 km from trailhead, about 4-5 hours).

N Face, Mt. Joffre.

North Face From the south end of Aster Lake, follow gravel flats west and then south around the end of Mount Marlborough's Northwest Ridge. Rather than go all the way up the outwash plain to a right-angling moraine, take a more direct line to the right up scree and rock to the toe of the much-receded Mangin Glacier. Follow the low-angled, lightly-crevassed glacier to the base of the North Face. Cross the berg-schrund and switchback up the right side of the face, to the right of a narrow cliff band, on snow or ice up to 35-40 degrees. At the top of the face, follow the West Ridge to the summit, the last section involving a short, exposed scramble on rock. Note: A direct line up the face to the summit, passing through a small rock band, can also be taken but is slightly steeper and more exposed to avalanches.

Northeast Ridge Follow the above route up the Mangin Glacier. Just before the North Face, traverse left and go up a narrow and sometimes icy gully that splits a rock wall (some risk of rockfall). Beyond, gentler snow slopes lead to a col to the right of a subsidiary summit on the Northeast Ridge. Follow the ridge to the true summit over snow and some rock.

Descend either route, the Northeast Ridge being slightly easier.

Mount Harrison

3359 metres (11,020 feet)

Seemingly banished to the southern reaches of the Canadian Rockies, Mount Harrison is literally out of sight from most high vantage points in the range. For decades, it was also off the radar screens of big-peak mountaineers, who were unaware there was a virgin 11,000-footer in southeast B.C. Once the mapmakers discovered this unknown mountain in the early 1960s, there was a brief, mad scramble to be the first up this last of the unclimbed 11,000ers that is definitely a separate peak.

Harrison barely qualifies as an 11,000er. At 3359 metres, it is the second lowest of the bunch and a mere six metres above the qualifying criteria, its credentials perhaps suspect to the measurement police.

It is certainly off the beaten path. It's the only 11,000er one drives well south on Highway 93 to reach. Indeed, one continues a fair ways south of Radium and then east into the Park Ranges to access it. Although Harrison isn't far, as the crow flies, from southern Kananaskis Country, it's in the middle of nowhere for most Canadian Rockies climbers. Still, it provides a good opportunity for exploratory mountaineering in a beautiful area where one is more apt to run across hunters than other climbers. The summit provides views of two other impressive but seldom climbed peaks—Mount Folk, to the near north, and Mount Mike, to the southwest.

Harrison offers two standard climbing routes. Though it involves some circuitous traversing, the normal route up the Southwest Face is a relatively straightforward fourth-class ascent, best done in early summer when there's good, firm snow cover. The North Couloir is a superb snow or ice line that climbs more steeply and directly to the summit. Getting to both routes involves a brief brush with B.C. alders, a reminder one is no longer on the east side of the divide.

The mountain was named in 1964 after Francis Harrison of Cranbrook, B.C. He was killed in World War II while serving with the Royal Canadian Air Force. It's somewhat ironic that this overlooked peak is the only big Rockies' mountain named for a local, Canadian military figure, while many of the brand-name peaks to the north commemorate British or French generals.

Mt. Harrison A. N Couloir route.

Mt. Harrison Access

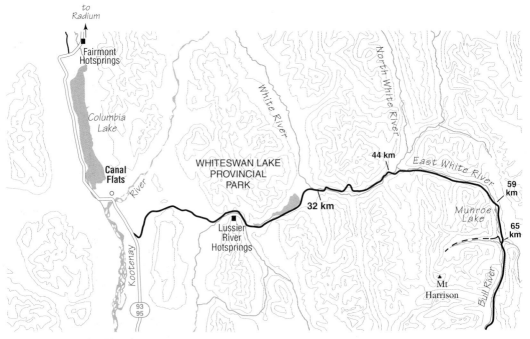

History

After Mount Andromeda was climbed in 1930, Monroe Thorington and Howard Palmer wrote in *A Climber's Guide to the Rocky Mountains of Canada*: "So much is now known of Canada's Rocky Mountains that no new peaks above 11,000 feet are likely to be discovered, although revisions of base levels or triangulation in future may raise some known summits into this category." Yet in the early 1960s, B.C.'s mapping branch indeed reported such a peak in an unexplored valley east of Canal Flats.

Aided by a fresh logging road that went as far as Munroe Lake, a Vancouver-based group set out in August 1964 to conquer Harrison. After eight hours of slogging in torrential rain up a trapper's trail that gave way to meandering elk tracks, they hacked a campsite out of willows in the headwaters of Bull Creek. Following a day of reconnaissance, they went up the valley to a col, crossed the Northwest Ridge and side-hilled on steep scree till they reached a ridge that opened onto a broad slope of debris under the Southwest Face.

"It was a huge face, open and seamed with many gullies. On the southerly side of it, a stream fell, obviously draining the snow ridge on the summit. We followed this up, partly in the gully, partly on ribs of rock that was rotten with occasional sound patches," wrote Paddy Sherman. This led directly to the summit, which had no traces of previous visitors and measured 11,050 feet on their aneroid.

"We weren't very impressed with the region as a climbing area," wrote Sherman, later president of Southam Newspapers and author of the mountaineering book *Expeditions to Nowhere*. "The rock was too rotten, and there wasn't enough snow and ice for our tastes. But as a venture in climbing history, the whole affair was quite delightful."

In July 1978, Frank Campbell led Pat Michael and Brian and John Darragh up the right-hand of two North Couloir routes. Because of excessively deep snow, they went up rock to the right of the couloir and then almost swam up the upper couloir before reaching the summit West Ridge late in the day. They returned, exhausted, to camp, nearly 24 hours after setting out. The same month, the left-hand North Couloir route was climbed, topping out on the East Ridge just below the summit.

Routes

First Ascent August 11, 1964: Werner Himmelsbach, Ralph Hutchinson, Joe Hutton, Don MacLaurin, Brendan Moss, Paddy Sherman – Southwest Face
Routes Described Southwest Face (II), North Couloir/West Ridge (III) *Recommended*
Gear Southwest Face: Ice axe, crampons, rope (optional)
North Couloir: Rope, crampons, two tools, ice screws, couple of pitons
Map 82 J/3 Mount Peck (NAD 1927)
Season July to early October
Time Trip – 2-3 days
Climb – Southwest Face: 8-10 hours return
North Couloir: 12-16 hours return

Access A low-clearance vehicle is fine for most of the approach, on good gravel roads that pass Whiteswan Lake and the East White River before swinging south past Munroe Lake (watch for logging trucks and recreational vehicles). A high-clearance vehicle is recommended for the last few kilometres up Bull Creek.

From Radium, drive 65 km south on Highway 93/95 and turn east onto the Whiteswan Lake Provincial Park Road, following the kilometre signs, which begin at 0. At 17 km, the road to the park passes Lussier River Hotsprings (worth a visit on the way out). After passing along the south shore of Whiteswan Lake, stay straight at a junction with the White-Blackfoot Road and, at 32.5 km, cross a bridge and turn right onto the White River Road, continuing straight ahead at several subsequent junctions. At 43.7 km, turn right onto Munroe Lake Road, cross the White River soon thereafter and at about 45 km take the middle of three forks (trending right) to follow the slightly rougher East White River Road. At a junction (59 km), go left towards the Bull River and at 65 km, turn right onto the much rougher Bull River Road, which climbs more steeply west up this valley. Drive as far as you can (rough crossing of a small stream at about 5 km), camping just before the road crosses a small creek (at about 10 km) and swings back east towards Smith Peak.

Southwest Face From the roadside camp, cross the creek and follow a hand-cut, flagged trail southwest up the upper Bull Valley drainage, thus avoiding most of an alder bash up the creek. Beyond, follow the creek up into a scree basin that leads southwest to a broad col between Harrison and the more visually arresting Mount Folk, to the north.

Traverse around the west side of Harrison on scree, crossing several shallow basins. Continue this long stretch of side-hill gouging, passing beneath a subsidiary summit, until below the broad scree basin and myriad shallow gullies of the Southwest Face. Though the upward view is somewhat obscured, try to pick a gully system that follows a slight stream descending from the West Ridge, just left of the summit. If you're in luck, you can kick steps in snow that steepens to 30-plus degrees. Otherwise, you'll have to deal with some scree, perhaps venturing onto loose rock ribs occasionally. The West Ridge is intercepted just below the summit, near where the North Couloir route tops out.

North Couloir/West Ridge It's best to start up the couloir early in the day, preferably after a night of frost, when the risk of rock fall is diminished. A crisp fall day is more likely to guarantee a safer, and icier, ascent.

From the campsite, follow the drainage southwest through the same bush as for the Southwest Face route until you are into the upper scree basin and below the North Couloir. Ascend snow to the bottom of the couloir and cross the bergschrund where feasible; yes, there is a small glacier here, unmarked on the map. If rockfall is a concern, the narrowest part of the couloir, at its bottom, can be bypassed by climbing up very loose rock to its right for about two rope lengths; a couple of pitons might be handy on this low-class fifth section. Above, the couloir rears up to 50-55 degrees, under a protective roof, with conditions ranging from good step-kicking snow to superb alpine ice, or something in between. If it's ice, expect six or seven pitches of climbing. The couloir tops out on the West Ridge, just below the summit.

For both routes, **descend** the Southwest Face route.

First Ascents in Chronological Order (guides' names in italics)

Mount Temple – August 17, 1894: Walter Wilcox, Samuel Allen, Lewis Frissell

Mount Hector – July 30, 1895: Philip Abbot, Charles Fay, Charles Thompson

Mount Lefroy – August 3, 1897: Norman Collie, Harold Dixon, Charles Fay, Arthur Michael, Charles Noyes, Charles Thompson, J.R. Vanderlip, *Peter Sarbach*

Mount Victoria, South Summit – August 5, 1897: Norman Collie, Charles Fay, Arthur Michael, *Peter Sarbach*

Mount Athabasca – August 17, 1898: Norman Collie, Herman Woolley

Snow Dome – August 20, 1898: Norman Collie, Hugh Stutfield, Herman Woolley

Diadem Peak – August 25, 1898: Norman Collie, Hugh Stutfield, Herman Woolley

Mount Victoria, North Summit – August 1900: James Outram, William Outram, Joseph Scattergood, *C. Clarke, H. Zurfluh*

Lunette Peak – September 2, 1901: James Outram, *Christian Bohren, Christian Hasler*

Mount Assiniboine: September 3, 1901: James Outram, *Christian Bohren, Christian Hasler*

Mount Columbia – July 19, 1902: James Outram, *Christian Kaufmann*

Mount Lyell, Edward Peak (2) – July 24, 1902: James Outram, *Christian Kaufmann*

Mount Forbes – August 10, 1902: Norman Collie, James Outram, Hugh Stutfield, Herman Woolley, George Weed, *Christian Kaufmann, Hans Kaufmann*

Mount Bryce, Southwest Peak – August 20, 1902: James Outram, *Christian Kaufmann*

Mount Alexandra – August 23, 1902: James Outram, *Christian Kaufmann*

Mount Goodsir, South Tower – July 16, 1903: Charles Fay, Herschel Parker, *Christian Kaufmann, Christian Hasler*

Hungabee Mountain – July 21, 1903: Herschel Parker, *Christian Kaufmann, Hans Kaufmann*

Deltaform Mountain – September 1, 1903: Herschel Parker, August Eggers, *Christian Kaufmann, Hans Kaufmann*

Mount Huber 1903: George Collier, Ernst Tewes, *Christian Bohren, Christian Kaufmann*

Mount Goodsir, North Tower – August 16, 1909: John Forde, P.D. McTavish, *Edward Feuz*

Resplendent Mountain – August 1911: Byron Harmon, *Conrad Kain*

Whitehorn Mountain – August 12, 1911: *Conrad Kain*, alone

Mount Robson –July 31, 1913: Albert MacCarthy, William Foster, *Conrad Kain*

Mount Edith Cavell – August 5, 1915: A.J. Gilmour, Edward Holway

Mount King George – August 10, 1919: Val Fynn, *Rudolph Aemmer*

Mount Sir Douglas – August 11, 1919: Joseph Hickson, *Edward Feuz, Jr.*

Mount Joffre – August 18, 1919: Joseph Hickson, *Edward Feuz, Jr.*

Mount Willingdon – 1919: Topographical survey party

Mount Brazeau – July 9, 1923: Howard Palmer, Allen Carpe, William Harris

North Twin – July 10, 1923: Monroe Thorington, William Ladd, *Conrad Kain*

Mount Clemenceau – August 9, 1923: Henry DeVilliers-Schwab, Henry Hall, Jr., Dana Durand, William Harris

South Twin – July 8, 1924: Fred Field, Osgood Field, Lem Harris, *Joseph Biner, Edward Feuz, Jr.*

Mount King Edward – August 11, 1924: Joseph Hickson, Howard Palmer, *Conrad Kain*

Mount Alberta – July 21, 1925: Seiichi Hashimoto, Masanobu Hatano, Tanezo Hayakawa, Yuko Maki, Yukio Mita, Natagene Okabe, Jean Weber, *Heinrich Fuhrer, Hans Kohler*

Mount Woolley – July 26, 1925: Seiichi Hashimoto, Masanobu Hatano, Tanezo Hayakawa, Yuko Maki, Yukio Mita, Natagene Okabe, Jean Weber, *Heinrich Fuhrer, Hans Kohler*

Mount Lyell, Rudolph Peak (1) – July 5, 1926: Alfred Ostheimer III, Monroe Thorington, Max Strumia, *Edward Feuz, Jr.*

Mount Lyell, Ernest Peak (3) – July 9, 1926: Alfred Ostheimer III, Monroe Thorington, Max Strumia, *Edward Feuz, Jr.*

Mount Lyell, Christian Peak (5) – July 9, 1926: Alfred Ostheimer III, Monroe Thorington, Max Strumia, *Edward Feuz, Jr.*

Mount Fryatt – July 10, 1926: Joseph Hickson, Howard Palmer, *Hans Fuhrer*

Stutfield, West Peak – July 2, 1927: Alfred Ostheimer III, *Hans Fuhrer*

Mount Lyell, Walter Peak (4) – July 8, 1927: Dyson Duncan, Twining Lynes, Jimmy Simpson, *Ernest Feuz*

Mount Cline – July 1927: J.H. Barnes, Alfred Castle, Alfred Castle, Jr., Jimmy Simpson, *Rudolph Aemmer*

Mount Kitchener – July 3, 1927: Alfred Ostheimer III, *Hans Fuhrer*

Tusk Peak – July 31, 1927: Alfred Ostheimer III, John de Laittre, W.R. Maclaurin, *Hans Fuhrer*

Tsar Mountain – August 8, 1927: Alfred Ostheimer III, Jean Weber, *Hans Fuhrer*

Recondite Peak – August 26, 1927: Howard Palmer, *Ernest Feuz*

The Helmet – July 1928: Georgia Engelhard, *Hans Fuhrer*

Mount Andromeda – July 21, 1930: William Hainsworth, John Lehman, Max Strumia, Newman Waffl

Twins Tower – July 29, 1938: Fritz Wiessner, Chappell Cranmer

Mount Bryce, Centre Peak – July 27, 1961: Jo Kato, Siegfried Bucher, Robi Fierz

Stutfield, East Peak – August 15, 1962: William Buckingham, Bill Hooker

Mount Harrison – August 11, 1964: Werner Himmelsbach, Ralph Hutchinson, Joe Hutton, Don MacLaurin, Brendan Moss, Paddy Sherman

West Twin – July 1975: Dane Waterman, alone

Mount Goodsir, Centre Peak – August 17, 1979: Don Forest, Gary Pilkington, Ian Rowe

Most First Ascents of 11,000ers

Peaks listed in order of ascent date (guides' names in italics)

Nine
Christian Kaufmann: Columbia, Lyell (Peak 2), Forbes, Bryce (Southwest Peak), Alexandra, Goodsir (South Tower), Hungabee, Deltaform, Huber

Eight
James Outram: North Victoria, Lunette, Assiniboine, Columbia, Lyell (Peak 2), Forbes, Bryce, Alexandra

Seven
Alfred Ostheimer III: Lyell (Peaks 1, 3 and 5), Stutfield (West Peak), Kitchener, Tusk, Tsar

Six
Norman Collie: Lefroy, South Victoria, Athabasca, Snow Dome, Diadem, Forbes
Hans Fuhrer: Fryatt, Stutfield (West Peak), Kitchener, Tusk, Tsar, The Helmet
Edward Feuz, Jr.: Sir Douglas, Joffre, South Twin, Lyell (Peaks 1, 3 and 5)

Five
Conrad Kain: Resplendent, Whitehorn, Robson, North Twin, King Edward

Four
Monroe Thorington: North Twin, Lyell (Peak 1, 3 and 5)
Howard Palmer: Brazeau, King Edward, Fryatt, Recondite
Charles Fay: Hector, Lefroy, South Victoria, Goodsir (South Tower)
Joseph Hickson: Sir Douglas, Joffre, King Edward, Fryatt
Herman Woolley: Athabasca, Snow Dome, Diadem, Forbes
Max Strumia: Lyell (Peaks 1, 3 and 5), Andromeda

Resources

Most of the historical accounts in this book have been culled from four sources: in order of importance, *Canadian Alpine Journal, American Alpine Journal, Alpine Journal* and *Appalachia.* These are the annual journals of the Canadian, American and British Alpine Clubs, respectively, along with that of the Appalachian Mountain Club. They are an invaluable resource, containing nearly all the accounts of first ascents of the 11,000ers and subsequent new routes. As a collection of amateur writings, they are uncommonly well written, with the contrasts in styles over the years in some ways paralleling the technological changes and evolution of big-mountain alpine climbing in the Rockies. It is an unexpected pleasure from the research of this book to bring portions of these often long-forgotten texts to a wider, modern audience.

While many of these journals can be found in local libraries and home offices of the various alpine clubs, perhaps the most complete collection is found in the archives of the Whyte Museum in Banff. Phone 403-762-2291. www. whyte.org

Some of the early major players in the exploration and ascents of the 11,000ers wrote engaging books about their travels through the Canadian Rockies. Prominent among these accounts, in order of publication, are:

Walter Wilcox, *The Rockies of Canada* (Putnam, 1900)

Norman Collie and Hugh Stutfield, *Climbs and Explorations in the Canadian Rockies* (Longmans, 1903)

James Outram, *In the Heart of the Canadian Rockies* (MacMillan, 1905)

Arthur Coleman, *The Canadian Rockies – New and Old Trails* (Scribners, 1911)

Arthur Wheeler and Richard Cautley, *Report and Atlas of the Interprovincial Boundary Survey* (three volumes, 1917-1924) – Excellent early topo maps and photos

Howard Palmer and Monroe Thorington, *A Climber's Guide to the Rocky Mountains of Canada* (American Alpine Club, 1921)

Monroe Thorington, *The Glittering Mountains of Canada* (Lea, 1925)

Conrad Kain, *Where the Clouds Can Go* (American Alpine Club, 1935)

William Putnam, Andrew Kauffman *The Guiding Spirit* (Footprint, 1986)

E.J. Hart, *Jimmy Simpson – Legend of the Rockies* (Altitude, 1993)

Alfred Ostheimer III, *Every Other Day* (Alpine Club of Canada, 2002)

Other useful references
Glen Boles, Roger Laurilla and William Putnam, *Place Names of the Canadian Alps* (Footprint, 1990)

Chic Scott, *Pushing the Limits* (Rocky Mountain Books, 2000)

Glen Boles, Robert Kruszyna, William Putnam, *The Rocky Mountains of Canada-South* (American and Canadian Alpine Clubs, 1979)

Robert Kruszyna, William Putnam, *The Rocky Mountains of Canada-North* (American and Canadian Alpine Clubs, 1985)

Sean Dougherty, *Selected Alpine Climbs in the Canadian Rockies* (Rocky Mountain Books, 1991)

Gregory Horne – Route descriptions and photos of the most prominent 11,000ers in seven pamphlets (1989 and 1990)

Ben Gadd, *Handbook of the Canadian Rockies* (Corax Press, revised edition 1995)

Backroad Mapbook – Kootenays (Mussio Ventures, 2004) – shows B.C. logging road approaches for some 11,000ers

In the Internet age, many recent accounts of 11,000er ascents can be found on the Worldwide Web. Some of the best sites are:

Bivouac.com – Offers detailed accounts, from various submitters, of many of the standard 11,000er routes, often accompanied by a photo or two. An annual fee is charged to obtain access to most of these accounts.

Peakbagger.tripod.com – Alan Kane, author of *Scrambles in the Canadian Rockies*, has brief accounts and pictures of a number of 11,000er ascents

Peakfinder.com – Dave Birrell's site offers no route descriptions but is an excellent source of historical and other information and photos about these peaks

Live-the-vision.com – A climbers' forum on Rockies' routes, conditions and minutiae

Where to stay
Alpine Club of Canada (Canmore) – Maintains a clubhouse in Canmore and oversees a number of alpine huts, which can be booked in advance by calling 403-678-3200 (www.alpineclubofcanada.ca). The ACC also sells backcountry wilderness passes, required for overnight stays in national parks.

Hostelling International-Canada – Maintains a string of hostels between Banff and Jasper: Banff National Park 403-670-7580, Jasper National Park 780-852-3215 or toll free 1-877-852-0781. Book online at www.hihostels.ca.

There are excellent campgrounds throughout Canada's Rocky Mountain national parks. While all have traditionally been available on a first-come, first-serve basis, Parks Canada in 2004 was introducing a reservation system (1-877-737-3783 or www.pccamping.ca.) Peter Lougheed Provincial Park has a number of front-country campgrounds, most first come, first served: 403-591-7226. B.C. logging roads, used to access some 11,000ers, usually have roadside forest service campgrounds, which are often free.

Useful phone numbers

Phone numbers, especially in parks, seem to change regularly. Check them for accuracy before you head out.

Banff National Park
Banff Information Centre 403-762-1550
Banff RCMP 403-762-2226
Banff Wardens 403-762-4506
Lake Louise Visitor Centre 403-522-3833
Lake Louise Wardens 403-522-1220
Lake Louise RCMP 403-522-3812

Jasper National Park
Jasper Information Centre 780-852-6176
Columbia Icefield Centre – Parks Canada 780-852-6288
Jasper Wardens 780-852-6156/5
Sunwapta Warden Station 780-852-5383
Jasper RCMP 780-852-4421

Yoho and Kootenay National Parks
Yoho National Park Information 250-343-6783
Yoho Wardens 250-343-6142
Kootenay National Park Visitor Centre 250-347-9505
Kootenay Wardens 250-347-9361
Radium RCMP 250-342-9292

Kananaskis Country
Peter Lougheed Provincial Park Information 403-591-6322
Peter Lougheed Park Rangers 403-591-7222
Kananaskis Country backcountry camping permits 403-678-3136
Kananaskis Country Emergency 403-591-7767

Golden, B.C.
Louisiana-Pacific Canada (Golden) – logging company that maintains logging roads northwest of Golden 250-344-8800
Golden RCMP 250-344-2221

B.C. Provincial Parks
Mount Assiniboine – Contact Assiniboine Lodge for all accommodation (including hut bookings) and helicopter flights 403-678-2883 or www.assiniboinelodge.com.

Mount Robson Visitor Centre 250-566-4325

Weather
Calgary 403-299-7878
Banff 403-762-2088
Jasper 780-852-3185
Environment Canada online forecasts http://weatheroffice.ec.gc.ca/canada_e.html.
Weather Network: www.theweathernetwork.com.

Helicopter and fixed-wing flights
Alpine Helicopters 250-344-7444 in Golden and 403-678-4802 in Canmore
Canadian Helicopters in Golden 250-344-5311
Yellowhead Helicopters (Valemount, B.C.) 250-566-4401
Alpenglow Aviation (Golden) Ski plane flights to icefields west of the divide until early summer, 250-344-7117 or toll-free 1-888-244-7117
BC Air Ambulance 800-561-8011

Avalanche Information
Canadian Avalanche Bulletin 1-800-667-1105 or www.avalanche.ca/.
Banff, Yoho and Kootenay National Parks 403-762-1460
Jasper National Park 780-852-6176
Kananaskis Country 403-591-6322

Lovely campsite below Mt. King George.
Photo: Nancy Hansen.

Top Bivy/Camping Sites

A major attraction of climbing the more distant 11,000ers is camping in spectacular, remote areas. After the effort of claiming the summit, it's nice to have some extra time to linger in camp and soak up the surroundings; it's sometimes the most memorable part of the trip. From north to south here are some of the most notable back-country camping/bivy sites. See the individual peak descriptions for access information.

Rearguard-Waffl Meadows (The Helmet) – A green oasis just off the Robson Glacier, but far from the climbing hordes, with fascinating rocks and families of marmots.

Mount Brazeau – A high plateau south of the Brazeau Icefield provides a stunning panorama, including Mount Alberta's North Face and much of the Columbia Icefield peaks.

Mount Fryatt – Hummocky meadows below the West Ridge offer a small stream, big boulders and fine views.

Mount Tusk – This rarely visited spot offers a bit of elevated greenery near the wildly fractured Duplicate–Tusk Icefall.

Mount Tsar – Truly remote shoreline site below the northern flanks of Tsar.

Mount Alberta – The horrible slog to reach the first ledge below the East Face is redeemed by arguably the most awesome view in the Rockies – the "Black Hole" and the Twins and Columbia beyond.

Stutfield Col (The Twins) – More than 3,200 metres high, this glacial col has stunning views of Mounts Alberta, Columbia and the Twins. Mind you, if the weather moves in, this is one of the worst camps to be stuck in.

Mount Alexandra The cirque at the head of South Rice Brook offers hanging glaciers, cascading waterfalls, splendid wildflowers and an ancient coral reef.

Mount Forbes – A streamside spot near the toe of the North Glacier offers dazzling vistas of the Mons Icefield and beyond.

Mount Cline – Perched above two small lakes, this alpine site is set amidst the barren beauty of the front ranges.

Recondite – You're almost guaranteed to have this scenic, elevated spot – with plenty of fresh running water – to yourself, if you can stagger the 37 kilometres in one day to get here.

Devon Lakes (Willingdon) – Lovely camping in an alpine basin near Clearwater Pass. Worth the fabulous hike over Quartzite Col and through the Upper Pipestone Valley, even if you don't climb.

Assiniboine-Lunette – This tiny, peaceful meadow south of the mountain boasts a tiny stream and lofty views to the south.

Mount King George – The verdant meadows south of the peak are truly sublime, fringed by alpine larch and bisected by a burbling stream.

Acknowledgements

Although I have climbed all the peaks described herein, this book is very much a collaborative effort. I leaned heavily on climbing partners, friends and experts to describe routes I haven't tackled, fill in gaps in my memory and casual note taking, provide route updates and generously offer many excellent photos.

Many thanks to long-time climbing partners Forbes Macdonald and Roman Pachovsky, the latter who provided many photos and read the entire text. Nancy Hansen and Doug Fulford went beyond the call of duty, providing photos, detailed descriptions of many routes and careful proofreading as well as opening their Canmore home to me on archival research trips.

Dan Doll patiently answered many technical and route questions. He, Alan Kane, Dale Cole and Kelly Adams also edited portions of the text, as did national park wardens Marc Ledwidge and Lisa Paulson.

Other photo contributors include Markus Kellerhals, Clive Cordery, Don Beers, Helen Sovdat, Peter Amann, Mike Mokievsky-Zubok, Nancy and Dennis Stefani, Isabel Budke, Thomas Choquette, Sandy Walker, John Shaw and the legendary Glen Boles, who also filled in some historical details.

Many thanks also to Gillean Daffern, Nicole Bauche, Gabrielle Savard, Marg Saul, Allan Main, Colin Jones, Paul Stoliker, Chic Scott, Bill Putnam, Frank Campbell, Raphael Slawinski, Chris Beers, Bill Marriott, Tom Fransham and the staff of Parks Canada, the Whyte Museum, the Alpine Club of Canada and Assiniboine Lodge.

Ben Gadd provided invaluable, concise information on the geology of the Canadian Rockies. David Jones, Fred Thiessen, Natural Resources Canada's Steve Westley and others steered me through the complexities of determining peak elevations.

Kudos to David Finch for his editorial guidance and to Ana Tercero, who produced fine maps and put up with my endless submissions of photos to be scanned. Special thanks to Tony Daffern for his expert layout and publishing wizardry under a tight deadline.

Index of 11,000ers